FINDING UNSHAKABLE

HAPPINESS

DONNA MARTIRE MILLER

JOSEPH BOLOGNA, EDITOR, CONTRIBUTING PHOTOGRAPHER

LINDA JACKSON, CONTRIBUTING EDITOR

Published by: e-Clements.com

Cover Design by: Kerry Enns

ISBN: 978-1-09839-438-7

For Online Purchases:
BookBaby
877-961-6878
https://www.bookbaby.com

Printed and bound in Location by BookBaby

FINDING UNSHAKABLE HAPPINESS
Table of Contents

Getting Comfortable with Yourself

-Megan McDonough

I could feel Jessica's anxiety through the phone. It was 2013, and I was on my way to the first immersion for the Certificate in Positive Psychology (CiPP). Jessica was having second thoughts. Her big concern: She was hesitant about the group work. "Can't I just learn the material on my own?" she asked me.

How often have we tried to make progress "on our own" thinking it will be easier that way? It's not.

Together is better, I assured her.

There is great power in being with a group of people committed to learning and living into their best self through activating the skills of positive psychology. That's what you'll see in the stories you're about to read–the combined good work of many practitioners making an impact greater than any individual.

I saw Jessica again months later, at the final CiPP immersion. Her radiant smile made me smile, too. She said, "Thank you for making me feel comfortable in my own skin."

Her words have stuck with me all these years. What does it mean to feel comfortable in your own skin–in good times and bad? How would you act, speak, and show up if you were really comfortable with who you are? Would you have less trepidation and more bravery to reach higher?

Once you get comfortable with your own self, it's oh-so-much easier to serve. You know what you have to give and the significance of this day.

As the founder of Wholebeing Institute, I'm in awe of how people grow when they begin to ask questions like: Who am I at my best? What are my strengths? What is there to appreciate in this day, in this relationship, in this work, in myself?

This book you hold in your hands is a treasure trove of such stories–people connecting with their best self. And, in doing so, inspiring you, dear reader, to connect to what is sustaining and nourishing within you.

Since 2013, thousands of people have studied positive psychology at Wholebeing Institute, representing 42 states here in America, and more than 45 countries worldwide. I'm grateful Donna spearheaded the effort to combine these real-life applications of positive psychology into this one book.

These stories are like water in the desert, filling us with possibilities when life dries us out.

My story with Donna started when she joined the Certificate in Positive Psychology–first as a student, then as part of the staff, supporting the students as they lived into what they were learning. Donna's authentic self is loving and zesty. You can feel her warmth in every interaction. She lived into the skills of positive psychology as the leader of a social service non-profit, and now as the driving force for this book.

She elevates us all with her loving leadership.

It's my greatest hope that as you read the stories of people at their best, you touch that place within yourself. And that, by using the tools you'll learn in this book, you stay connected with that best self as you reach even higher.

Megan McDonough | Founder, Wholebeing Institute

Hardwick, MA May 2021

What is Unshakable Happiness?

-Donna Martire Miller

I will start this section the same way it will end with this core belief. YOU deserve to be happy. YOU deserve to live your life in the way that your deepest desires have been leading you throughout your life. YOU *are* your greatest asset, resource, and best friend ... Let me explain.

Recently my sister Sandra gave me an ancestry kit as a gift. I followed the directions and sent it in. The outcome was surprising. My parent's families are from different parts of Italy, Naples, and Sicily. My ancestry, however, determined that I was 85% Italian, 10% Turkish, and 5% French! Ooh, La, La! Currently family members are American too. I began to think about that. I started to do the math. I have two parents, four grandparents, eight great grandparents, 16 great, great grandparents, 32, 64, 128, etc., into the hundreds of thousands of ancestors that I suddenly felt blessed and sustained by.

Ater all, many stories have been passed down in this lineage. How it all began, our faith and a creation story. Stories of love and love lost, those that lived as heroes and those that led a simpler life. From these stories came our family traditions and rituals. Genealogy had me imagining my ancestors living by the ocean or in the mountains. Ancestors that lived in Europe or worldwide, all interwoven with this bloodline that eventually became my inheritance. I no longer felt alone.

At each stage of my own development, I perhaps have unknowingly played out a part of their life's adventure as they pursued happiness. And the beat goes on as I offer the learning and experiences life offers, what I know about pathways to happiness on to my loved ones, children, and grandchildren.

Sonia Lyubomirsky et al. explains that 50% of the variance in our happiness level is determined by our genetic factors. It seems that some of our ability to be happy is built into our DNA. Ten percent of our ability to be happy is determined by "Our life circumstances," such as living during a global pandemic. This research also claims something that I find to be amazing! Up to 40% of the ability to increase or achieve sustainable happiness can be attributed to our moment-to-moment choices! This means that our thoughts, words, actions, and the activities we choose to engage in can increase our well-being and joy in our day-to-day existence!

In his book "Choose the Life You Want," Tal Ben-Shahar writes that we as individuals can *choose* to affect our own happiness and well-being substantially! The 40% of a person's happiness that, by this account, can be improved upon, by our own choices, gives us hope and optimism! Learning this from the team leaders at Wholebeing Institute, Tal Ben-Shahar, Megan McDonough, Maria Sirois, and Phoebe Atkinson (where I earned my Certification in Positive Psychology, CIPP), was the impedance for a radical change for the better to begin in my life.

How many times have you heard someone say that they needed space to go and find themselves? This is where I found myself as I joined Wholebeing Institute at Kripalu in my search for happiness. It is as valid a search as any. I would like to share a poem that explains this journey. It is a beautiful perception of how life can be until we find out who we are and how to grow from our life experiences.

Autobiography in Five Chapters

By Portia Nelson, from her writing in 1977, There's a hole in My Sidewalk. The Romance of self-Discovery

I

I walk down the street. There is a deep hole in the sidewalk
I fall in. I am lost ... I am hopeless. It isn't my fault. It takes
forever to find a way out.

II

I walk down the same street. There is a deep hole in the
sidewalk. I pretend I don't see it. I fall in again. I can't believe
I'm in the same place. But it isn't my fault. It still takes a long

time

to

get out.

III

I walk down the same street. There is a deep hole in the
sidewalk. I see it is there. I still fall in... it's a habit. My eyes are
open; I know where I am; It is my fault. I get out immediately.

IV

I walk down the same street. There is a deep hole in the
sidewalk. I walk around it.

V

I walk down another street.

It stands to reason that everything we do in life is somewhat motivated by this inner knowing of our true self, our best self. We just pay attention to so many other things that years can go by before we stop long enough to listen. We get spun around like a top by hardship, trauma, or misunderstandings.

Years can go by before discovering the resources that will help us to build resiliency. Knowing who we are when we are at our best will help us overcome the negative bias in our thoughts. To replace that bias with evidence of positivity, we need to recognize our strengths and develop more positive emotions. These happiness strategies help us clearly define our resources and natural supports and shift from a fault-finding mindset to a more growth-oriented benefit-finding mindset.

I firmly believe we were all born with a special "something" that we are meant to have and share. Our personalities' talents or beautiful gifts can include gratitude, kindness, love, creativity, courage, or compassion. These gifts of our character were bestowed upon all of us to use them to navigate life's challenges and share them in support of those we love or others to help with the greater good.

Today we live in a global community. One of the lessons Covid has taught us is that people around the world are not so different. We are all joined in the fight against this pandemic. That is why I hope we come out of this experience, learning to embrace each other's differences, to understand the complex nature of diversity and to see the blessings in our everyday existence ...

Happiness strategies help us gain critical personal perspectives that will bring about a way to engage in life authentically. A way to live on purpose. A way to know why we are here, a "knowing" that will give our life meaning. Until we engage in this self-discovery and deep listening to our heart and soul, we will habitually continue to fall into that same hole where we feel stuck and helpless. The good news is that many researchers have been testing strategies proven to get us out of these ruts. Strategies to help us spiral upwards instead of sinking into our experiences of learned hopelessness. I became aware of these strategies in my 50's, after I realized that I was at one of my lowest points and no one was coming to save me. I am now 66 and have been applying them in my own life, and it has saved me from several physical health and mental health disparities. I can personally attest to the increased wellness, wholeness, and happiness that directly result from using these strategies and practices that you will discover while reading these chapters.

In this, book two of the "Unshakable Happiness" Trilogy, as you turn the pages, you will hear the voice of many authors as they tell their stories. You may find yourself laughing with them as they use humor to know how to face a challenge or courage in their wild adventures. You may feel the thrill of elevated, excited emotions witnessing their shared encounters as they helped themselves and others. You will see how they navigated through their life before and after using these strategies. You may recognize parts of yourself in them, in our shared experiences of humanity at its best, and sometimes, learning from challenges they have faced. In a conversation I had with Tal Ben-Shahar recently, he reminded me of one of the books he wrote called *Short Cuts to Happiness*. In his book, he writes of gaining substantial learning from others who told their stories while getting his hair cut! I hope that you, as the reader or as one of the members of the team that helped this book to come to fruition, gain from their stories a new understanding of the many opportunities we have to become happier, to laugh more, and to live a life worth living filled with all the love your heart can hold. I hope you will listen to your inner calling, to love one another, and honor the gifts bestowed upon you with joy and gratitude. I hope one of the stories will inspire you to draw closer to those you love solidifying the bonds between you. I hope you will discover opportunities to draw closer to our global world community in our shared human experience of happiness and well-being.

Today's society child is experiencing an acceleration of loss and fear, a relapse in depression, loneliness, addiction, anxiety, and suicidal ideation. We are living in challenging times. I am not discounting that. I am saying with sound conviction and optimism that we can make choices to focus on what truly matters to us. In doing so, we will build self-efficacy. Dear reader, you are one choice away from becoming happier. Choose to believe you can. With the help of some science backed strategies we can find ways to be more resilient. We can find happiness in discovering our best self, authenticity and sharing our gifts with others.

You deserve to be happy. You deserve to live your life in the way that your deepest desires have been leading YOU throughout your life. You are your greatest asset, resource, and best friend. Quietly listen, you will hear the whispers of your soul gently calling you to your best life, a life filled with unshakable happiness. *"You hold the power to be the Change."* It starts within you.

INTRODUCTION TO THE SCIENCE OF HAPPINESS

Crafting a Life Where Every Day Counts: Living InSpired in Uncertain Times

-Hanna Perlberger

When the Heart of the World Skips a Beat

I was about to give a talk to a philanthropic women's organization in South Florida. I was shaking, but it wasn't from the usual nerves that precede every time I speak in public. Four days earlier, on Valentine's Day, the deadliest of all school shootings occurred at the nearby sprawling suburban campus of Marjory Stoneman Douglas High School, leaving 17 dead and just as many injured. One of the news segments struck me as especially poignant. The reporter observed that the day's expectation – festivities, love, balloons, hearts - surprises of the "right" kind – was in utter contrast to the horror that the day actually brought.

For a moment, I flashed on Mina, my mother-in-law, who, as a teenager in 1942, was celebrating Passover in Tyczyn, a little village in Poland. As the family sat down for the Seder, the front door was broken down in an explosion of violence. Purposely deciding to liquidate the village on this holy night, the Nazis pulled Mina's father out of the house by his beard and thrust the family into the Rczezow Ghetto. Soon after that, Mina's parents were deported to Auschwitz, never to be seen again.

When evil stops joy in its tracks, we feel violated in our depths, sometimes where we feel most sacred. It shakes us to the very core, and we may wonder – what do we really know? On what can we ever rely? And for younger people, like those Florida high school students, the sudden encounter with the unspeakable can change their perceptions of reality, their decisions about the world, and even their place in it - forever.

How can we face reality that turns on a dime, irrevocably shattering our world in an instant? On the other hand, is it any easier, I wonder, when the shift occurs over time, when the collective world inexorably slides into the unimaginable for weeks - and then months?

This Can't Be Happening!

The first U.S. cases of non-travel-related COVID-19 were confirmed. Suddenly, the new weird virus that was "over there" was now here, and soon everywhere. Every encounter with another person, object, or surface became a possible life-threatening event by an invisible enemy that lurked in everyone and on everything. "Shelter in place for two weeks," we were told, and be prepared for a death toll that could possibly exceed 250,000 (a catastrophic number at the time). But after that, we were reassured, the curve would flatten, summer would come, and we could resume a "normal" life.

While we still presumed that life would return to "normal," some of us wondered, however, whether that was the goal. Did we want to go back to the way it was or move forward with a better way of being? After all, what was the point of it all, unless there was a lesson to be learned? We were still under the impression that there was even a choice in the matter, that waking up from this nightmare to a normal and fully functioning society in the near future – or ever - was even an option.

Maybe that's why in the early months of the pandemic, some people seemed to be coping remarkably well, gleefully posting on social media how they were using their downtime to learn a new language, master a new cuisine, study opera, etc. I wasn't one of them. I lowered my hopes of thriving and settled for surviving. I hunkered down with Netflix, Insta-cart food delivery, and a "wake me when it's over" attitude. I absorbed my daily dose of COVID-19 briefings on TV, watched the numbers soar worldwide, and searched online for hand sanitizer and toilet paper while pretending to be happy on my daily Happy Hour on Zoom with friends (Zoom-tinis, anyone?)

Resilience 101

Most people can get used to just about anything except for constant and relentless change. We're simply not wired for it – it affects our happiness and wellbeing. The antidote to uncertainty, surprisingly, is not certainty but resilience.

For that very reason, to aspire to craft a life of everyday meaning takes on new urgency. It's not just a cliché, platitude, or mental luxury – it's a lifeline back to sanity, and yes, even to thriving. At one time or another, we've all known grief, despair, and hopelessness. As the lyrics go, "*Hello darkness, my old friend, I've come to talk with you again...*" Sometimes, however, a dauntless soul fires up a torch so brilliant it lights up the way for the rest of us for all time. Viktor Frankl is one of those souls.

The Search for Meaning Starts with the Biggest Question

According to Freud, man's primary drive is the pursuit of pleasure. Nietzsche disputed that theory when he proclaimed that man's primary drive is the pursuit of power. Meet Viktor Frankl, the world-famous Viennese psychiatrist and philosopher, who pioneered a new approach to psychology. Having endured three years of concentration camps in Germany, where his entire family and pregnant wife were murdered, Frankl founded "logotherapy," positing that man's primary pursuit is neither pleasure nor power but the search for meaning. It was not in Vienna's cafes but in the very inferno of man's most depraved inhumanity to his fellow that Frankl formulated his most inspiring and transformational theories.

Who Am I – in the Presence of This?

Will I be beaten today? Will I eat today? Will I die today?

In taking away his every freedom, Auschwitz had shrunk an intellectual giant into animalistic thinking. But Frankl came to realize that he had, in fact, one freedom left – and it was by far the most important freedom of all – the freedom to choose. In his incomparable book, "Man's Search for Meaning," Frankl famously wrote, "Everything can be taken from a man but one thing: the last of the human freedoms – to choose one's attitude in any given set of circumstances, to choose one's own way." It would not be the little questions of survival, or even pondering the unfathomable and unanswerable question "why?" that would give him moral fortitude. Instead, Frankl distilled his search for meaning into one powerful and prevailing question, *"Who am I – in the presence of this?"*

While this question may well have helped Frankl survive, he was not looking to live at any cost. In a place where his identity was taken away with the prisoner numbers inked into his arm, Frankl knew that he was still an immutable "I." And in the place where humanity itself had died, the most significant challenge, Frankl knew, was, nevertheless, how to remain fully human.

We all have a "this" in our lives that tests our ability to respond with our highest and best capacity. Once we decide who we are, or want to be, however, the choices that align with that identity become clear.

Response-ability

Just as the vaccine was starting to become available, a friend of mine lost both her father and her husband to COVID-19 within four days of each other. "People have asked me whether this has shaken my faith," she mentioned to me on the way to her father's memorial. With a wisdom that surpasses understanding, she answered rhetorically, "I just lost the two people I love the most. Why would I want to lose my best friend on top of that? If I didn't have God in my life, I would really be alone."

Notwithstanding the age-old question of why bad things happen to good people, shaking our fist at heaven may be a natural response to tragedies, but it's not a long-term solution or strategy for wellbeing. Choosing our way – responding from a regulated and centered sense of self, especially during dark and uncertain times - can move us from victim to chooser, from helplessness to empowerment, and from inconsequence to significance. *Who am I?* What do I want to manifest in this – or any given set of circumstances? I was listening to a talk on resilience by Maria Sirois, positive psychologist, author, and faculty member of the Wholebeing Institute, who said:

> *When we get that every single day is ours to shape, that our day and how we shape it is significant, when we retrain our perspective away from being a victim and towards the understanding that our lives add up to the series of choices that we make every day, we get that our days matter. Our lives are meaningful and important because we matter.*

That's the challenge. How do we increase our resilience and self-compassion to give ourselves permission to matter - *no matter what?* Sorry to say, but we can't think our way out of this; we have to do something. The very word "craft" is a verb of action and deliberate process. To craft something is to create a new form from raw materials or shape an existing structure into revealing a new identity. And it doesn't happen on its own. A life of meaning doesn't happen to us or for us. We can't be passive in this endeavor.

A Whole-Being Approach to Happiness

What's in an Acronym?

Martin Seligman, often referred to as the father of the positive psychology movement, came up with the acronym PERMA, comprised of the five building blocks that promote what we would call the "good life," namely flourishing, as the path to well-being and happiness. These elements are: Positive Emotions, Engagement, Relationships, Meaning, and Accomplishments.

Tal Ben-Shahar, one of the world's thought leaders in positive psychology, and Meghan McDonough, founder of the Wholebeing Institute, where I obtained my positive psychology certification, co-created a model for a whole-person approach to happiness: SPIRE - which stands for: Spiritual, Physical, Intellectual, Relational, Emotional.

SPIRE departs from PERMA in significant ways. Instead of "A" for Accomplishments, SPIRE has "I" for Intellectual, which is defined as "engaging in deep learning and being open to experience." By emphasizing the dynamic learning process and growing through experience over the achieving of fixed goals, sustainable happiness in this domain is achievable by anyone.

The physical realm has gotten little attention from mainstream positive psychology, but it is one of the foundations of SPIRE. The "P" of SPIRE stands for "Physical," as in, "caring for the body and tapping into the mind-body connection." Even more overlooked is the realm of the soul. But the first element of SPIRE, the "S" stands for "Spiritual," and is defined as "leading a meaningful life and mindfully savoring the present."

SPIRE holistically synthesizes "doing" with "being" to create a mind, body, heart, and soul experience that considers the whole person. While we can discuss each dimension of SPIRE on its own, this model posits that they are all connected and interdependent. At the heart of the Wholebeing Institute is its teaching that the greatest well-being and happiness can only be realized by taking the whole into account.

Living In-SPIREd.

"S" - Spiritual: Leading a Meaningful Life and Mindfully Savoring the Present

Leading a Meaningful Life

If I asked you to define "spiritual," some of you would draw a blank, and others would jump right in. For our purposes, "spiritual" is not to be confused with "religious," although those terms can undoubtedly overlap. Joan Borysenko, a Harvard physician who is one of the pioneers of integrative medicine, recognized the role of meaning and the spiritual dimensions of life as an integral part of health and healing. She says: "Spirituality is a commitment to a life of depth and compassion that connects each of us to a larger whole. Our personal spiritual development must ultimately serve others for it to be an authentic unfolding of the heart of spirit in action."

And so, part of crafting your life around the dimension of spirit is to become your genuine self while at the same time expanding your consciousness to connect to others or something larger than you. It is becoming aware of the undeniable yearning of your heart and its infinite generosity and then making choices in alignment with this sacred awareness. And there are times in life, in the spiritual maturation process, when this calling just happens more naturally.

To Everything, There is a Season

If you are 45 or older, you're going to be happy with what I'm about to tell you. In his book, *What You Can Change and What You Can't*, Seligman explains there are basically two great seasons in a person's life. The first season is when we discover the demands of the world: schooling, finding a mate, children, embracing the values of your place and time, embarking on your life's work, etc. "And if you're lucky," Seligman says, "you master these things."

I would never suggest that any of these things are not meaningful – to the contrary! But this phase of life is characterized by being extrinsic; namely, you learn what is expected from you by society, culture, parents, etc., and you comply with those norms that come from the outside, that are external to you. Inwardly, you may be insecure over what other people think of you, how you look, whether you are successful, and so on. You may fall into the trap of status and the hell of social comparisons. You're trying hard to "make it," but you may be climbing someone else's idea of the ladder of success. You may reach the top only to find you're on the wrong wall.

In the second season of life, gradually, you become less and less what others expect of you and more of what nourishes you intrinsically, from the inside. In her TED talk, "The Art of Being Yourself," Caroline McHugh says when you get to the stage in your life, when there are more summers behind you than in front of you, everything intensifies. You become more honest. Less compromising. "When you're a wrinkly, you can't be arsed." (That sounds great with a Scottish accent.) "We call our oldies eccentric," she goes on to say, "when in fact, what they are being is authentic."

So, what is authenticity? There is no one answer, but Seligman characterizes it as the willingness to arrange your life to fit what you have discovered about who you really are and that you will now pursue what your inner world demands of you. To be authentic, Seligman explains, means that you do not quiet the whisperings of your heart.

For some, responding at last to what is intrinsic can mean self-indulgence, frivolity, or emptiness. But that certainly doesn't have to be the case. An astonishingly large part of what is "genuinely you" coincides with old notions like duty, service, generosity, guiding young people, and mentoring others.

Whether you already have a spiritual practice in place or are coming to these ideas for the first time, crafting your life to strengthen, expand, or discover new ways to deepen your connection to what creates meaning for you will optimize your happiness.

Mindfully Savoring the Present

After ten months of the Certificate Course in Positive Psychology (CIPP) at the Wholebeing Institute, the program concluded with a five-day on-site immersion that culminated in a graduation ceremony. During our last night together, the students put on a talent show, and one of the selected participants announced that her talent was "swimming." Since there was no swimming facility other than a dreary hot tub in the basement, I couldn't imagine how she would showcase that for us. The student's name was Soni, the significance of which was lost on me at the time. Some of you, however, may recognize the name of this American six-time Olympic medalist who set a new world record at the London Olympics in 2012.

Soni talked about what it was like from the moment she touched the wall and lifted her head out of the water to hear she had won the gold and shattered the previous record - to arriving at the podium a mere twenty minutes later. In that time, she had to get back to the changing room, dry off, pull on some sweats, and run a comb through her hair. Then she had to run through the gauntlet of a long corridor where one interviewer after another thrust a microphone into her face as she anxiously made her way to the ceremony stage. The whole experience from start to finish was a mindless and harried blur. Had she known, Soni told a mesmerized audience, that the instant when she touched the wall was "her moment - the moment" - she would have slowed down, taken a breath, and savored it for just a moment more.

Mindfully savoring the present means slowing down to appreciate life's pleasures, big and small. Travis Bradbury, who writes about the habits of happy people, explains how important it is to savor the taste of a meal, revel in an amazing conversation, or even just step outside to take a deep breath of fresh air. A friend of mine told me that her young son loves gummy fish. She cuts each fish in half, and he gets to eat one tiny piece a day. But it takes him a full half-hour to finish because he sucks on it to make it last. That's savoring!

It's not the glorious gold medal moments that happen to you, but the moments you seek out to relish and enjoy. It's not deflecting or brushing off a compliment but taking it in and letting it settle in a grateful heart. Take a cue from wine connoisseurs who know how to get the most pleasure from a sip of wine: from the visual appreciation, breathing in the aroma and bouquet, swishing the wine in the mouth for the most complex taste sensations, and then, finally, to being silent for a full minute to allow the aftertaste to emerge. Imagine becoming a connoisseur of your own life and enjoying and appreciating your experiences in the richness of all of their complexity and nuance. Research even shows that mentally reliving our positive experiences in a sensory way locks them in and deepens their effect.

With that, we move into the domain of "P" of SPIRE.

"P" – Physical: Caring for the Body and Tapping into the Mind-Body Connection

Caring for the Body

"The problem with psychology today," says Martin Seligman, "is that we focus on the neck up, whereas most of what happens to us is neck down." Sitting at a computer most of the day, I am one of those "above the neck-ers." Except for the neck and back pain I get from sitting for hours at a time, I forget that I have a physical body. Furthermore, I also tend to forget that my body is inseparable from me, that it is the very place where I live, and that caring for the body incorporates caring for the self. I was listening to a talk by Borysenko on the importance of self-care:

> *If you don't nurture yourself, you can't be your best, and you have much less to offer to others. The basis of your power is to take the time to eat well and sleep well, to stop and savor. When you take time to say "wow – that's beautiful," and you sit with it and absorb the experience, your brain manufactures new circuitry – you become happier and more grateful. Gratitude*

*is one of the keys to mental health and the single best
predictor of physical and psychological health.*

As a holistic model, all of the elements of SPIRE overlap,
engage each other and can be used to support new ways of
thinking. For example, when I am tapped into "an attitude
of gratitude," I am in my favorite domain, "Spiritual." There
is a Jewish custom to try to say 100 blessings a day, one of
which is the blessing *"Asher Yatzar"* (literally meaning the
One who forms), which is recited after going to the bathroom.
This unique blessing acknowledges God's Divine wisdom in
fashioning the body with its many intricacies, openings, and
cavities, each of which must operate appropriately for survival,
and we are thankful for the miracle of allowing our bodies to
function daily.

But we have to do our part. Cultivating physical wellbeing is
not just good for the body; it's good for the soul. Rather than
coming from the familiar place of resistance or resentment,
making choices that promote health can become an
expression of gratitude to my Creator while honoring the
physical vessel with which I have been entrusted. Bringing
awareness to mindless habits and behaviors that honor
your values is the first step in shifting to a more holistic
consciousness.

Tapping into the Mind-Body Connection

Dr. Patricia Hart, who writes on the mind-body connection,
explains that we can have emotional reactions to situations
without being aware of why we react. That is why the mind-
body approach focuses on becoming more conscious of our

mental states and using this increased awareness to guide our mental states in a better, less destructive direction.

Holistic physician, Lakshmi Menezes, describes the mind-body connection as the link between a person's thoughts, attitudes, behaviors, and physical health. Negative thinking patterns, such as assuming the worst, jumping to conclusions, and self-criticism, can make it more challenging to deal with health problems. "For example, a patient diagnosed with prediabetes may think since everyone in her family has diabetes, there's nothing she can do to prevent it, even after being told that prediabetes is reversible with diet and exercise."

This negative inner voice can have serious health consequences, and those types of thought patterns are difficult to break. That's where mind-body therapies that help us get centered are helpful, such as mindfulness meditation, yoga, centering prayer, qi gong, or cognitive therapies, etc.

The holistic approach to the mind-body connection is to understand the impact not just on physical health but recognizes the interconnection and intersection across the domains of life. As Borysenko explains, "Bodily sensations provide feedback and guidance about every aspect of your life. By acting on this information, you can reduce stress, balance your life, and maximize your innate potential for health, creativity, and spiritual growth."

Whether you choose to strengthen a practice already in place or experiment with new methods to get more aware of the mind-body connection, try making a commitment for a full 28 days and put it into your schedule, preferably at the same time every day.

"I" – Intellectual: Engaging in Deep Learning and Being Open to Experience

"As we become adults, paying attention to what we find naturally interesting is a key part of our overall well-being," says Ben-Shahar. "What captivates our curiosity feeds our inquisitive nature as much as food feeds our physical nature."

If you are unfamiliar with the VIA (Values in Action) Character Strengths, I strongly encourage you to go to www.viacharacter. org and take the online survey to learn about the "24 VIA Character Strengths" and identify which are your top five. According to my results, "Love of Learning" is one of mine. As a lifelong learner, I was especially gratified to learn that this trait is associated with healthy and productive aging.

But this dimension of SPIRE goes beyond what typically comes to mind when you think of the term "learning" and engages our fundamental approach to how we process our experiences. While engaging in deep learning can be rewarding for its own sake, it is the transformative aspect of learning – being open to new experiences - that engages us more profoundly and creates wellbeing.

"Growth-Mindset" Versus "Fixed-Mindset"

Carol Dweck is a pioneering researcher at Stanford in the field of motivation. By explaining why some people succeed while others don't, Dweck's groundbreaking work changed the field of education. Like Seligman's explanatory styles of pessimism and optimism (discussed in the section on Emotions below), Dweck demonstrated that there are two mindsets that foster or inhibit success: a "fixed-mindset" or a "growth-mindset."

With a "fixed-mindset," you believe you are who you are, and you cannot change. This creates problems when you're challenged because anything that appears to be more than you can handle is bound to make you feel hopeless and overwhelmed. People who are open to deep learning experiences, on the other hand, have a "growth-mindset." People with a "growth-mindset" embrace challenges, treating them as opportunities to learn something new.

An article by the Peak Performance Center enumerates the characteristics of each mindset:

The Characteristics of a Fixed-Mindset:

1. Believes intelligence and talent are fixed
2. Sticks with what they know
3. Believes putting forth effort is fruitless or worthless
4. Believes personal failures define who they are
5. Hides flaws so as not to be judged as a failure
6. Avoids challenges to avoid failure
7. Tends to give up easily
8. Ignores feedback from others
9. Views feedback as personal criticism
10. Feels threatened by the success of others

The Characteristics of a Growth-Mindset:

1. Believes intelligence and talents can be developed
2. Believes effort is the path to mastery
3. Believes mistakes are an essential path of learning
4. Views failure as an opportunity to learn
5. Believes failures are just temporary setbacks
6. Embraces challenges
7. Welcomes feedback from others in order to learn

8. Believes feedback is a guide to further improvement
9. Views feedback as a source of information
10. Views other's success as a source of inspiration and information

If you identify with any of the characteristics of a "fixed-mindset," it would naturally follow that you might feel helpless to change. Give yourself a great deal of compassion and gentleness around exploring a new way of being. The key is the willingness to look at failure as an opportunity.

A few maxims were drilled into us in CIPP, one of which was the famous saying of Ben-Shahar, *"If we don't learn to fail, we will fail to learn."* Understandably, in times of uncertainty, you may want to cling even more strongly to what you know. A pandemic would seem like a time to hunker down, not take risks, or try anything new. As counterintuitive as it may seem, I am suggesting that the more you can embrace vulnerability and uncertainty, the safer and happier you will feel. And the more you can accept imperfection and failure, the more you will be at peace. Take heart, for these are learnable skills.

"R" – Relational: Nurturing a Constructive Relationship with Self and With Others

For some people, the pandemic has been a lonely time of isolation. While it scared me that my eighty-three-year-old mother was taking chances that I was unwilling to do, I knew that living alone in total seclusion could also negatively affect her health. I read a statistic that some inmates on death row will forego lengthy appeals and choose death over remaining indefinitely in solitary confinement. For better or worse, humans are relational beings, wired for connection. So, it's heartbreaking when we make a hash of things and destroy or damage the relationships that we cherish, often without intending to do so.

I Should Have Said Something

My husband and I were out to dinner with a couple. It was their second marriage, and they remarried late in life. But based on the constant bickering, they sounded as if they had been married for decades. Unpleasant as it may be, squabbling alone is not the death knell of a marriage. Instead, the conversation I witnessed that evening was a real sign their marriage was in danger, and it's not one people imagine would be such a problem.

When we think of classic communications issues, we think about managing stress, negativity, and disagreements in a constructive manner. "Learn to fight fair," the therapists tell us. And of course, working to reduce reactivity and learning to turn conflict into growth and intimacy is vital. But according to prominent marriage expert John Gottman and other researchers, one of the best predictors of a successful relationship is not how we react to the negative experiences of our partner (or family members, friends, etc.) but how we respond to their positive experiences.

The 4 Ways We Respond to Good News

When someone shares good news with us, we usually respond in one of four ways: Active Constructive, Passive Constructive, Active Destructive, and Passive Destructive. In our couple's case, the wife is very artistic and has had a lifelong love of handmade jewelry. After years of wanting to create a business, she announced that she had finally launched her online jewelry store on Etsy and was exhilarated as she shared the news. This could be a typical response in each scenario:

- **Active Constructive** (Shows interest and enthusiasm, shares the joy, and asks questions to relive and amplify the experience)

  "That's amazing. I'm so excited for you. I can't wait to see the website. You've been working on this for a long time and I'm happy you finally launched it. How did you feel when you finally saw it online? Waiter – bring a bottle of champagne – my wife and I are celebrating," says the husband as he leans towards his wife.

- **Passive Constructive** (Shows a little enthusiasm, but it's no big deal)

  "That's nice, dear," says the husband with a head nod and gentle smile.

- **Active Destructive** (A total buzzkill, actively creating doubt, pointing out problems or feigning concerns that kill excitement)

  "What do you know about wish fulfillment? People want things right away. How will you handle delays? What if someone calls and you're on vacation? Stick to your hobby – you don't know the first thing about running a business," the husband says in a demeaning and authoritarian way.

- **Passive Destructive** (Disinterested, and unresponsive or changes the topic)

  "I didn't have lunch, so I'm really hungry," says the husband, not looking up from the menu.

In our couple's case, the husband's response was "Active Destructive" – he said those very words. They have since divorced, and like other couples I have known whose marriages have ended, I can think back on having witnessed similar types of painful conversations. Knowing the consequences of this behavior now, I will never again be silent in the face of active destructive or even passive destructive behavior.

But it doesn't have to be as extreme as this couple's example. For instance, your sister gets a job promotion. You respond with congratulations, followed by asking her if that means she'll have to be away from her family for more hours – and - is that really a good thing? It can be subtle. You may even mean well and not even be aware of the harmful effect you are creating.

Be My Hero

If the Active Constructive Response (ACR), as it is called, or "Be My Hero," which is my preferred moniker, does not come naturally or easily for you, then make the conscious effort to respond with heartfelt enthusiasm, even if you feel it's a bit forced at first. Over time it will come more naturally to you, and you will cherish this straightforward and accessible tool. The positive emotions you will generate in yourself and the other person build trust, intimacy, wellbeing, happiness, stability, and even self-esteem.

Sometimes, if we are feeling down, stressed or preoccupied, it may be hard to respond with genuine vitality to the child who is jumping for joy over a new toy, the friend whose daughter just got engaged, the coworker who got a new dog, the nephew who won a scholarship, etc. But studies show that when we can bring a positive response and celebrate other people's wins, the joy is contagious and, they in turn, lift our spirits.

And since this dimension of SPIRE is about nurturing a constructive relationship with self, do unto yourself what you would gladly do to others. Be your own hero. Don't deflect or diminish a compliment when it comes your way, and celebrate, savor, and own your wins and victories. Write down a list of all your accomplishments over the past year, list the ways you have grown, the lessons you've learned, the challenges you have met or overcome - and see your worth come alive on paper.

"E" – EMOTIONAL: Reaching Towards Resilience and Positivity

What's Your Explanatory Style?

In his ground-breaking book, *Learned Optimism*, Martin Seligman explains two ways of looking at life: either as an optimist or a pessimist. Where they differ is their explanatory style, how they go about explaining the events that take place in their lives.

The pessimist tends to "awful-ize" events, takes situations personally, views harmful conditions as long-lasting, if not permanent, and allows the ensuing upset to permeate all areas of life. The optimist, on the other hand, doesn't anticipate defeat, but when it happens, sees defeat as a challenge to be surmounted, limits the setback to a pertinent and present situation, and sees the cause as something external – not as a fundamental flaw or irredeemable defect of character.

Note the correlation between pessimism and the "fixed-mindset" as well as optimism and the "growth-mindset." People who have an optimistic explanatory style as their default way of seeing life will view setbacks as a learning opportunity, and vice versa. I must confess that I am by nature (and probably nurture) in the latter category. Fortunately, as we now know, optimism is not just awarded to the winners of the happy gene lottery, but that anyone can learn the skills that will create more optimism.

It may be unrealistic for pessimists to completely flip their nature, especially when they have experienced many years of ingrained habitual ways of thinking and processing their experiences. A realistic goal is to move towards optimism while decreasing the symptoms of pessimism. You don't have to compare or measure yourself against other people; rather, the idea is to make incremental changes.

Here is one tool that may help. Drawing on the cognitive, emotional, and behavioral techniques of Aaron Beck and Albert Ellis, Seligman developed the "ABCDE" model of learning optimism:

- **Adversity**: The situation that calls for a response
- **Belief**: How we interpret the event
- **Consequence**: The way that we behave, respond, or feel
- **Disputation**: The effort we expend to argue or dispute the belief
- **Energization**: The outcome that emerges from trying to challenge our beliefs

When you catch yourself regressing to a pessimistic explanatory mode, you now have greater awareness. You can engage your thoughts and check in with what you are making the experience mean. And by challenging the validity of these thoughts, you can redirect to a more positive and constructive range of responses.

To Conclude

It is precisely when life is out of control, and when you feel unmoored, as if you have lost your bearings that it is the optimal time to turn your attention inward and work on yourself. One of the essential qualitative differences between humans and the rest of creation lies in the ability to go against instinct and grow when it would be so much easier to shrink. And so, we end where we began: *"Who am I in the presence of this?"* The SPIRE model for whole-being answers that question by helping you grow towards your highest and best self. When you craft your own life, you are the fashioner and the object, the potter and the vessel. The elements of SPIRE are merely the tools that wait for your hand, your heart, and your soul to shape.

The next 24 hours contain 1,440 minutes. You will never relive these moments again, and if you waste them mindlessly, you will never get them back. My hope for all of you is to savor life, surrounded by loving people that lift your soul, doing what makes you authentically happy, harvesting meaning, and making a difference. May you live life every day to the fullest, while increasing your capacity to live with hope, optimism, and joy.

Hanna Perlberger | Miami, Florida
https://www.ayearofsacredmoments.com

Hanna is the founder of the Shalom Bayit Project, on the web at (www.shalombayitproject.com), a worldwide movement devoted to helping Jewish singles and couples transform their lives by learning the skills that nurture constructive and positive relationships with self and others. She is a former divorce attorney and graduate and former teaching assistant for the Certificate Program in Positive Psychology with the Wholebeing Institute. Hanna brings a holistic approach to finding solutions that are "heart-based and soul-driven."

Hanna is the author of *A Year of Sacred Moments: The Soul Seeker's Guide to Inspired Living* (available on Amazon), which takes readers of any background on a guided interactive journey of self-discovery. She is a regular contributor to Chabad.org, and TheJewishWoman.org, Hanna writes on topics from a fresh new perspective that combines Judaism with positive psychology.

SECTION 1: WHAT IS HAPPINESS? | DONNA MARTIRE MILLER

Joseph Bologna

Current neuroscience shows that our brain, at any age, is malleable! We can learn, grow and change!

WHY NOT YOU? This is the question to ask yourself. Why not? Why can't you be happier? Why engineer smallness in your life versus giving yourself permission to live a big, colorful, more comfortable, healthier life. Research now proves that we are capable of much more than we think in our lives; it can be everything and anything that we can imagine.

Setting an intention to begin a new habit that will help you to become happier actually starts a brand-new neuropathway. This pathway enables you to change, to transform, and to manifest the intention. All we have to do is take some action steps, and the impossible becomes possible. I know this to be true from my own experiences!

Happier people benefit in many ways, as we have mentioned. Good health is one of the side effects. Good health alone will not make you happy, but research shows that happiness affects your health significantly!

In the following chapters, you will meet Shawn, Jane, Alice, Sue, and Christine. You will see how our *IDEAL* self, our best self, is discovered from what we have learned from our life experiences, the demands in our society that we strive to live up to, the character strengths that help us to rise up no matter the challenge and ways to move towards an idealized version of ourselves created from what we admire most in people, especially our role models. Realizing these things gives us a road map to our own authenticity.

You will begin to see "what's right with me." As a counselor, I remember working with a young man who had many hardships to face. I worked with him on his *IDEAL* self and his character strengths … I will never forget the day he looked up from the table at me with tears in his eyes and said, "I am really a good person, aren't I." It was the first time he met his IDEAL self, the first step towards his ability to believe that he mattered, he belonged, and he deserved to be happy.

> *"If you want to awaken all of humanity, then awaken all of yourself. If you want to eliminate the suffering in the world, then eliminate all that is dark and negative in yourself. Truly, the greatest gift you have to give is that of your own self transformation.*
>
> - Lao Tzu

The Journey Home to My Ideal Self

-Shawn Fink

It was a beautiful sunny day. The leaves were falling from the trees and I had a skip in my step that I hadn't seen in a while.

As I walked with a playlist playing in my earbuds, I had a distinct feeling of hope in my heart.

The world seemed perfect at that moment. But most of all, I was happy with myself and my life.

It was the week after I returned from Kripalu for the WholeBeing Institute's retreat for the Certification in WholeBeing Positive Psychology program. I was on the Kripalu campus along with 25 other women who were all working toward certification. I had spent a week tending to myself in a way I hadn't done in years.

I woke up early and caught the sunrise over the lake. I ate healthfully and mindfully in silence each morning in the cafeteria from a fresh buffet of nourishing foods and fresh apple cider as dessert. I moved my body joyfully throughout the week as well. I hiked each day around the Kripalu campus. I danced in classes called Let Your Yoga Dance. I did yoga. I walked through the woods and spent a lot of time outside in nature. Best of all, I connected with like-minded women who were traveling a similar journey as I was and so the conversations were deep and fulfilling. That week was my happy place, in other words. And, the after-effect lingered. For the first time in a long time, I felt … whole. I felt strong. I felt extraordinary. I felt confident. I felt fearless. I loved who I had become.

Something Was on the Horizon

But there was this curiosity forming. Why did I feel so different, I wondered? What was I doing differently to feel so good? Why was I suddenly feeling amazing rather than just OK? And, most of all: Could I make it stick? I felt desperate to understand what I was doing to feel so good and what I could do to make sure that feeling stayed with me indefinitely. Now, I look back and see that at that moment I was living life as my *Ideal Self*, a positive psychology term that defines the best self that we aspire to be in our lives. That day, I was able to see myself as someone content, resilient and, confident.

What worried me, though, was the fear of not being able to keep it all going for myself. As a busy working mother and activist and volunteer in my community, I worried I wouldn't be able to keep this magic going for myself. I worried old patterns of fear and ignoring myself and my needs would return and I would fall into a downward negative spiral of feeling low more frequently.

Embracing the Fearless Inner Kiddo

That elated, confident feeling that day on my walk reminded me of when I was a child and my best friend Mary Anne and I would run around my grandparent's huge 50 acres of woods, or her family's farm pretending we were Supergirl. We were fearless. We climbed rock walls and trees. We leapt from rock to rock in the creek. We ran through fields imagining we were chasing villains. Mary Anne always had a superpower of vision. She could see anything, anywhere. And I always had the superpower of being able to hear anything – even the inaudible sounds of the imaginary world we were creating.

We spent hours and hours running through fields, forests, and creeks pretending we were superhuman and, therefore, could do anything, save everyone and be anywhere. Oh, if that were only possible as an adult.

The superpowers must have worked wonders because we always managed to rise from the pitfalls of our adventures such as the ravenous teeth of dogs chasing us through the woods and even my great fall squarely into a manure pit, losing a shoe in the process. We definitely got into some trouble back in those days.

But we were fearless and confident and anything was possible. Sometimes I feel so desperate to go back to feeling that way. We didn't question ourselves. We just acted on our intuition and trusted ourselves immensely. We were happy and content playing and using imagination that allowed us to feel free and courageous.

Somewhere, though, along the way, I lost sight of that little girl, the one who felt she could do anything, the one who wasn't afraid to take risks and live out loud. The one who wasn't afraid to step into her personal power and claim her voice. Anxiety, fear, and self-doubt took over.

On Losing My Authentic, Courageous Self

Somewhere along the way in my life, I lost my authentic, courageous self. I grew up, started adulting, became a mother of twins, lost my entire sense of self, and, with that, my unwavering courage and confidence as well.

Over the years I poured my heart and my soul into my children, my family, and then eventually my work. I lost my ability to surrender to courage and allow anything to be possible. I forgot what it was like to dream bigger. I forgot what it was like to want to fly. I forgot what it was like to believe in yourself so wholeheartedly that anything is possible.

Instead, I was caught on what many women experience as life on the hamster wheel. I was busy getting up each day doing everything I needed to do and serving my family and my clients but not as much for myself.

Life has a way of taking over even when we know better, even when we know something needs to change. Small inconsequential urgencies become the daily to-do list and the next thing you know you haven't fully lived your life the way you truly wished. The truth is, though, I was living a life with a lot of beautiful moments filled with stress and responsibilities. I cared a lot about everyone and everything – and this is part of who I am – and I struggled to take quality time for myself to do what matters most for me, my health and my well-being.

As a result, I was not as carefree and relaxed at times. I knew I wanted to work on that side of myself. If I allowed myself, I would lean too far into over-thinking, perfectionism, and over-planning a perfect life that never pans out.

The result was that I was always living just one tier away from thriving. I would have thriving moments but then I would slip into a downward spiral of negative thinking and seeing myself as someone who wasn't good enough. I was so close to being who I wanted to be except for how I treated myself. I wasn't kind to myself. I wasn't good to myself. I wanted to become my own best friend. Realizing that I may be able to change how I experience happiness is exactly what led me on the journey to positive psychology.

Learning about and applying the strategies in positive psychology allowed me to finally embrace all of me. The whole of me. The good and the bad. This is what we refer to as the authentic self.

The Bumpy Journey to my Ideal Self

I'll never forget the tears that fell from my eyes that day sitting on the floor at Kripalu while beginning our work on resilience – a crucial exercise to help us understand our authentic and ideal selves a little bit better. Our instructor, Maria Sirois, asked us to write about a challenging time in our lives and what inner resources we used to get through it. I didn't have to think twice about my difficult moment.

I instantly began writing about the loneliness and isolation that I had felt 13 years prior – when I was a brand-new mom of twin baby girls and I had very little outside help or support and no time to take for myself to be a whole person.

My family had just moved 700 miles away and even though I read a ton about being pregnant with twins, I didn't actually know how to soothe two crying babies at once or how to feed two babies at once or, how to find time for myself when there weren't any breaks. My husband, who was also sleep-deprived, worked long hours out of town each day.

That first year was so hard and exhausting. I cried a lot. To me, when I looked back at those early years, I saw nothing but failure, weakness and, that I was not enough as a mother.

I remember every moment of not being enough such as when I realized it was not possible for me to breastfeed and when I couldn't soothe my baby who cried and cried for hours seemingly every night.

I remembered the long, lonely days. It was just me and the babies and how I wished someone would offer to bring me a coffee from the cafe or just stop by and ask how I was doing. It was the most beautiful time of my life because I was becoming a mother but it was also a very challenging time in my life.

And so, sitting on the floor that October morning at Kripalu, journal and pen in hand, writing about a stressful time in my life when I was also at my best, was truly a powerful exercise for me. It was on that day of our retreat when I realized that my ideal self is already within me – and always accessible in any challenging moment. I had already been using my *Ideal Self* all of these years – I just wasn't aware of it until positive psychology brought it to my attention.

The *Ideal Self* exercise begins by thinking about the people in our lives who we admire and are inspired by because of their qualities and characteristics. These can be strangers or people we know. We take time to list the qualities they exhibit that we like and appreciate in them.

Once we have that list, we start to imagine ourselves with some or all of those qualities that we appreciate in them and we write out a personal list of *I AM Statements*. This vision of who we could be is our *Ideal Self*.

I Am Statements can be anything from I am kind to I am present to I am courageous and anything you can imagine for yourself.

THE IDEAL ME WAS BEGINNING TO EMERGE

I sat there on the floor writing an exhaustive list of the strengths and values I used as I navigated those long, hard three years of early motherhood. I began to see proof of my own resiliency. And as I wrote the list, tears ran down my face.

I realized just how much I gained in my life from that very challenging time when I felt depleted and exhausted and alone. In fact, it was those years that led me to the confident, courageous, and wise woman I have become now. I am strong, resilient, and wise.

It was back then during those early years of motherhood I was searching for hope and joy in challenging times when one of the lifelines that showed up for me was a book on mindful motherhood where the author wrote about how hard motherhood was and how to stay present and mindful through the challenging moments.

This book and my love of learning and spirituality saved me and led me on a spiritual quest to learn more about mindfulness, Zen living, and Buddhism, a religion I hadn't known much about before those desperate days.

I also began to study other religions and spiritual practices – I became grounded in learning and infusing my life with spirituality as a main source of strength.

Spiritual well-being continues to be one of my strongest assets as a life coach for women who are trying to cultivate unshakable resilience and well-being to do courageous things in their life. I am still passionate about spiritual rituals, practices, and routines and keep these in my daily work and personal life as a source of strength and hope.

Back in those early motherhood days, I also began a daily gratitude journal practice where I write at least three to five things down that I am thankful for each day. One of the more powerful lists I created in my first journal was a list of 50 people I was grateful for to help offset the feelings of isolation and loneliness. My daily gratitude practice is one of my favorite practices that I have kept up with now for 11 years.

I like to tell people that gratitude is my superpower – It's a practice that I have taught to thousands of women around the world. Immersing myself in the power of gratitude turned all of my hurt about my family moving so far away when I needed them most into a softened awareness of complicated grief.

But there was more, I realized, sitting on the floor that day at Kripalu. Being a mom of twins required so much of me that I did effortlessly and without thought or striving. It required self-trust, self-compassion, and perseverance. I learned not to give up even though there were many times I wanted to run away from the crying, the hard work, the sleepless nights, and the incredibly long days. I learned not to give up on myself, too.

It required creativity and resourcefulness to navigate through the boring, mundane moments of sitting around, waiting for babies to get to their next stage, or watching them sleep or waiting for them to fall asleep, or waiting for them to wake up.

And, even more powerful, was this fact: I eventually built a business during those years showing other moms how to cultivate unshakable resilience and well-being. I started blogging and eventually starting leading online classes. I showed courage and appreciation for beauty and excellence. I demonstrated social intelligence and leadership.

And, of course, there was so much love. Love that drew me to staying home with my babies. Love that led me to create fun activities and explore the world. And, with that, a love of learning. I loved showing them the world. I loved teaching them and encouraging them to learn.

Those hardest years where I felt so lonely and alone and exhausted were how I learned to be so resilient.

Grounding into the Authentic | Aspiring to the Ideal

Those years were what made me "me," and suddenly I saw parts of my ideal self as being exposed. And then again the tears fell. I felt seen. I felt raw. I felt vulnerable. And I felt empowered.

Those years had been the hardest years of my life – at least until navigating a pandemic with those beautiful twin girls – now teenagers – made me focus even more strongly as to what it means to visualize my best possible self.

The ideal self-concept is about visioning a future self that is the person you most aspire to be. And, part of the process of determining your best possible self is understanding who you are right now – your authentic self – and who you could be at your best and living into your best self. I like to think of this best possible self as my extraordinary self. When I operate from the traits and strengths of my ideal self, I am always at my best in the present moment as well.

There are many pathways to discovering your best possible self – or ideal self. One is what we did during our retreat where we looked back at a moment in our lives where we struggled and yet managed to get through it.

Another pathway to your ideal self is to imagine yourself in the future when you are living your best possible life. Who are you at that moment? What are you doing? How are you living and being in your life?

For me, the most profound work begins with the grounding work of uncovering who we are at our core – unlocking the messy and the magnificent. It helps to know our shadows and our strengths before we start envisioning something more for ourselves.

The aspirational work of living into a higher, or best self, is where we get to be the change we want to see in our own lives or in the world. This appeals to me as a high-achieving woman who values personal growth. The ideal self-work that we learn in positive psychology has not only empowered me, it has also changed how I show up every single day for my life, for my clients and, for my community.

The ideal self – or the best possible self-concept is about visualizing and naming who you want to be in the future. One of my favorite ways to encourage my clients to find their best possible self is to think back to a time in their life when they handled a challenging time well. A time in their life they look back on as being a very successful moment and asking themselves what they were doing and experiencing to thrive at that time.

You might be wondering how you can identify your Ideal Self. I offer a lot of journaling prompts to my clients to help them dig a little deeper below the surface to figure this out.

Here are three prompts that one can use to get started with a personal Ideal Self-awareness journey:

1. When you are your best self, who are you and what qualities do you share with other people?
2. Thinking back to a memory from your past when you were at your absolute best, what qualities did you demonstrate that stand out strongly for you?
3. If you could be your best self for someone who needs you the most right now, what qualities would you need to tune into?

The ideal self is aspirational, but it's also based on reality. So often my ideal self traits are already within me. I just need to wake them up and focus on them. I find, too, now that I know myself so intimately that my ideal self doesn't change that much. And she's almost always a lot like that little girl playing Supergirl on the farm in the early 1980s.

She is courageous, serving the world and helping others, strong, and listens very well to what others are experiencing.

She is patient and adventurous and spends a lot of time outdoors. And she listens to her intuition and practices a lot of self-trust to do the hard things in life.

Anyone who wants to feel more empowered, be their best self, or who is struggling with a challenging situation can use the ideal self-concept. I work with my high-achieving clients on developing their extraordinary superpowers so they can live and lead with more courage and creativity.

That day on the floor at Kripalu, I realized that now, in the present moment with twin teenage girls, I have everything I need to get through the hard situations unfolding in my life now.

I realized that during that first year as a mother, I relied on so many inner strengths to get me through – strengths that I still carry inside and can tap into any time I want when I tune into my Ideal Self.

My ideal self – the one I aspire to be and the one that is already within me if I allow it to lead – is grateful, courageous, tenacious, loving, kind, and resilient. And so when the pandemic hit and life grew increasingly harder and harder, I found myself creating powerful exercises to keep tuning into my ideal self.

I came to see my ideal self not as aspirational but rather as a bridge to the inner strengths and resources I already have within me – traits I've had since I was that little girl running through the fields free and happy. I only need to trust myself and imagine my adult self as a powerful woman with superpowers that are always at her fingertips, ready to be strong, courageous, and able to do anything. I only need to believe in myself – and that my best possible self is there already within me. Always.

Shawn Fink | York, Pennsylvania

https://shawnfink.com

Shawn Fink Strategics LLC

Shawn Fink is the host of The Brave Yes, a podcast that explores the intersection of resilience and authenticity.

She is a Brave Life & Leadership Coach. She graduated from the CiWPP program in April 2020 – amid the world's shut down from the pandemic.

She is a mom of twin teenage girls and loves to be in nature.

"That day on the floor, I realized that I had everything I needed to get through the present moment of any hard situation."

- Shawn Fink

To Be Spiritual Is To Be Amazed

-Sue Knight Deutsch

The train rumbled along the tracks through the English countryside, the dot of trees in the distance quickly coming into view, then passing by in a flash. The clouds in the sky changed shape and color as my eyes instinctively darted back and forth to watch the scenery as I looked through the windows. The carriage gently rocked from side to side to the rhythm of clickety-clack, clickety-clack, lulling me into a hypnotic space. It was 1968. Not quite yet thirteen years old, I was accustomed to this one-hour train ride I had been making by myself for a year from my foster family in Letchworth to spend each weekend with my birth mother in London. This Friday, however, was a rare Friday. I noticed there were no other passengers in the rail carriage and found myself alone between stops. I had the entire rail carriage all to myself with its bench seats facing each other and open spaces to walk on.

I had boarded the train feeling rootless and homeless, unsure of my mother's mood that awaited me at my final destination. Now here I was, cradled in the warmth of the carriage, my body in rhythm with the motion of the train, and suddenly, a song came into my head. Without the judgmental eyes of an audience and with all the conviction, commitment, and strength of my young body, I stood up, flung my arms out to the side in an embrace, eyes turned toward the sky outside the train windows, and belted out Paul Anka's song "You are my destiny/you are what you are to me/you are my happiness/ that's what you are." I was now blissfully happy standing there in my school uniform, singing at the top of my lungs.

After a while, the train slowed; instead of the trees moving quickly by and the landscape changing by the second in neat squares of farmland with the odd cow grazing, buildings came into sight. A platform with people on it came into view. I sat down again, shifting my school satchel and little suitcase as passengers boarded the train to end my reverie.

Back in the 'real' world again, the sense of not belonging anywhere or to anyone returned, and yet there was something inside of me that had reached out through music and foreshadowed the life I would create, which would take me along my spiritual path to find my happy place.

The weekly train ride continued for the next three years back and forth, back and forth. Although I would never have a carriage alone again, and it was the same train, the same countryside, the same departure and destination, with the same foreboding of what might happen that weekend, the journey itself was always different by how I chose to pay attention. I noticed the little details with a sense of wonder at the world and the beauty of nature passing before my eyes when I looked out the train window. Although the bench seats of the carriage had been empty that day, in a sense, they had allowed me to have something greater as my witness.

I did not know on that train ride that I would leave my foster home for good and be sent to live with my mother a mere three years later. Yet somehow, I 'knew,' simply in the words "you are my destiny." Not that my mother was my destiny, but rather, the force I reached out to through the music would be the home I was so desperately looking for to be my anchor. It seemed like every time I felt lost or that I didn't belong anywhere, I would turn to that force that often spoke to me through music. Sometimes, I called it "God," and yet it was beyond the God I had read about in the Bible. It wasn't confined to the synagogue of my first home, the church of my next home, or the Friends' Meetings of my next home, or any of the other homes I grew up in. Year after year, as I searched for my real home, the one where I would feel secure, where no one could tell me upon waking that it was time to move on, there was this energy that seemed to follow me. That nameless, faceless Source I sang to; all I needed to do was pay attention. Always, I would be amazed by the joy I found in it.

There would be many other journeys on trains, planes, boats, and ferries to many other countries. Each of them held the wonder of other worlds to discover within my world. In America, I would find the family I had been born into; in Israel, I would find a whole people who spoke the Hebrew language to communicate; until then, I had only used Hebrew in its archaic form as a language of prayer. More importantly, I felt like I belonged to a people there, no matter my beliefs. In Cyprus, I found that same happy force on the shores of Paphos, looking out at the ocean where Aphrodite was said to have arisen from the sea. Eventually, home became the one I created with my husband and children in California. I continued to think in terms of music and learned to pay attention to that little voice inside and follow what my spirit urged me to do. I discovered that I had many voices. After I turned forty, I trained my singing voice, studied and trained to become an ordained Cantor, a Jewish Spiritual Leader. I thought I had finally found home. And then, my husband died. It was the same year that our youngest child had left home. I was alone again, in the same house, and yet it no longer felt like home. Eleven weeks later, I joined the mission to Poland with the Cantors Assembly, a trip that had been planned before my husband died. I was asked to chant from the Torah in the barracks of Auschwitz, the infamous Nazi concentration camp. Fresh with grief over the loss of my husband, standing in this terrible place, I felt the added palpable grief of the murder of millions of my people so many years ago, which included family members of my foster parents in Letchworth. Yet, I was alive to chant from the Torah in the midst of this devastation. I thought of Viktor Frankl's central question, "Who am I in the face of this?"

It still took me a year to break open. I asked myself, how could I be happy again? I went out running and threw on a shirt that my husband had given me twenty years before when he returned from the Esalen Institute, a retreat and adult education center in Northern California. Again, I turned my eyes to the sky and, through tears, asked, "Where should I go?" I looked down at my shirt, and written across it was the word "Esalen." I took it as a sign, and five weeks later, I drove along the California coast to the Esalen Institute in Big Sur, listening to music along the way, both in my head and on the radio, and sometimes just the music of ocean waves that accompanied me on my journey. I remember calling a friend on the way and leaving a message that with every mile I drove, it was as if my shoulders became lighter, and I was starting to feel that joy again. He told me later that he could hear something akin to ecstasy in my voice.

Immediately upon my arrival at Esalen, I felt my soul expand. I was given my own room with a waterfall outside my window, and I began my workshop "Water in the Desert: Faith, Hope, and Awe in a Time of Loss" with Dr. Maria Sirois that evening. Over the next five days, I felt a shift. In an experiential and storytelling way, Maria introduced our group to the basic principles of Positive Psychology. In them, I recognized that all along, I had been using my character strengths of Spirituality, Appreciation of Art and Beauty, Honesty, and Perseverance to build resilience. Only now was I being given strategies to create a thriving life after loss, and I experienced my first guided meditation from Maria. Most importantly, I learned that the qualities of being peaceful, centered, and home were inside of me and were something I could always return to. At night, I would go and soak in the mineral hot tubs overlooking the ocean, listen to the crash of the ocean waves below, and look up at the stars. Here, with no artificial light, the stars were more breathtaking than I had ever seen. I was astonished to clearly see the Milky Way and felt like I was an integral part of the universe and yet a tiny, infinitesimal particle of it. I would later have a similar experience while at Hollyhock and on the island of Kauai with people I had met at Esalen. When I returned home, a Rabbi colleague reached out to me to ask me how I was. I told him that I was concerned. "Here I am, Jewish clergy, and I'm finding solace in Buddhism!" I confessed.

"Oh, that's fine," he said. "Buddhism and Judaism work well together. Read *The Jew in the Lotus* by Rodger Kamenetz." I was relieved.

My experience at Esalen that week was the beginning of another journey that would take me to other spiritual centers and discover other spiritual guides. When I saw that Maria would be teaching a workshop at Hollyhock (another retreat and learning center in British Columbia) and wanting to reconnect with her as well as further my knowledge and experience of Positive Psychology, I took a seaplane to reconnect with her there. When first at Esalen, after I had seen an Intuitive and shared with the group, Maria mentioned an Intuitive, Bev Martin. After a phone session with Bev when I returned home, I took another plane to Portland, Oregon, to meet her, forming a connection that would lead to Bev bringing my first book out of me and continues to this day. At Esalen, Maria introduced me to the poetry of David Whyte and his poem, *Sweet Darkness* whose ending lines, "sometimes it takes darkness, and the sweet/confinement of your aloneness/ to learn/anything or anyone/that does not bring you alive/is too small for you" so resonated with me, that I flew to Seattle, Washington to meet the poet himself. There were many return trips to Esalen, where I learned from other teachers and furthered my practice of meditation with Dr. Rick Jarow. He would lead me to discover the Ananda Ashram in New York. Through these travels, I was on a quest, paying attention and finding my writing and speaking voice to tell about it.

Being accepted into the Clergy Leadership Program at the Institute for Jewish Spirituality gave me permission to bring it all together in my calling as a Jewish Spiritual Leader. During four retreats on both East and West Coasts interspersed with online learning over an eighteen-month program, I was able to connect with other leaders of like minds. I was introduced to spiritual texts, sang wordless melodies in community, meditated both sitting and walking, and ultimately realized that it was time to leave my sixteen-year pulpit.

On our four five-day retreats in the Institute for Jewish Spirituality's Clergy Leadership Program, we spent 18 hours out of every 24 in silence. At first, I hated it. I was used to living alone and being in silence. It was difficult to be around people and not even gesture to them. Something fascinating happened, though. My physical senses became more acute, my attention heightened, and my sense of wonder and amazement grew. Sometimes, as we sat in silence eating our meals, it seemed that the food tasted more intense. I ate more slowly. While I was used to saying a quick prayer of gratitude before eating, now I would stare at the food and consider where it actually came from, who prepared it and served it, and gratitude swelled throughout my being. I would pay attention to the people at the table and swore I could 'hear' what they were thinking, and later during speaking hours, I discovered I had been correct.

After our final retreat at the Pearlstone Retreat Center in Maryland, everyone had returned home, and I was waiting for the shuttle to take me to the airport. On this particular day, while I was waiting, I was thinking about my journey home and what my next steps might be when I got back to California. I took a walk through the beautiful Pearlstone grounds. There were signs here and there, sometimes with an explanation of the flora and fauna, and sometimes with a quote. With my ears attuned to the silence, the buzzing of insects and the chirping of birds' songs seemed loud and harmonious. I recorded the sound so that I could meditate to it later. Along the grass path, I came upon an archway to a garden with a quote by Abraham Joshua Heschel:

> Our goal should be to live life in radical
> amazement ... get up in the morning and look
> at the world in a way that takes nothing for
> granted. Everything is phenomenal; everything is
> incredible; never treat life casually. To be spiritual
> is to be amazed.

Ah yes! I thought. This is what it is! Time seemed to slow down in that moment. My heart was beating in rhythm with the sounds of nature around me and the pulse of the earth, which grounded me where I stood.

I don't believe in coincidences. When I returned home, there was an email from Maria Sirois announcing another yearlong course for a Certificate in Positive Psychology through the Wholebeing Institute in Massachusetts with an invitation to register. I knew that Maria had been teaching this course along with Dr. Tal Ben-Shahar and Megan McDonough for years, and it was never the 'right' time for me to take it. I had left my pulpit three months prior, and now I had no full-time pulpit to constrain my time, even though I was in the middle of becoming certified as an ICF coach. Although now wasn't the time to be spending money, I knew in my gut that the moment had arrived. I listened to that inner voice, registered, and five months later, taking more planes, trains, and taxis, I flew to my first Positive Psychology immersion at Kripalu, another retreat center on the East Coast. As I danced my yoga with Megha, chanted Om and breathed deeply on a meditation cushion, listened to Maria talk about resilience, Megan talk about the Wholebeing concept of SPIRE, the "S" representing Spirituality, I knew in my bones that in the Science of Happiness I was about to learn, and the people in my cohort I would get to know, that my life would be changed. I had made the right choice.

When Tal spoke about the connection between Buddhism and Positive Psychology, I thought back to my conversation with my colleague after Esalen. I had come a long way. Studying psychology in college in London decades ago, I had been trained to look for what was wrong and work to fix it. With Positive Psychology, I learned to pay attention to what was working well and grow more of it while at the same time holding space for what was not working. Moreover, I could teach it to others, as this capacity is open to anyone who chooses to pay attention and build on their strengths. The fact that there was research and even conventions on happiness amazed me.

All faith traditions have built within them a mindfulness practice, all of them tapping into that quiet inner space where the spirit is born. And there's scientific research to show that it makes us happier, with strategies to implement them.

During this past year of the pandemic, even living by myself in my home, the same one I raised my children in, I have never felt alone. When I became sick with the Coronavirus, what I noticed most was the kindness of others, from the doctors and my family who called me every day after I was discharged from the hospital, to the friends and neighbors who brought me food; I took none of it for granted. I was simply amazed.

Although I instinctively look to the skies for inspiration, be it the moon and stars at night or the rising and setting of the sun, now I have made it a practice to go out each night to look at the stars and the moon, and the sunset and sunrise of each day. No sunrise or sunset is the same, and I never take for granted that it happens, even though I know the sun will rise and set each day. Light always follows darkness, just as darkness follows light. Each day amazes me. I'm betting that my not quite thirteen-year-old self would sing about that, being home at last.

Sue Knight Deutsch | Laguna Hills, California

www.CantorSue.com

Sue Knight Deutsch is the author of *The Healing Hand: 5 discussions to have with the dying who are living* and is an internationally acclaimed speaker. Originally trained as a psychiatric social worker in her native England, she is an ordained Cantor, and received her hospice training while serving as the spiritual leader and chaplain of an Assisted Living facility in Orange County, California for sixteen years. With all her training, it was the experience of losing her husband to cancer in mid-life that deepened her calling.

Sue is an alumna of the Institute for Jewish Spirituality, an ICF credentialed Coach, and holds a Certificate in Positive Psychology through the Wholebeing Institute. She travels to speak and teach workshops on how to be present for those who are ill and their families, and grief resilience workshops based on Positive Psychology, as well as serving clients in her coaching practice while she continues to write. She can be reached at www.CantorSue.com.

Strength Based Living

-Jane S. Anderson

I cannot make my days longer, so I strive to make them better.
- Henry David Thoreau

If you could add hours to your day, what would you do with them?

I used to think having more hours would simplify my life. That it would relieve the guilt I felt as a single parent, allow me to spend more time with my two young children, and ease my demanding work schedule. It would hasten my recovery from cancer and allow my return to "normal" life more quickly. In short, I thought it would shift me toward better relationships, more accomplishments, and good health.

Right?

Unfortunately, no. In hindsight, this constant focus on what was wrong – problems, illness, and lack - kept me at a high stress and anxiety threshold. It often prevented me from building toward what's strong.

This shift from wrong to strong is pivotal to making our days better. It's not about ignoring or minimizing difficult emotions or circumstances but bringing balance to our lives by also focusing on what's positive and possible. I've learned firsthand that it's possible to lead a resilient and meaningful life even during the bleakest of times. Even during hardships like a global pandemic, a serious illness, or the heartbreaking loss of a loved one.

The toolbox I use is filled with tools from the scientific field of positive psychology, the study of human flourishing. By practicing these tools, virtually any moment, hour, day, week, even month can become better. We become better versions of ourselves as we face new possibilities, challenges, and everyday life. Not by manipulating external forces, but by relying on our own unique character strengths to build and sustain a life of substance.

Why Your Character Strengths Matter

These strengths are part of a scientific framework you can view on the internet at tinyurl.com/strengths-graphic. They include 24 capacities like perseverance, kindness, or fairness that reflect what's best in humans around the world, over time, and across religions. Deliberately engaging these character strengths helps you build what's strong – positive relationships, meaning and purpose, fairness, goodness, and excellence. They build your reserves of energy and effectiveness during times of ease. They also buffer you against the effects of stress when those reserves become depleted.

Whether you're a parent, young adult, leader, team member, retiree, student, or unemployed person facing an interesting challenge, a transition from one life phase to another, or a significant loss, character strengths are already part of your toolbox. It's a matter of discovering and applying them deliberately.

My Character Strengths Transformation

I discovered the power of my unique blend of character strengths while enrolled in an 11-month positive psychology certificate program at Wholebeing Institute.

I was at a crossroads in my life and feeling burned out by the demands of single parenting, a long recovery from cancer, and earning a living. I knew what I didn't want, but I had no clue what I did want.

At first, I wasn't able to recognize my own blend of strengths, much less figure out how to engage them deliberately. Nor did I have the language to describe them. I remember feeling profoundly sad. I could easily name things that needed improving. However, I couldn't acknowledge my best qualities or describe how they helped me cope, connect, and excel.

Through study, reflection, and practice, I began to experience how essential they are to happiness and success. As I gained confidence in knowing who I am and what I do when at my best, I began to craft my work and life around my own character strengths. Teaching, coaching, publishing a book, and launching a business around character strengths have transformed my life. By sharing character strengths work with others, I've witnessed countless others transform their relationships, work, and lives too.

Now It's Your Turn

To experience your own transformation, you don't have to do what I did. You can just start by launching or deepening your own character strengths journey. The results can seem magical at times, but it really boils down to science and practice.

Below are three short, research-based strengths practices for you to try. They're from my blog *A Series of Short Practices to Cultivate Strength and Resilience*. The blog was launched during the global COVID-19 pandemic to offer moments of respite, but the practices can apply to almost any situation you face. Many have found them eye-opening and helpful.

Each blog post has an introduction, context for the post, a short practice for you to try, and a reflection to help you process your experience. I hope you enjoy practicing these as much as I do!

BLOG POST #1 – SHIFT FROM WRONG TO STRONG

Published April 23, 2020

In these extraordinary times, we're encountering a dizzying array of unwanted challenges and disruptions in daily life. Many of us cannot connect in person with family, friends, and teammates. Others have lost work and opportunities. Sadly, there are even more tragic repercussions. It's enough to create a sense of hopelessness in even the most positive people.

Fortunately, research around character strengths shows us how to shift into what's strong to help us face virtually every situation with strength and resilience. Character strengths reflect who we are and how we contribute.

Since COVID-19 entered our lives, I've noticed that my top strength, creativity, is calling my name to help navigate difficult situations. For instance, during a stressful text exchange with my sister, I offered a few novel ways to solve a family problem. I was tempted to avoid replying – it was late on a Sunday evening, and I was tired. Creativity gave me the capacity to engage. Channeling creativity didn't change the stressor, but it shifted me toward my best, kept me grounded and allowed me to contribute from a position of strength.

Most likely, your signature strengths look different than mine. Your top strength might be hope, giving you the power to envision a positive, yet realistic, future. Or, your number one strength might be bravery, making you a force that gives a voice to the voiceless.

No matter your signature strengths, your unique contributions are sorely needed in your home life, work life and community.

But here's the thing: although the idea of engaging strengths seems appealing to virtually everyone, not everyone practices living into them. The value comes from putting them into practice.

The Inspiration

In my work with individuals and groups, I've noticed a variety of obstacles to living into one's strengths. Below are two of the most common:

- We don't have the language to describe what's good and strong within ourselves. Growing up, many of us learned to avoid speaking of ourselves in positive ways due to modesty concerns. We're good at describing what's wrong and what we can do better, but not who we are at our best.
- The human brain is hardwired to attend to what's wrong – problems, challenges and weaknesses. We're often not aware this is happening. What doesn't work attracts us like a magnet.

Luckily the first item can be addressed by taking the free, scientific character strengths assessment found at tinyurl. com/your-character-strengths, taken by more than 13 million people globally. In about 15 minutes, you can discover your unique strengths profile.

The second is more complex. Humans have a natural instinct dating back to ancient times to scan the environment for threats. This instinct remains active in us today. Although helpful in some circumstances, it's also a reason we can over-invest time and resources dwelling on what's wrong at the expense of what's strong.

There's so much that feels wrong about life during this pandemic, but you can shift into what's strong to feel a greater sense of ease, energy and flow. Research shows that building strengths is where our greatest contributions lie.

I invite you to experience for yourself how shifting from wrong to strong can create positive results. The following practice is inspired by the work of Michelle McQuaid, an expert in positive organizational leadership.

The Practice

For this practice, you'll need a pen and some paper.

1. Place a pen in your dominant hand, then write your full name.
2. Switch the pen to your non-dominant hand. Again, write your full name.
3. Describe the differences between your two experiences.

Many people describe writing with the non-dominant hand as more effortful, difficult, and time-consuming. They aren't as pleased with the outcome.

Often, this is what it feels like to improve a weakness. If you practiced writing with your non-dominant hand, you could probably improve over time. However, it would likely take many hours to progress, let alone achieve the same results.

Conversely, writing with the dominant hand typically has an ease and flow. It's faster and requires less effort. The results are pleasing. Often, this is what it feels like to build, and live into, our strengths.

The Reflection

Begin by bringing one of your strengths to mind. If you don't know your strengths, use the graphic at tinyurl.com/strengths-graphic as a reminder of all the strengths, and choose one that resonates with you right now. Then return to the reflection.

As I tackle my next challenge today, my strength of _____ can help me by _____.

Think of one way you can put this strength into action and then try it as you go forward. As you go about daily life, I hope you will remember this experience of shifting from wrong to strong and the positive differences in outcomes.

BLOG POST #2 – PRACTICE STRENGTHS-SPOTTING

Published September 11, 2020

If you've been around awhile, like I have, you'll probably remember Bobby McFerrin's 1988 award-winning hit song, "Don't Worry, Be Happy." It's also known among younger generations. Bobby McFerrin is famous for his a cappella songs. He gave a popular TED talk at the World Science Festival in 2009 in which he turned the whole audience into his musical accompaniment using just their voices.

The TED talk offers a clear example of someone in "the strengths zone" doing what he does best and being his most authentic. I sometimes use it in presentations to introduce strengths-spotting. Strengths-spotting is a powerful practice that helps us focus on the good and see ourselves and others through a lens of what's strong, rather than blame or what's wrong.

One of the best gifts you can give throughout the day is strengths-spotting. It's easy and intuitive to do. Find out why and how below, then practice strengths-spotting in your own work or life.

The Inspiration

Strengths-spotting is a gift we all deserve to receive more often, especially when confronted with times of high anxiety. This practice is about naming and valuing character strengths in each other, elevating who we are and what we do best. When someone else notices and values you for these qualities, you get the added bonus of feeling seen and understood for who you are. It's like looking through a magnifying glass, where the image on the other side suddenly becomes clear and true to its nature.

My clients consistently highlight strengths-spotting as a practice that changed their lives the most. They notice improvements in difficult relationships, better teamwork, and more confidence.

You can practice strengths-spotting each day, no matter the circumstances. You can apply this practice in a family, work, or social setting. You can also practice it with acquaintances and people you just met, like the cashier at the grocery store, or your favorite movie or book characters. You can even practice it with that person that constantly rubs you the wrong way.

To easily learn and practice strengths-spotting, Dr. Ryan Niemiec, education director at the VIA Institute on Character, suggests using the SEA approach (spot, explain, appreciate).

First, pause to notice and name the strengths you see. In other words, **spot** them in action. This can be within yourself or others around you – your kids who picked up their toys without being asked (kindness) or your co-worker who supported your idea even though others didn't (bravery).

Next, **explain** the details or context in which you spotted the strengths in action. What was the person doing? Who were they with? What was happening?

Last, describe the impression this person's strengths left on the situation at hand, on others, or you. Why did you **appreciate** the use of these strengths? How did this person's strengths create a positive result or affect you personally?

It's always nice to have someone recognize you for a positive contribution you've made. For example, "Jane, that blog post was really creative." But it's a richer experience when put into context and made personal.

> *Jane, your creative blog post "The Mindful Pause" gave me an easy but powerful tool I've shared with clients and friends. I also use it throughout the day to reduce anxiety. It helps me face what's next with clarity.*

It feels so good to hear about the impact I had on someone using my top strength creativity in my work!

Most people find spotting other people's strengths to be quite intuitive. Naming our own strengths, however, is a bit more difficult. Many of us don't feel comfortable describing ourselves in positive ways. Others don't have the language to describe our positive traits. For some, the discomfort is grounded in cultural norms.

Another challenge arises when someone in your life constantly tests your patience – that relative who gossips about family members or the co-worker who never seems prepared for the Zoom calls. Guess what? They have character strengths, too! Can you acknowledge them for their strengths?

Remember that strengths-spotting is a practice that can be practiced. Over time, you will become more effective and comfortable strengths-spotting yourself and others. Are you ready to practice? Follow the simple SEA approach below.

The Practice

1. Watch this 3-minute clip of Bobby McFerrin's 2009 TED talk at tinyurl.com/B-McFerrin-2009-TED.
2. Write down all the character strengths you see in Bobby, the gentlemen behind him, or the audience before him. Try to spot all 24. As a reminder, you can see all 24 strengths at tinyurl.com/strengths-graphic. Practice with your family or team if you like. Up the ante and create a reward for the person who spots the most strengths.
3. Use the SEA approach to spot, explain, and appreciate the strengths.
4. Next, apply the SEA approach to a personal situation in which you are interacting with your team, family, or others as you are out and about in your day.

The Reflection

As I practiced strengths-spotting, I noticed that _____.

What did you notice about shifts within yourself -- what were you thinking, feeling, or doing? What did you notice about others or how the situation shifted?

May you "SEA" a new perspective as you practice strengths-spotting today!

BLOG POST #3 – AMPLIFY A SIGNATURE STRENGTH

Published May 20, 2020

> *You can't be anything you want to be – but you can be a whole lot more of who you already are.*
> – Tom Rath, author and expert on workplace strengths

In a recent spring-cleaning project, I discovered a bin in the back corner of my basement. It held my high school yearbooks from decades ago. Feeling nostalgic, I picked one up and flipped through the colorful markings and handwritten notes left by my classmates.

Throughout the stories of misadventures, brief confessions of feelings, and bursts of teen-aged wisdom, I noticed one predominant theme: Never change.

"Stay who you are honeybuns," said one. "You're so fun – stay that way," said another.

Never change? Really?! It turns out, this is some of the best advice I've ever received.

The Inspiration

We often hear that one of the only constants in life is change. Through the ups and downs of my life – navigating single parenthood, overcoming cancer, and transitioning into a new career – I have found this to be true.

However, we can choose to keep what's best within us the same, and even develop those qualities. Then, "never change" truly is great advice. We know this to be true from research about signature strengths in the field of positive psychology.

Signature strengths are personality traits that reflect what's best within you. Research shows that people who focus on their signature strengths are more likely to flourish in their work; have less stress, anxiety and depression; have more confidence; and experience more positive outcomes in virtually every facet of life.

So, what are your best traits? If you aren't aware of your unique signature strengths, I invite you to discover them by taking the character strengths survey at tinyurl.com/your-character-strengths. Your signature strengths will be in the top 5-7 of your results.

I find it ironic that during my high school years, when everything seemed to be changing, my classmates and I urged each other to stay the same. Many yearbook comments reflected my signature strengths, which I lean on every day to face daily challenges and opportunities.

For example:

"You were a great listener when I had problems with my love life." (Perspective)

"No, seriously you are…always fun to be around." (Humor)

And a favorite: "… your personality is a rare, but good one."

That last comment was a testament to how a friend appreciated my uniqueness. It made me laugh out loud!

You don't need to make yourself over to transform your work or life. By focusing on your signature strengths, you can not only grow and change but also live more deeply into who you are. In Tom Rath's words, "… you can be a whole lot more of who you already are."

So, never change? Absolutely!

The Practice

Try living into a signature strength by following these two simple steps:

1. Develop an awareness of your signature strengths.
2. Practice engaging them with intention.

This practice will help you accomplish both.

I invite you to choose one signature strength. If you wish to skip taking the survey, choose one strength from this graphic at tinyurl.com/strengths-graphic.

Practice using the strength you've chosen in a new way. To challenge yourself, try engaging this strength in a new way each day for the next week to help you relax and de-stress, achieve a meaningful goal, overcome an obstacle to a goal, or make a deeper connection with someone important.

If you get stuck, please do not hesitate to reach out to me. I love helping people live into their signature strengths!

The Reflection

When using my signature strength of _____, I noticed that _____.

Take your time with this reflection. Perhaps journal about it or talk it through with someone you trust. You might notice that you felt more confident or energized, had an "aha" moment for an obstacle you faced or approached a situation or person with a different perspective.

Just notice what happens when you engage a signature strength, and feel free to try this practice with other signature strengths.

Keep Living Into Your Strengths

Whether you're new to character strengths or a seasoned strengths enthusiast, I hope you will continue practicing and living into your strengths. The world needs what you uniquely have to offer, so go forth and make each day better. May your presence in the world be fueled by your strengths.

Jane S. Anderson | Glen Ellyn, Illinois

www.StrengthBasedLiving.com

Jane S. Anderson is the founder of Strength Based Living, LLC (SBL), a business dedicated to helping people craft their work and lives around their character strengths. From the field of positive psychology, the scientific study of human flourishing, character strengths are 24 personality traits - like fairness and bravery - that lead to living a life of substance, even during dark times.

She is also the author of *30 Days of Character Strengths: A Guided Practice to Ignite Your Best*. This one-of-a-kind workbook offers a guided character strengths journey spanning 30 days with activities, reflection questions, and real-life examples. Jane offers strengths-based coaching, workshops, and presentations that demonstrate how character strengths can become pathways to transformation in personal and professional settings. Her blog offers strengths-based practices that can be put into action immediately.

As a seasoned positive psychology practitioner, workshop facilitator, speaker, and coach, Jane has helped hundreds of people apply their character strengths deliberately, introduce positive changes that last, and build more meaning, happiness, and success.

Her signature strengths are Creativity l Humor l Perspective

Choosing to Look, Learning to See

-Alice Dommert

It was a 30-day Challenge. I had a sinking feeling. Thirty days seemed like an eternity.

In the big picture of life, it's the blink of an eye. How much could happen? I'd made a choice and already come this far.

Chasing "success" had failed to deliver the happiness I'd dreamed of. I'd carefully designed a plan for my life that started on the pages of a pink-covered spiral notebook in 2nd grade. Over time I checked the boxes next to many of my goals. The plan was an excellent one...until it wasn't.

Sometimes life comes crashing down. Significant events mark clear turning points. For me, it was a slow erosion, and then the sudden realization that something had slipped away.

Lost Muchness

One night, on the couch with my two teenagers, we were watching the new version of Alice in Wonderland with Johnny Depp as the Mad Hatter. In this version, 19-year old Alice, feeling the stifling expectations of the society of 1871 London, receives an unwanted marriage proposal. Her heart sinks.

Out of the corner of her eye, she catches a glimpse of a white rabbit, says a polite "excuse me," and follows the rabbit down a deep rabbit hole. A disoriented Alice finds her "old" friends, though no one in Wonderland is sure she is "the right Alice" who had been there years before.

The Mad Hatter challenges a tiny, shrunken Alice, saying, "You're not the same as you were before. You were much more, *muchier*. You've lost your muchness," replies the Hatter. "My muchness?" Alice asks. "In there," the Hatter says as he points to her chest, "something's missing."

The Heroine's Journey

Over the next few days, I began to see the parallels in my story to Alice's. Somewhere along the path of my perfect, expected life, I, too, had lost my muchness. For the first time in my life, I had no plan.

The ancient Greeks to modern movie makers utilize a similar template for the stories we love the most–the hero's journey. The unexceptional girl is living life. Disruption arrives as the gateway to an adventure. Against the odds, she finds guides and experiences challenges along the way to the victory of transformation before finding her way back home.

Choosing to Look

Positive psychology gets misunderstood. It's not about constructing a life where you live in your "happy place" in eternal bliss, peace, and harmony with all sentient beings. It is the scientific study of how people can flourish and thrive. Positive psychology practices support personal agency, a leaning in to focus on what's working balanced with the reality that every human life will include episodes of disruption, challenge, and change. Tal Ben-Shahar shared in the early months of the COVID-19 quarantine that we can enter these episodes with fear or openness because these are "periods of time ripe for expedited growth."

To me, thriving means living a life of health, purpose, and joy. It means understanding my genius, my gifts, talents, and strengths. Then, there is a crevasse across the path. I can know my gifts, talents, and strengths. But then, what would it be like for me to step courageously into living my strengths fully for my joy and then offer them in service to humanity, *as my life*.

What might the world be like if we all did that?

As I stood at the precipice of my own heroine's journey, it felt much less glamorous than the way it's described in the stories. Fortunately, I was not alone. I'd been infected as I walked alongside my fellow CIPP sojourners as we spent a year together in the Wholebeing Institute's Certificate in Positive Psychology program. Their courage had been contagious.

We'd explored our character strengths by using the VIA Character Strengths assessment, www.viacharacter.org. It identifies what makes you feel authentic and engaged–the positive parts of your personality and aspects of your character, your innate abilities that you perform with ease. The results of my assessment arrived as a map I did not yet recognize that would guide me on my journey.

The 30 Day Challenge

I knew the basic tenets of a 30-day Challenge. Design a habit that would move me toward thriving. I'd pressed myself into some exercise and eating 30-day Challenges, which had become part of my life. This go-round, I wanted to find muchness. With these few clues, I decided to tap into the spirit of Alice and venture outside. I had a new iPhone and a newly discovered woods near my home. Maybe I'd find a rabbit to follow.

I decided I'd go outside for 30 days, take photos of "something" in Nature and then share one image a day on social media.

Curiouser and Curiouser

On day four, I charged out the door, phone in hand. With the looming pressure of an over-packed schedule for the day, I calculated I could be in the woods within a few minutes, snap a photo, edit it, and post it as I walked back.

Then I saw her–a tiny masterpiece. She looked like an artist's sketch. I dropped down flat on the ground to meet this tiny mushroom, eye to eye. The smell of the earthy mulch under her wrapped around me. I knew her kind. She had a life span of only a few fleeting hours. As I took the photos, the details of her underside gills, tinted with black ink, came into focus. My curiosity grew. Time slipped away. Something within me lit up and flickered like a sparkler.

Curiosity was the first quiver of my muchness that woke up in me that morning. I recognized that feeling of excitement from playing as a young child enveloped in a green room of the branches of a weeping willow on my grandparent's farm. It was a brightness of being fully in my senses and bolstered by the desire to explore the next discovery and delight. As a child, I was bold, wondering about why and how it all worked. I loved looking closer and following vibrant, bright colors and patterns to understand what was within.

The days ticked off on the calendar. On some walks, I'd focus on the tiniest of things. I wanted to get low, to zoom in, look at all the details. Other days, my eyes would shift, my perspective would broaden, and I'd take in the forest and the trees. With each day I spent in my woods, among the trees, my curiosity flamed into a steady fire. My serious, over-packed adult life had squelched my curiosity over the years. In my woods, over time, looking so closely, my curiosity came back to life.

Among the Trees

New guides arrived daily. The scent of honeysuckle, the bright black-eyed Susans, the sweet songs of the birds, the rustle of a red fox under the brush collected my attention and attuned me over and over again to look, to seek out the fleeting treasures being offered. Within the first few days I found a perfect sitting spot among the roots of a magnificent katsura tree.

The flotsam and jetsam of the to-dos and shoulds of daily life had in the past regularly littered my life. They kept me caught in the constant churning tide of my mind, forgetting that my body had senses. In the woods, the waves of my mind would settle and release me back into my body. Sight, smell, taste, and touch became invitations for alternate ways to experience life free of my thinking mind. Something was shifting in me, nudged by the tiny mushrooms, fliting butterflies, blooming flowers, and intricate trees' roots.

Mary Oliver's words arrived one day, bringing a voice to what was happening.

> *When I am among the trees,*
> *especially the willows and the honey locust,*
> *equally the beech, the oaks, and the pines,*
> *they give off such hints of gladness.*
> *I would almost say that they save me, and daily*
> *I am so distant from the hope of myself,*
> *in which I have goodness and discernment,*
> *and never hurry through the world*
> *but walk slowly, and bow often.*
>
> ~Mary Oliver

When I was among the trees, I fell quickly into a rhythm matching theirs. With my open attention and a choice to look, I saw no rushing or struggle for things to be different from what was. The fleeting and the permanent, the sturdy and the flexible all flowed together within each day. In this absence of resistance, I could sense their hints of gladness and feel it spreading within me.

Beauty and Excellence

Each day the scenes shifted, and I took it all in. There were arcs of fractal patterns reproducing the perfect proportions of the Golden Ratio. A leaf's vein pattern, the trees' bark's colors, and endless shades of blue sky–it was as if I was studying a prolific and magnificent artist.

At home, after my walks, I'd look to see what my photos had captured in another round of surprises. Details I had not noticed before came clearly into view. Each image was a slice of the story of my time in the woods, a glimpse of nature's beautifully choreographed dance.

Appreciation of beauty and excellence was another one of my strengths. It's the ability to seek out beauty and experience feelings of wonder and gratitude. It's also about appreciating excellent craftsmanship and mastery of skill in self, others, and the world. As my collection of images grew there were ripples of positive emotions that rolled through me in waves–as I took the photos, as I worked to prepare the image, as I looked at them weeks later. I was in awe of the mastery of design that nature delivers, day after day.

In positive psychology, I learned about the power of positive emotions. We talk a lot about the chemical cascade of hormones that happens when we are under stress that can negatively affect our bodies. The body is a brilliant system, and it works both ways. Curiosity, wonder, awe, gratitude, and love are all positive emotions, and they trigger the feel-good hormones that enhance health and wholebeing. As I spent more time experiencing positive emotions, I was strengthening my ability to balance my nervous system, which helped me work with challenges, change, and life's daily stressors more effectively.

I also began noticing the ripple my images made as I shared them. Instantly people would respond. Friends I'd see at the gym or the grocery store would tell me they loved seeing the daily images. They looked forward to them and felt as if they were there with me, in the woods. My desire to keep sharing the images, to extend what nature offered me daily, pushed my strength of appreciation of beauty and excellence even further.

Everyday Creativity

I was learning to look with less expectation and more patience. In that state of mind the fleeting treasures arrived. As I composed a photo each day, I remembered how much making was a part of me.

Creativity is the act of thinking and making. Life and work are a continuous stream of challenges. To dream, envision, and innovate in life, then pull together the resources to bring those ideas alive amidst the challenges requires practice. Being creative in any way–painting, drawing, writing, cooking, gardening, and taking photos–requires trial and error and builds problem-solving skills.

A study found that people who engage in everyday creative activities, like I was doing, also fostered and reflected psychological health. However, I didn't need a study to know that this daily creative act brought me joy and much more. Then I knew what Mary Oliver meant–these trees, these walks, these photos were saving me, and daily.

Falling in Love

Thirty days turned into 60 days and then stretched into 120 days and then 150 days. The daily walks were no longer a to-do on my task list. I slowed down. Each day I anticipated that moment when my breath would catch as I spotted the beauty.

The time in the woods shifted from producing an image to a practice of gratitude. I would pause and bow to the people who had left this little patch of green, to this daily practice, to the pines, the maples, the dogwoods, and the katsura. In walking slowly, getting to know, receiving what nature offered, and bowing often, I fell in love. Another strength surfaced.

The VIA defines love as "the ability to invest in reciprocal loving and the capacity to receive love from others in romantic, friend, and companion, as a compassionate patron or a parent-child relationship." The love I found was a love of nature, a love of life. It, too, was reciprocal. As our familiarity with each other grew, I would cross the threshold of pavement that turned to soil in the woods, and it was as if nature was waiting for me.

Eckert Tolle's small book, *Stillness*, describes it best.

> *Nature can bring you to stillness. That is its gift to you. When you perceive and join with nature in the field of stillness, that field becomes permeated in your awareness. That is your gift to nature.*

> *Through you, nature becomes aware of itself. Nature has been waiting for you, as it were for millions of years.*

Millions of years. When I sat at my beloved katsura tree, I could feel this deep stillness, deep peace, a deep and life-giving feeling of love. That feeling spread over me like the wandering honeysuckle vines that I watched grow in the early summer months of my walks. I could say yes to this gift. I could be in love with nature, and with life. When I felt this love for nature, I felt happier, and I responded to life with more ease, less struggle, and more peace. But there was something that mattered to me beyond being happy.

Radical Hope

What started as a 30-day Challenge became a life-giving daily ritual. Days built on each other like deposits of sediment, and another of my strengths became a sandstone rock and anchor. For sandstone to form, sediment collects and solidifies due to pressure across time. Life can be like that too. When things shift, we feel stress, and while it may not be comfortable, it can solidify the foundation for the next step in our growth.

The waves of shock and the deconstruction of life began in March 2020 as COVID-19 cracked open our lives. By this time almost four years had passed since I began the 30-day Challenge. Homebound for two weeks and then months upon months upon months, we shared a growing sense of isolation, and oceans of uncertainties.

In the woods, nature carried on. The seasons and cycles played out with expansion, contraction, energy, and then rest. Like beautiful, vivid illustrations I could see nature's relentless resilience. As a grand tree falls, it takes on the next phase of its life as home for new occupants. The space left behind opens possibilities for new growth. As the months collected and the world continued to feel like it was falling apart, nature continued to display these signs of leaning toward the light, and growth as an ever-expanding, interconnected, and interdependent system.

With life deconstructed, the underpinnings of disfunction of so many of our systems came more clearly into view. What happens when you realize the world no longer makes sense, and to move forward, so much of it must first come undone? Seeing these signs in my woods built my sandstone of hope. Not just the everyday kind of hope that things will work out, a radical hope, as defined by Philosopher Kyle Robertson. "It is a commitment to live a meaningful and good life according to standards of meaning and goodness that we haven't created yet together. It is a hope that will survive in a world we don't yet understand."

Against all the odds, I could see this radical hope in the tiny mushrooms that grew and delicate flowers that bloomed in a web of interconnected diversity. Not because they wished for it. Because that is the way of nature. People spoke of being in it together. In nature, together is the only way.

In this small pressure across time during a pandemic, I had a choice again as to what I would look for and what I might see–loss or opportunity, death or rebirth, despair or hope. This last character strength of hope, radical hope, became my rock, anchoring all of my strengths.

The Way Home

> We depend on nature not only for our physical survival. We also need nature to show us the way home, the way out of the prison of our own minds. We got lost in doing, thinking, remembering,

anticipating–lost in a maze of complexity and world of problems.

We have forgotten what rocks, plants and animals still know. We have forgotten how to be–to be where life is: Here and now.

~Eckert Tolle

I had started my search for muchness as if it was a holy grail, a solid object to repossess. In the slivers of time in the woods each day, I walked and sat still. I looked at the forest and the trees, the rain, and perfect cloudless blue skies following the voices of the poets. Yet, it was the framework of positive psychology that eventually allowed me to see what had happened along the way.

My muchness was the collection of my character strengths–curiosity, appreciation of beauty and excellence, love, and radical hope. These were the parts of me that made me feel alive in the here and now and my navigation tools for the stormy and sunny days. With this collection of treasures in my pocket, I learned to see my right path and found my way back home.

Alice Dommert | Drexel Hill, Pennsylvania

https://www.prasadawholebeing.com

Alice Dommert is the Founder and CEO of Prasada and a Wholebeing Architect with a unique background as a licensed architect and exhibit designer, writer, speaker, and consultant with training in yoga and mindfulness, breathwork, positive psychology, and organizational development.

In 2009 she founded Prasada, a group of health and wellness professionals, to deliver skills and practices for Wholebeing to the workplace so individuals and their organizations can thrive. Ms. Dommert leads the Prasada team working with clients across the country to build positive cultures for human sustainability through professional development and wellness programs.

Destination Resilience: The Value of Persistence Through Life's Storms

- Christine E. Agaibi

An exhilarating rite of passage for many children around the world is being able to independently ride a bicycle. According to many parenting and biking enthusiast websites and magazines, most children learn to ride a bicycle between ages three to seven. The freedom that comes with learning to ride a bicycle is an important developmental step and a point of pride for parents and children alike. In learning to ride, children learn lessons in both balance and perseverance, and it gives many children autonomy as well as the opportunity to interact with their peers from a young age.

At ten years old, I did not know any of this information, but by the age of ten something felt different for me when many of my peers were zipping around the neighborhood on their bicycles while I watched from the sidelines. Imagine my intense disappointment when at ten years old I had not only not learned to ride a bike, but I did not even own one! My dad was a Certified Public Accountant who worked in several large corporations in many states. This caused us to move many times, in my early childhood, and this certainly contributed to my not being able to own or learn how to ride a bike. By the time I was ready to start school, we settled in Indianapolis, Indiana. Yet, despite my parents wanting me to learn, we did not have space to house a bicycle, so I continued to not learn. So, the years went on, but the opportunity never arose for me to have a bike. By the time I was ten, I was different than my peers and friends, I had never learned to ride, and I certainly felt like an outlier.

Then one day the tide turned in my favor when an amazing thing happened! A childhood friend told me she was getting rid of her bike to buy another one and offered her old bike to me. I finally had an opportunity that could not be turned down. Despite my excitement, a part of me thought, "Wow she's already on to her second bike and I haven't even ridden one." Doubt began to creep in regarding my ability to ride since she was clearly so much more advanced than me. She had been riding for years but this was brand new to me. What would she and my peers say about my inability to ride when we were together? Though I was young, I vividly remember these thoughts of apprehension and fear. Yet, there was a small voice deep inside me that pushed past the trepidation and I focused on the fact that I finally had the opportunity to have my very own bike! My excitement did not silence my fear but pushed back against it. If I wanted to get out of the sidelines and into my group of friends, I had to push past those misgivings.

Though storing the bike was still a concern, my parents agreed to find the space for the new bike, and I was elated! I wanted to get to riding right away! We took the bike out and my dad, who taught me many simple and profound lessons, taught me how to balance that day. He balanced me and pushed me on the bike for hours. He was not tired and seem overjoyed at my happiness and determination. I went from not knowing how to ride, to being pro at riding in just seven hours! I surpassed other kids that often spent weeks on training wheels. However, my determination and excitement, my dad's encouragement, and my friend's kindness in giving me her old bike combined and paid off and were a big source of inspiration that allowed me to bypass the training wheels step. In just a few short hours I had forgotten that I was a ten-year-old outlier who had never ridden a bike. My uncertainties were gone, I had faced my doubt and apprehension head-on, and I was riding independently! It is a memory that I still cherish decades later.

However, as with most life situations, excitement waxes and wanes, and my delight in riding a bike was short-lived. After this remarkable and uplifting day, the weather changed. It was almost as a metaphor for the ups and downs of life; my excitement was replaced with rain. I could not go back out the next day but was determined to do so when the weather improved. After the rain lifted, I was eager to go back out again and show off my new skills. However, two incidents after this rainy day could have halted my progress forever had I chosen not to persevere.

A few days after learning to ride when I was still a new rider and some trepidation continued to surface, I was riding alone, and a neighbor's dog started to chase me. I was frightened and rode faster and faster trying to get away. I did not realize at the time that the dog was simply playing with me. Instead, I had thought he was trying to hurt me, and I peddled faster and faster trying to get away. The dog eventually realized my fear and stopped because my dad saw what was happening and came to my rescue, shooed the dog away, and calmed me down. My dad was always a source of calm and comfort.

In another incident, I was riding after a rainstorm with my friend that had given me the bicycle. My bicycle slipped on some smooth gravel and I flew off the bike and onto the hard pavement right on my knees. There was blood everywhere and I was embarrassed and in a lot of pain. My dad scooped me up, placed me on the counter at home, washed my cuts, and bandaged me up. He could have told me I should take a break then and there but instead he asked me what I wanted to do. He said that we all fall but it is important to not give up or let my pain deter me from doing something I enjoyed so much – riding.

These stories seem to be simple memories of a young girl learning, overcoming her fears, and coming into her own while riding a bike. However, these are not just simple stories surrounding riding a bike. They are stories of how my father laid a foundation of life lessons that continue to unfold for me even decades later. These lessons turned out to be much deeper and more profound lessons about perseverance and life.

A few short years after this summer with the bicycle, my dad passed away suddenly from natural causes while we were on vacation. This was of course traumatizing. However, for a young girl who loved her dad and looked up to him in everything, this was especially devastating and heartbreaking. Losing my dad meant losing my biggest cheerleader, my place of comfort, stability, and support, the place that taught me about integrity and faith, and the place that gave me confidence and belief in myself and my ability to do all things. It has been many decades now since his passing, and the lessons he taught me continue to unfold, and my memories of him are renewed by my mom's consistent discussion of him and the man he was and continues to be in my heart.

My mom, also devastated by the sudden loss of her husband and life partner, was thrust into the difficult task of raising a teenage daughter alone, managing her grief as well as mine, and stepping into a new dual parenting role she never imagined would be part of her life. Looking back now as an adult, I am amazed at the strength and resilience we exhibited at that time. She not only held it together, but within three weeks of my dad's passing, she packed up our home in Indianapolis and moved us to Cleveland Ohio where we had a family. Being near cousins, aunts, uncles, and my grandmother as well as being close to a church we loved was the greatest blessing to come out of this time.

Though grief never truly ends but only evolves, and though times certainly were not easy emotionally or logistically after this, and there was much to adjust to, the life lessons embedded in this time in my life set me up for an adulthood bent towards service, resilience, faith, and integrity. As an adult now who has experienced many things since my father's passing, I understand that mobilizing resources and facing times of crisis with faith and perseverance are not easy to come by when difficulty hits. However, these are some of the greatest assets and gifts we can give ourselves in moments of difficulty.

As an adult I have learned that no one is immune from pain and tragedy. It is a part of the human condition that unites and touches each of us at some point. While we cannot escape tragedy, it is what we do with those times that matter. In the several decades since my dad's passing, I have of course faced many challenges as well as times of unshakable happiness and joy. Looking back at these decades retrospectively and with many decades of life experience, and positive psychology training, practice, and research in my toolbelt, I see that I have used many of the tools of positive psychology, even as an adolescent and also as an adult, without even realizing. This tool belt along with perseverance and faith have been the greatest instruments for coping and thriving no matter what storms were surging around me. These tools gave me confidence that things will be alright and that I had strengths within not only to balance challenges but to surpass them. I learned that meaning comes from facing challenges head-on, acknowledging that at times difficulties exist, but not allowing such difficulty to consume me. I also found value in serving others who are attempting to overcome their own hurdles and found that altruistic compassion also coupled with perseverance goes a long way in the quest for thriving. In the next few pages, I will address what these times of challenge have illuminated for me and how times of challenge need not be forgotten to be surpassed. We can thrive despite any difficulty, and the principles of positive psychology lie within each of us if only we spotlight them and cause them to grow.

Look for Opportunities

> When things do not go your way, remember that
> every challenge – every adversity – contains
> within it the seeds of opportunity and growth.
> – Roy T. Bennett

Those early days on the bicycle taught me that trepidation will always come with new and unfamiliar territory. Of course, a ten-year-old who had never been on a bicycle would be afraid. So was the teenager entering a new town, circle of friends, and a new school. So is an adult dealing with a family crisis, a relationship ending, or a health or financial issue. Our fears do not go away simply because we have gotten older. In fact, they often are more complex, convoluted, and more is at stake. Yet, we should have confidence that we are equipped to deal with challenges because we have dealt with every challenge before the present one. Therefore, if we look for opportunities within the fear, we will realize the tools to work through challenges are within us.

The answers may not be simple, but problem-solving can begin when a situation is seen as a challenge, not as something insurmountable. In my own life, I was fearful of the prospects of learning to ride a bicycle at ten years old when most of my friends had been riding for years. Yet, I found my friend's old bicycle to be an opportunity and I was perseverant

FINDING UNSHAKABLE HAPPINESS

in trying to ride despite my apprehension. Likewise, when I had to move from Indiana to Ohio after my dad's passing, it was a frightening prospect to leave behind my friends, school, and all that I had known as a child. These feelings were made worse knowing I would be leaving my childhood and my city behind and starting a new chapter as a teenager and without the guidance of support of my beloved father.

Once again despite my apprehension and fear, I put one foot in front of the other and embraced the potential of a new town and the occasion of being near family. The move and my time in Ohio were not without challenges and the challenges came as I navigated a new world. However, the mindset of opportunity allowed my thinking to shift to possibility rather than difficulty. Indeed, "in the middle of every difficulty lies opportunity" (Albert Einstein) and it is in that opportunity that challenge is transformed to possibility and hope.

Savor Stillness

> *I savor life. When you have anything that threatens life... it prods you into stepping back and really appreciating the value of life and taking from it what you can.*
>
> — Sonia Sotomayor

> *Nature does not hurry, yet everything is accomplished.*
>
> — Lao Tzu

Anxiety creeps in during times of uncertainty and in the valleys of our life. The stressor we are facing may already be causing havoc and chaos. Our anxiety about the unknown need not add to the commotion. Stillness allows for a pause from the disarray and confusion and allows us to fully appreciate what is happening in this moment and this season of life, so we can glean from it what we ought to know. When there is no peace surrounding us, savoring allows us to find peace within, and it is within this peace that we can value the extent of the experience and evaluate the next steps with wisdom, discernment, and contentment.

In positive psychology, savoring allows us to increase the intensity and appreciation of a positive experience and emotions to help manage negative emotions. In that regard, savoring allows us to stay in the present moment without focusing too much on the past or the future. Instead, our focus turns to the present and allows us to fully take in the moment we are in. Savoring allows us to focus on all we are grateful for and this allows us to shift our perspective from the struggles to the micro-moments that bring us joy. Savoring allows us to hold on to positive moments that transcend difficulties.

Viktor Frankl, the Austrian author, psychiatrist, and Holocaust survivor said, "Between stimulus and response there is a space. In that space is our power to choose our response. In our response lies our growth and freedom." When we savor, we remain in that space for a little longer and allow for positive emotions to increase as we consider a response, and that response can come from a more positive position.

During times of challenge in my life, savoring certainly allowed me to hold positive emotions in view. Savoring helped me to remember the things that I am grateful for and prevented focus from shifting to the negative. When times were difficult as a teen and as a new adult, it was helpful to remember the relationship I had with my father, the trips I had enjoyed, him teaching me to ride a bike or simple moments like enjoying a good meal or coffee with friends. Those moments are precious, at times fleeting, and are often swept away with the busyness of life. That is all the more reason, to take intentional time to savor and remember that while there may be challenges there are many positive moments as well that should be honored and revered.

Nothing is Insurmountable

We are surrounded by insurmountable opportunities.

- Bill Mollison

The American Psychological Association's Public Education Campaign put together a statement of "10 Ways to Build Resilience" in 2009. The second thing on that list tells an individual who is trying to be more resilient to "avoid seeing crises as insurmountable problems." We cannot prevent high pressured or stressful events from happening. We cannot stop illnesses, people from passing away, relationships from ending, job losses, or financial crises from occurring. Our attempts to control uncontrollable situations often lead to even more stress. Stepping out of an old life that no longer fits is fear-provoking and takes immense courage to overcome. However, bravery lies within us and appears when we make connections, when we accept that change comes with life, when we take decisive actions towards goals we set for ourselves, when we do not see problems as the only thing in our life and instead when we keep a hopeful perspective, and when we engage in self-care and self-growth. Difficult times often put into hyper-focus who we really are, what is truly important, and what we truly want out of our lives. Challenges tend to eliminate the "noise" that prevents us from discovering who we truly are. All that does not matter falls away in times of challenge, and all that matters becomes the central focus that should be paid attention to.

When faced with these situations, we need to look within and change our fear to faith. We cannot change the situation, but we can interpret the event as surmountable. If we are willing to let go of what is temporary and focus on what is meaningful, if we accept that challenges are a part of life, if we accept that things do not always go according to plan but that does not mean it is hopeless, if we can be patient while being goal-oriented, then we can adapt to circumstances that arise and we can attract new and healthier things. Things do not always go according to plan, but we can thrive if we see situations as surmountable and are flexible and adaptable to overcome.

I recently took a stroll in an arboretum and park in northeastern New Jersey and was astounded to see a very unique tree. I have dubbed this tree "The Resilient Tree" for its distinctive and unusual sideways growth. There was a sign nearby that visitors should not sit on the tree. However, people stood around mesmerized by it. I meditated on this tree as providing very interesting lessons to the humans observing it. The tree does not rush about or complain that it is sideways. It has certainly adapted to growing this way. It has let go of the notion that it should grow upright like its neighbors but still has deep roots and growth. This tree was not conforming to our idea of what a "normal" tree should look like. Yet, by adapting to the way it was destined to grow, it fulfilled its true potential and became a source of wonderment for all who saw it. People were flocking to see this tree more than any other in the arboretum! Likewise, the ten-year-old bike rider now has a story to tell that I may not have had if I had ridden at five years old like everyone else. When we adapt to the challenges rather than succumb to them, we have a story to tell. We can accomplish much as humans if we are flexible to adapt to the challenges rather than surrender or concede to them. Nothing is insurmountable in nature. Nothing is insurmountable to us either.

Permission to Be Human, You Are Worthy, and Challenging the Negative Scripts with Strength

Connection is the energy that is created between

people when they feel seen, heard, and valued –
when they can give and receive without judgment.

- Brené Brown

Humans are social beings. Humans crave interaction, love, identification with others, acceptance, and deep lasting connections. One of the greatest sources of joy is being deeply understood by another while the juxtaposition of that is being rejected. Think of a time you were rejected from a job, a university, a partner, or a friend. It was probably one of the most intensely saddening experiences of your life. It is deeply memorable, and the wound and scars remain long after the event has ended. I have felt that deep sorrow on many occasions in my life and indeed it left a memorable and existential injury that lingers and lingers. We are left with more questions than answers. Am I good enough? What could I have done differently? How can I improve in the future? Sometimes we do not have answers. However, as with most challenges these crossroads are points where growth can develop.

In the days of the bicycle, I wondered how a non-rider like myself would fit in. Would my friends reject me because they could ride, and I could not? Maybe it would be an intentional rejection because my nonriding status made me different. Maybe it was just a matter of logistics. They could get places faster since they could ride, and I would just hold them up. When I moved to Ohio, those fears arose again. I was the new kid at church and school. I was the kid that lost her father on vacation. Would people feel pity? Would there be whispers? Would I be able to fit in with others?

I have learned along the way that there will always be these questions. I have lived in five states now and have learned to adjust to making friends and connections along the way. I do not see these as hindrances but as opportunities to grow my circle of beloved people. I have worked in three states and have learned what it takes to make myself marketable and beneficial to an employer. I have learned what it takes to "fit in" and it has taken work.

Every failure, every rejection, and every disappointment brought me closer to my goals because it taught me much about myself and what it means to be human. Humans need to give each other and themselves permission to be human. We are not meant to be perfect, but we are to persevere and strive for our best. We are meant to be loved through this process and despite it, and that aids in our growth whether we are or are not. We have strengths (24 of them to be exact!) and we can lean on those strengths to achieve our greatest potential. When we focus on our strengths rather than our faults, we stop being hard on ourselves and we learn, grow, and thrive.

My strengths as a ten-year-old, and even now decades later, have always been around perseverance, hope, awe, transcendence and spirituality, and a love of learning. I looked for opportunities in times of challenge and I did not let a time of difficulty hinder my growth – even in the most disappointing of moments. Rejections were times to learn, to grow, to listen intently, and even to cry but to eventually emerge whole and ready to give again. That is what leads to my resilience and to resilience in general. That perseverance similarly leads to the resilience of many I work with.

Understanding the unique profile of our character strengths can help us to feel and experience the authentic nature of who we are. According to the VIA (Values in Action) Institute on Character, applying our strengths helps us to: "boost confidence, increase happiness, strengthen relationships, manage problems, reduce stress, accomplish goals, build meaning and purpose, and improve work performance." These strengths reside in a unique constellation in each of us and leaning on them and applying them can help us to reach our fullest potential and to thrive. When we examine ourselves in this way, we will see our rejections and failures not as character flaws but as parts of our humanity that can be adjusted for a better and more lasting outcome.

> *In the confrontation between the stream and the rock, the stream always wins – not through strength, but by perseverance.*
>
> > - H. Jackson Brown

In Conclusion – Emerging from the Winter of Our Lives into a Glorious Spring

> *Spring brings new growth. Weed out of the bad, and makes room for something beautiful.*
>
> > - Anonymous

> *The signs of spring are all around us. Acknowledge winter. Shine a light. Feel the warmth. Foster Growth.*
>
> > - Luke Boyes

Spring is the perfect season of rebirth after a dead and dreary winter. We have seasons of winter and spring in our lives as well because such cycles are the nature of life. Do not linger in winter. Permit yourself to be human. You are worthy just because you are a human. Despite challenges and mistakes, understand that we all have character strengths within us that will help us to bloom come spring. Blooming takes time but is a beautiful reminder that winter does not last forever.

In winter, there should be a mindful looking for opportunity despite the bleakness. What can I learn? How can I grow? Where are the prospects of hope? To achieve this, savoring times of stillness will help to identify the areas that need bolstering and will enhance positive emotions and gratitude which will help in making the best and clearest decisions. Perseverance in moments of difficulty is key to prevent hopelessness and the key to seeing the problem as surmountable. Small steps every day towards the goals we set helps lead us on a path towards resilience. Resilience is a muscle to be built. Resilience is an aspirational and inspirational journey to embark on and to mindfully walk towards every day. Resilience does not develop overnight and there may even be missteps. However, even with missteps along the way, permit yourself to be human, to experience the emotions you face but not be overcome by them, to understand your value as a human, to identify your purpose and develop meaning, and strive to engage your character strengths to thrive and achieve your greatest potential. Thus, resilience is not the absence of difficulty. Resilience is the conscious choice to experience the full spectrum of human emotions, to not be consumed by them, and to persevere to thrive despite them

That little girl so many years ago eventually did learn how to ride a bike and riding was not insurmountable. Every time I get on now, I remember the value of perseverance, the lessons of my father, learning how to takes the scrapes and bruises along with the achievements, and to reach the pinnacle of resilience through determination, self-acceptance, growth, and perseverance. The lessons of my father were timeless. Faith and perserverance from above and within have always illuminated all the strength I have ever needed to thrive. My resilience and thriving will continue so long as I continue to persevere.

Victory is always possible for the person who refuses to stop fighting.

- Napoleon Hill

Christine E. Agaibi | Akron, Ohio

https://www.caresilience.com

Christine E. Agaibi, received Masters and Doctorate graduate training in Counseling Psychology in Ohio.

Christine is the current Chair of the Special Interest Group on Religious and Spiritual Issues in Counseling Psychology in the American Psychological Association's (APA) Counseling Psychology Division (Division 17).

Christine's professional research and clinical interests are in the area of Resilience and Positive Psychology, Religion and Spirituality, and Diversity. She has presented on these topics at nearly three dozen Regional, State, National, and International Psychology conferences. She has also presented on these topics over 150 times at various invited community presentations and to Coptic Orthodox Churches and programs in Ohio, Pennsylvania, New Jersey, New York, Florida, Wisconsin, Virginia and Canada. Christine has also been an invited speaker to the Eritrean Orthodox Community, and to Jewish Community Programs. She has also published over 15 journal articles (national and international), book chapters, and APA Division and State Psychological Associations newsletter articles on these topics.

Christine completed her APA Accredited Pre- Doctoral Internship at the Ohio Psychology Internship, a consortium, where she had comprehensive and diverse didactic and practical training with children and adolescents, families, couples, and adults, in assessment, forensics, substance use issues, and individual and group therapy.

Christine is the Past-President of Ohio Women in Psychology (OWP) and Past OWP liaison to the Ohio Psychological Association (OPA) Board of Directors. She has also had several leadership and committee roles within the OPA and the OPA Board of Directors. She has also served on several committees in the New Jersey Psychological Association, the South Jersey Psychological Association, the Ohio Psychological Association, and is the Past-Vice President of the Akron Area Professional Psychologists. She has also been the Practice Representative for the Section on Positive Psychology within APA's Division 17. Internationally, she has served on the Board of Directors for the Students of the International Positive Psychology Association.

Christine has advocated for the profession of psychology and for clients of psychology at State Leadership Conferences in Ohio, Pennsylvania, and on Capitol Hill. She has been invited to National State Leadership Conferences four times and has twice served as the Diversity Delegate from Ohio.

Currently, Christine serves on two Task Forces within The Society for the Psychology of Religion and Spirituality within APA's Division 36, and she also sits on the Community Engagement Committee of APA's Division 17.

Christine has taught a variety of undergraduate and graduate psychology courses at four Universities in Ohio and Pennsylvania.

Christine has most recently conducted evaluations and provided therapy in a large community mental health clinic, a private practice, and at a leading national Child and Adolescent Behavioral and Mental Health Clinic in Philadelphia Pennsylvania and New Jersey.

Christine can be reached at: www.caresilience.com , or via email at: Christine@caresilience.com

SECTION 2: INCREASING POSITIVE EMOTION: FINDING THE "AND" IN CHALLENGING TIMES
- DONNA MARTIRE MILLER

Joseph Bologna

How we interpret the world we live in has a great effect on our well-being. Developing skills to deal with challenges will help us become more resilient and positive. When we can name what we are feeling, the monster of negativity that we feel inside becomes manageable. If we keep it inside, we often fall into a thinking trap, attaching this emotion to an old painful story that prevents us from seeing what is going on in the larger picture. If we use our character strength of curiosity, we can put our negative thoughts into perspective and then take positive action. This will propel us into an upward spiral of more positive emotions versus going the other way.

It is proven that the positive emotions connected to our experiences, especially when shared with others, can have a tremendous lasting impact on our feelings. Mindfully savoring these experiences and reminiscing about them will build positive emotions. Pausing to celebrate even the smallest of achievements is another way to climb the upward spiral. Helping others and being kind are also joyful ways to bring more positive emotions into your life.

In this section, you will meet Susan, Dawn, James, Lisa, and Phoebe. They will share their stories about benefit-finding mindsets, resiliency, overcoming challenges, and self-agency. Maria Sirois from WBI teaches in her lectures to always look for the AND. In every challenging situation, there is an and… for example, I was once stood up by my date, (who I was enamored with and really looking forward to seeing)…AND… I decided to look for something positive in the situation, I had the best lunch that day, I ordered my favorite things on the menu and enjoyed sitting where the sun was streaming in the window just enough to warm me. Yes, this happened, my heart was broken, *and* I really enjoyed the food, the hospitality of the server, and the restaurant's ambiance . . . I left smiling.

In this world that focuses on so much negativity, positive thinking is a skill that develops and builds in us when we notice the good in our life. Tal Ben-Shahar says, *"When you appreciate the good, the good appreciates."* Research shows that our attitude, when we shift it towards more positivity, can build our immune system, reduce anxiety, and increase our positive emotions . . . including happiness! There are many ways to improve your mindset. One way is to associate with people who have positive attitudes and keep encouraging you even when you fall, IF we can get into the habit of choosing to see situations with a more positive attitude, we will set into motion a remarkable chain of reactions that will lead to resilience, better coping skills, and increased joy and hope. Another is to walk a bit in nature or to read something inspiring. I like to listen, dance, and sing along to my favorite music. That has the power to lift my spirits and improve my attitude every time.

> *With everything that has happened to you, you can either feel sorry for yourself or treat what has happened as a gift. Everything is either an opportunity to grow or an obstacle to keep you from growing. You get to choose.*
> - Wayne Dyer

Mindset in Action

-Susan Neustrom, Ed.D

"I can't do that", "I'm not good at that", "Way beyond my intelligence", "I might fail so I'm not going to even try". For over thirty-two years, those phrases were a constant reminder of who I was and those negative thoughts directed my life. How I behaved, spoke, and interacted with others was driven by the voice inside my head whispering and sometimes shouting, "Failure, you're never going to be anything else". I grew up believing I was a failure because I dropped out of school at 16 and nothing was going to change who and what I was. That is, until one day I heard another voice, unrecognizable, but a voice so different I had to listen. I disregarded the voice at first because, well because I'm a failure. Why was this voice suddenly giving me words of encouragement? I was confused, bewildered, and astonished at the same time when I heard, "Just try, you can do it." Where was that voice coming from? The more I resisted that strange voice the more persistent it became. I would hear whispering in my ear in the quiet moments of the morning while sipping my coffee and daydreaming (did it a lot), and even while watching the sun rise from the clouds. The same whisper occurred in the midafternoon when I could barely stay awake at my desk because of boredom with my work, my routine, and my mediocre, less than exciting goals. However, by the end of the day, as I lay awake in bed wondering if anything will ever change, I would argue with the voice because I knew I was destined to fail again and again. Why try? In the hope that I was wrong all these years, I finally gave myself an ultimatum, NOW or NEVER! Not that I doubted my belief, I think I was looking for confirmation to prove to the voice I was right all along. When I decided to follow the directive of the strange voice and took the first step I never anticipated that I was embarking on a life-changing, twelve-year journey of discovery of who I am igniting my purpose, passion, and calling.

Of course, little did I realize when I began my journey, that in reality, I was transforming my beliefs from limited abilities to growing and developing, and wisdom was the result of the effort I put into changing my mindset from fixed thoughts to growth thoughts. Given that I wanted to make a change, a big change in my life, I became aware of the many "I can'ts" that directed my behavior, my motivation, and my ability to move beyond what I believed about who I was. I struggled with two conflicting stories, the external story, and the internal story. The persona others saw was a person with a successful career, probably well-educated, and passionate about the work I was doing. However, the story I told myself over and over centered on everything I can't do, being inadequate, an imposter, and far removed from doing work I love. For safety, I crafted my life to be risk-free. To put it differently, I guarded myself against failure. If I do nothing, I can't fail again. My fixed mindset formed a wall around my life vision and I was happy being in a safe place. Or so I thought.

Truly, the best decision I made was to return to school, obtaining a GED, and continuing to earn a Doctorate. It took me 30 years to commit to the decision because I was frightened to move forward. My fear was coming from my fixed mindset thinking I am a failure with no intelligence and I cannot grow anymore. I was at my peak so why try? Today, when I look back at the path I walked because of finally deciding to take the first step, I am in awe. Never had I dreamed I would be a Doctor, a Professor, a life coach, a CEO, an author, and a speaker! I have now experienced many exciting things in my life that I could only admire from afar earlier in my life. I still have a long way to go and fear is always present but not the same as when I began my journey.

For so many years I felt like I was climbing a mountain and even though the terrain was rocky at times each step got me closer to achieving a goal, then another, and another. The wall of "I can't" was no longer holding me back and I continued to surge toward my ideal self, always pushing just a bit harder. I almost reached the top of the mountain–my ultimate dream, then I began sliding down and I couldn't stop. Life has a way of changing course just when you think you have a clear path and set direction. Suddenly, I found myself at a point in my life where my thoughts were reverting to a fixed mindset and I didn't like what was happening. My happiness was being tested in a very disturbing way.

To me, happiness is a feeling of contentment, of being in the present and knowing everything is working as planned. The voices in my head cease to whisper and I don't worry or stress. It's sunshine in my face even when the sun isn't shining. Happiness cannot be seen only felt deeply and intently. While I have experienced happiness in the past, something was now blocking its existence and I began a search to uncover where happiness may be hidden.

A while back I subscribed to Wholebeing Institute's newsletter because I am fascinated with positive psychology concepts. Much of my graduate work focused on leadership strategies and the practical aspects of positive psychology in relation to organizations. I have applied the tools I learned in my personal life and my leadership of several human service organizations. As a life-long learner, I continue to read, research, and share new perspectives and ideas. While this may be true, slowly my energy level shifted ,and the excitement of learning also faded. Then I opened the Wholebeing Institute email and the 2019 spring session of Certificate in Wholebeing Positive Psychology was accepting applications. Should I? No, I shouldn't. There's is that voice again, sharing the "I can't. Well, maybe I'll think about it. The fact that I didn't like where I was in my life kept gnawing at me. Instead of moving toward my ideal life I was moving away and joining a group of individuals who are sharing similar journeys would be an opportunity for me to take control of my destiny. I decided to lock my inner voice in the closet so I was not interrupted when I registered for the nine-month Certificate in Wholebeing Positive Psychology program.

While I was very familiar with the concepts introduced throughout the program, in my quest to rediscover my happiness, I was introduced to the SPIRE model and asked to measure my strengths of the spiritual, physical, intellectual, relational, and emotional aspects of my life. As I reviewed my chart, it hit me, "I'm out of balance". Not just a slight imbalance but a big-time imbalance. The SPIRE chart was a snapshot of my life now and I didn't like what I saw. When I began my journey so long ago to transform my fixed mindset to a growth mindset quieting the voice that continually told me I was a failure, I focused my attention on obtaining an education, strived to advance my leadership role in human services to help people because, after all, it was my passion, and learning, always learning. Happiness was derived from my satisfaction of breaking down the walls of a failure mindset that held me captive and unable to move.

In the hope of recapturing my energy, I reflected on my journey and the changes I experienced. I reached what I thought was an unattainable goal from dropout to doctorate, led several nonprofit organizations, authored a book, became faculty at two universities teaching adults, coached individuals in life transition, and invited to speak to many groups and organizations. While all of the changes are still active and present I'm in a different place now- my life changed. The shift in mindset occurred when I lost my husband, my best friend, leading me to the stark realization that my biological clock is winding down as the years fly by. I'm getting old. I have always been a visionary, even when failure was all I knew. I spent my life looking forward and dreaming of the future. Suddenly, looking ahead is far less exciting than looking back. No wonder my energy was depleting and my mindset was resorting back to limiting beliefs.

SPRIRE was an awakening to the big gaping hole in my life providing deeper insight about what I missed on my journey to discover who I am. I could easily see that I neglected many aspects of who I am and it was time to revisit if I wanted to truly capture happiness again. It became clear that the habits I created for success were no longer working. Throughout the program, I learned the process of designing new habits. Considering both my strengths and values I could create a unique and personal SPIRE balance enabling me to move toward my best self.

However, I worried that my inner voice would be too strong to sustain the habit change I desired after the program was complete. I also knew changing a habit is hard, no less changing many habits because it is too easy to give up when a new habit feels uncomfortable and awkward. All the while I could imagine the new habit and visualize how I would feel after the habit led me to a better place. But taking an action to make it happen, well, I was stuck. Even with an accountability partner, I would probably find 100 excuses why I can't do something now. There is my inner voice again! So how was I going to meet the challenges and move forward? Too often having a motivating thought, "I am going to do it" is not strong enough to actually create an action step because too many other things get in the way. I'll get around to it someday. For me, it happens all the time. I write a to-do list, put post-it notes everywhere, put a reminder on my phone, and still nothing happens. That is until I met the challenge head-on. Knowing the challenges were just like a brick wall holding me back, I created the "Mindset Challenge". Not a bigger-than-life movement but rather a one thought at a time action step I take, see, feel, and admire.

To change habits, "The Mindset Challenge" project is a daily practice to break down the overwhelming task of transforming from a fixed mindset to a growth mindset. The Challenge is designed to recognize when a fixed mindset thought emerges and act upon the thought. With recognition, choices become viable options, resilience and grit can be developed, and old habits, that no longer work, are replaced with new habits. Changing one thought at a time supports a life-long journey of growth, development, and discovery.

While only holding a growth mindset is not realistic, researcher Carol Dweck, Ph.D. In her book, *Mindset, The New Psychology of Success*, (Penquin Random House, LLC, 2016) believes having a fixed and growth mindset is normal. Attaining more of a growth mindset to achieve success is a choice and with effort and a reasonable level of grit, can be learned. Similarly, In their article "Beyond Willpower: Strategies for Reducing Failures of Self –control," (*Psychological Science in the Public Interest*, 2019), Duckworth, Milkman, and Laibson suggest self-awareness is not a sufficient enough approach to maintaining self-control when working toward a goal, especially if self-control failed in the past. Instead, applying a strategic approach that considers both situation and mindset can lessen self-control failure.

The Mindset Challenge offers a playful visual for changing one thought at a time. Employing a strategic approach to grit and mental contrasting for goal achievement, the daily practice can change a fixed mindset thought to a growth mindset thought helping you move closer to your ideal self.

How the Mindset Challenge Works

Step one- Begin with taking three evidence-based assessments to measure the level of your fixed mindset. This is helpful information to know because you may be surprised to learn you are more inclined to a growth mindset than you may have thought.

First, take the mindset assessment to determine where the fixed mindset is strongest. (mindsetworks.com/)

Second, measure your grit scale/ to assess your current level of self-control. (angeladuckworth.com/grit-)

Third, apply the mental strategy for contrasting the challenge. (woopmylife.org/woop-1)

(What is your wish, what is your best outcome, what is your main inner obstacle, make a plan). This assessment is simple, yet a powerful way to identify challenges you encounter during change and prepares you to take action to combat the urge to give up.

Now that you have an honest measure of your mindset, grit, and challenges, identify the areas of your life, spiritual, physical, intellectual, relational, and emotional where you want to form a new habit to increase involvement moving you closer to your ideal self. For each area, consider what you need to do to increase by 5%. Design incremental movement that helps you walk toward your goal without feeling exhausted, overwhelmed, or burdened. Choose a feel-good action. For example, if you desire to increase your physical self, an action might be dancing in your kitchen to your favorite song for 3 minutes. I do this action quite often, especially when Bob Seger is singing "Old Time Rock and Roll", as my dogs stare at me in disbelief. Keep this thought in mind as you move to step two. Well, not the thought of me dancing but you dancing.

Step two- Set up five jars and label each one a letter of SPIRE to represent Spiritual, Physical, Intelligent, Relationship, and Emotional. Get a bag of colored stones (a different color for each element of SPIRE). Let your creativity go wild. I painted fluorescent letters on each jar and decorated the top with rhinestones, bling, bling!!

Step three- Every time a fixed mindset thought emerges, ask yourself three questions:

1. Where is the thought coming from?
2. Is it true?
3. Would people who know you say it's true?

Now answer the questions. Then make a choice to replace with a growth mindset thought and create an action based on the new thought. As the thought changes and you take action, a colored stone is placed in a corresponding jar for one of the elements of SPIRE where the thought originated.

Step four- At the end of the day take a few minutes to reflect on what worked well and how grit and WOOP were present.

Step five- Pay attention to the stones in the jar to see which letter of SPRIRE seems easier to have a growth mindset and determine if more effort is necessary as indicated by fewer stones or perhaps a fixed mindset is sufficient. You determine the pace of developing new habits and the stones represent your accomplishment of changing your life one thought at a time.

If you find one jar or all of the jars filled to the top, insert a silk flower as a reminder of the beauty of your life, the strengths you possess, and the ideal life you created, one thought at a time. Most importantly, celebrate the wonder of you, your success, and your happiness.

It's important to realize that changing a habit is no guarantee of happiness. The jars only represent movement. Happiness is like the wind, you can't see it but you can feel it. Sometimes, it will sweep you off your feet and at times be still. It is always present and appears any time of the day. The wind analogy was a profound lesson learned and my final journal entry after receiving my Wholebeing Positive Psychology certificate is a reminder: Here is the entry I wrote:

"Sitting at the airport waiting for my departure home after the immersion I reflected on the experience. I pushed my inner critic down throughout the week and still the old ways, the fixed mindset thoughts surfaced. I was surrounded by love and support and as hard as I tried happiness did not emerge or even attempt to make a breakthrough. I showed up with an open mind and resisted going back to my habits and fixed mindset thoughts. I let it flow and although I internally criticized myself, I did not dwell. When I needed time alone I took it especially when my thoughts were ready to sabotage me with questions, "Why did I come?" "Why was I sent here?" I came because I thought I would find direction, a new path to happiness. Instead, I'm leaving with the simplest of a task. I learned that I need to go backward, not forward, back to the basics, breathing and meditating. I did not learn something new, I learned something old. I reflected on that thought, then argued with the voice that is telling me "this was a waste of time". I reflected again, I know, I started to cry and tried to hold back tears that wanted to stream down my face while sitting at the bar and the server is giving me a long stare, then pacing back and forth waiting for me to order. I have been staring at the Caesar salad on the menu since I sat down but my mind was preoccupied with trying to make sense of what I experienced. I still have a few hours before my departure so including a glass of wine with my dinner seemed like the right thing to do. Besides, I'm not flying the plane, just a passenger, and I can honestly say a happy passenger. I took a celebratory sip of my wine and declared I am on a mission to change most profoundly with the realization that the direction I was seeking for happiness is not something to be found. Instead, the direction is right in front of me and all I have to do is follow with my head, heart, and whole being".

Surprisingly, it has been two years since I began the Mindset Challenge and some jars are a masterpiece and others are filling at a slower pace. I introduced the Mindset Challenges to my coaching clients and we share many high fives with every ping of a stone in a jar. I'll admit there are days when I don't feel like taking action and just let my thoughts float by. At that moment I don't panic, I'm not fearful, or frustrated. Instead, I sigh, smile, and permit myself to do a happy dance. I have even boldly twirled beyond my kitchen.

Susan Neustrom | Lisle, Illinois

https://www.susanneustrom.com

Dr. Susan Neustrom is a life, leadership, and career coach, Compassion Cultivation Trainer (©CCT), and author of *The Comfort Zone Illusion-Leaving Your Comfort Zone is Not So Hard After All*. She is dedicated to helping people take control of planned and unplanned change, eliminate fear, uncertainty, and anxiety, and ignite self-motivation for life-long success and happiness.

Susan has over 25 years of experience leading personal, professional, and organizational change including work in the disability field, the jail system, and senior services. She is faculty at National Louis University and DePaul University and is a keynote speaker, presenter, trainer, and facilitator at many universities, conferences, and organizations. When not filling her SPIRE jars with stones, Susan spends time with her two dogs, Milk and Snoopy both rescued from a local shelter, and making plans for future books.

Overcoming Obstacles
Through the Practice of Resilience

-Dawn Stidd

Mother Nature teaches us about resilience every spring. It reminds us that no matter how harsh and brutal winter is, there is an opportunity to move forward with beauty and grace. Every experience, even those as brutal as a northern winter, is a blessing that can help us to grow upward. Positive Psychology graces us with the tools to not just cope but shine in these times. Through these tools, we are able to see that we have the ability to bend towards the light. The idea, however cliche, is that this too shall pass! I love the reminder of spring, it's something that I strive to mirror during times of transitions and challenges in my life. By being confident in oneself and the ability to grow through challenges we build our resilience. We learn that our challenges and transitions can be overcome by coping and utilizing the control we have over our path forward. During this, we must permit ourselves to be human and allow time to process and cope. We acknowledge these feelings, allow them to be there, and then make the conscious choice to move back upward. This process requires work and practice.

While we are all born with different levels of resilience, there is an opportunity within our upbringing to either encourage or impede this character trait. For me, resilience was something that was expected at a very early age. I come from a family of pull yourself up by your bootstraps and get it done kind of folks. The blessing that I had growing up was that this was always done with love. My aunt would say it as, "Life is tough, wear a helmet." This would be said with a hug. My Pop-pop would say it as, "That's the way the cookie crumbles." This would be said with a smile. My kids repeat these along with many others. Sometimes it is, "You get what you get and you don't get upset." And sometimes it's the words of Tal Ben-Shahar they echo, "When you appreciate the good, the good appreciates." While all of these sayings essentially mean the same thing, the more we hear them, in different ways and contexts, the greater the chance that they will actually sink in. Similarly, when approaching a yoga pose, I like to have as many ways into that pose as possible. One way in may not work for all of us. And this is the case with Positive Psychology as well.

Part of resilience for me as a child was learning independence and always being respectful. While independence has an obvious way of building up a child's resilience, respect is one that I didn't connect until later as an adult. I see so many instances where people push back against challenges and discomfort. When we respect and trust the path the universe has laid out for us, we can better find a way to build resilience. Yoga is a wonderful way to learn to sit in discomfort. Growth in a yoga practice only comes when we tolerate the discomfort of placing ourselves into poses. We learn to breathe into the pose and in this way, we find our way back to comfort. Putting up a wall to any discomfort doesn't allow for the engagement with a challenge that builds character, strength, and resilience. Through yoga, we learn how to flow through poses and breathe even when there is a challenging sequence or pose. Or when we have a lot on our minds but we need to balance in a pose. Yoga teaches us that we smile into any falls and the concept of beginning again in times of failure. When we invite in challenges and discomfort instead of putting up walls against them, we are able to build our ability to overcome. The more we practice this grace and tolerance through the learning process on our mats, the more seamlessly we can do it off our mats.

At a very young age, I was drawn to music. By the time I was in high school, I wasn't the best but I had the best work ethic. At the end of high school, I wasn't good enough to get into a music conservatory as I had hoped to. I then went to community college, worked hard, reapplied, and transferred to a music conservatory the next year. The resilience I had grown up with allowed me to continue on my path despite many roadblocks. After graduating, I was always just one step behind and realized that the lifestyle that continuing to travel and audition was not making me happy. I decided to obtain my master's in music education to stay in the field I loved so much. As the universe continued to test my resilience, I managed to graduate at a time where the economy took a turn and arts programs were being reduced. Music teachers who were already working were laid off. I was lucky and got a leave replacement for a year and loved almost every minute of it. I felt fulfilled and on a path of growth, two things that are essential to my happiness.

In the meantime, I had been involved with yoga since high school. My oboe teacher at the time had said it would benefit my playing and she was right. There was a focus and a nurturing aspect to yoga that I adored. It helped me with performance nerves and breathing and discipline. I noticed that I had a similar feeling doing yoga that I did playing music. Later in my positive psychology studies, I learned that this feeling is Flow State. I could just zone out, or more correctly zone in. I decided to get my yoga certification during the summer break after my leave replacement and was immediately teaching yoga. This was a time where there were very few yoga studios and people didn't even really understand what yoga was. I quickly noticed that there were so many ties between music and yoga. I excelled at sequencing as I saw the correlation between musical phrasing and yoga sequencing. I was also used to being on stage and speaking. My natural rhythm allowed me to get students into a flow and moving together. I was also able to put just the right song at just the right time or integrate a theme through my playlist and my class. By the time I was teaching yoga successfully it was fulfilling me completely. I continued to do some music performances but eventually decided to open up my own yoga studio which has thrived for 10 years now. If I had turned away from the resiliency that was taught to me growing up, I would have been stuck on my first path instead of making changes until I was in a place where my needs were being met. I feel grateful that I continued to adjust my path until I found the thing that brings me the most happiness and at the same time allows me to support myself.

Resilience is something that I love to share with my yoga students. For some, resilience is something that can best be learned through a power class. Power classes remind us that we do have the power, control, and strength to surpass any challenge that comes our way. Challenge contains the word change and reminds us that it is an opportunity for reemergence, just like spring. Alternatively, for some of us, having a class that is restorative and asks for surrender is the best place for us to learn resilience. Resilience is many things but I think the one talked about the least is surrender to the universe. Trusting that things are as they should be and that they will work out as they are meant to. For those of us who like to feel as if we are in control this task that resilience asks of us can sometimes be the most challenging. There is a quote about yoga that says, "Blessed are the flexible for they shall not be bent out of shape." This is the core of resilience. The comparison of an oak tree versus a willow tree in a strong wind. Do you remain stuck in your ways and risk breaking? Or do you choose to bend with the wind and survive?

When I am teaching yoga, I strive to never teach the same class, sequence, or theme twice. While there may be similarities or transitions I reuse, the class as a whole is sequenced in a way that there is a build, unpredictability, and a requested receptiveness to the journey. All of these things I ask for during class allow for the building of neuroplasticity and strength. When challenges come up in our lives, we generally don't get to pick when they show up. They come to us and we need to quickly adapt and overcome to not get stuck in a downward spiral. The practice of releasing frustration, expectations, and faltering on our mats and growing through them is a practice in resilience that is priceless. This release and continuance into self-growth, while being grateful for the challenge to do so, is what allows us to continue on an upward spiral back up into happiness in times of challenge.

I aim to create a space in my classes where students enter moving meditation. Any form of meditation will grow resiliency. This is because when we allow ourselves to drift from the present and our thoughts go to the past or the future we have a tendency to lose touch with our present strength. We allow mistakes we've made in the past to stunt the strength we have gained. And we allow our fears of the future to shelter ourselves from growing into the person we can be tomorrow. By practicing meditation we are better able to sit in the reality of the present including our present strengths and a deliberate path forward. When we lose the reminder that we have control over our emotions, thoughts, and actions we enter fear, distrust, and despair. Meditation gives the reminder that we are ok as we are and releasing from the monkey mind brings the mind to a calm state. A calm mind allows you to settle into your best self as you approach any challenge that will come your way. A calm mind allows us to approach a challenge without the clutter of chatter that moves the situation from reality. This is why tricks like sleeping on it, and having the best breakthroughs in the shower do work.

One of my favorite things about Positive Psychology is that there isn't an emphasis on being tied to your past. There is instead a desire to move forward with tools and a desire to grow. As Buddhism teaches us, the root of all suffering is attachment. Being stuck in our past and limiting ourselves because of the failures of past experiences does not allow us to show up as our Best Selves. Additionally, if we are stuck on the things that we are attached to achieving, it can be hard to find a path forward. Goals are to be kept light with the journey towards that goal being the place where growth happens. It's not the achieving of the goal where the greatest levels of happiness are found. It's those steps along the way and small micro achievements along the way. It's the times we overcome the inevitable steps backward and make the conscious choice to continue forward that our heart fills most with happiness. Attachment can also be seen in tying our happiness to a certain situation or change in circumstances. When we realize that happiness can be attained without these attachments we truly thrive. To be happy in the here and now, as things are showing up for you is truly the best gift you can give yourself.

I began my exploration of positive psychology as something that I was called to do. When some of the topics came up during my coursework, I could feel a tug in my heart as if it was something that I knew but hearing the words from someone else just cemented it and allowed me to better translate it to those around me. It became not just something that was helping me to live a happier life but something that I could see changing my yoga students' lives as well. With every class, we explore themes and quotes which allowed each student to explore how to be happier in their lives off of their mats. Yoga practice is a safe place where we can try things on and learn about ourselves. These times of reflection are imperative for growing into your Best Self. I've seen countless times where students discover a tendency in themselves that's keeping them from achieving more time in a happy state through their practice. Those students who strive for perfection on their mats are most likely the same way off of their mats. To them, I echo the words of Tal, "Good is good enough." Those students who resist challenge most likely do this in their day to day as well. By exploring these tendencies on our yoga mats, we find a way through them off of our mats as well.

One of the themes which I love is the idea of exploring Gratefulness through Reframing. While many of us can list things we are grateful for, this theme encourages us to look at something we wouldn't normally be grateful for through the eye of growth. An example of this would be a time of hardship that allowed us to make shifts or growth that will serve us in the future. All challenges are an opportunity to make choices. We can choose to push into the pain and grow. Or to turn away from it and have to keep coming back to it until we deal with the lesson the universe insists we deal with. I like to give the lighthearted example that I am grateful for Vermont's mud season because it gives me a chance to clean, which is like therapy for me, and makes spring all the sweeter when it arrives. This practice of gratefulness through reframing grows us into resiliency by showing us the benefit of challenges and discomfort. It teaches us a path to making lemonade out of lemons.

I am now blessed with two beautiful daughters. My daughters are 4 and 6 now but my 4-year-old was born right as I was completing my positive psychology course. I believe that wearing headphones while I was pregnant with her allowed her to absorb these beautiful concepts. She is the epitome of happiness. This doesn't mean that she doesn't have her moments of what I call "fire breathing dragon." But she is able to hit the switch and regain her composure quicker than many other children I have seen. She was born with compassion and empathy that fills my heart with pride. I am frequently using Positive Psychology with both of my children. When something upsets them it is talked about on a scale of 1 to 10. This allows them to ascertain how bad it is when they are upset about something. Having an open opportunity to cry when something is very hurtful for them but not allowing them to get into a downward spiral when it is something that isn't so terrible. Resilience feeds happiness by allowing us to get out of a downward spiral towards unhappiness quicker. It allows us to regain our spiral upwards towards happiness which is something that we do have the power to do!

As a parent, I think it's important to create opportunities for children to be uncomfortable. So many times we want to make them comfortable, partly so we don't hear complaining which children master at a young age. But partly because it's a parent's role to help a young child with basic tasks. At a certain point, I began to step back and let my children be uncomfortable and annoyed at having to do things themselves. By doing this they have built confidence and independence within them which allows for a transition into resilience. I'll never forget Tal saying to us in our Positive Psychology course, "No one is coming to save you." At first, this sounds harsh and frightening. However, when it settles in there is a realization of Self Sufficiency and Independence. Children tend to get stuck in the downward spiral when discomfort and annoyance appear. They need to be taught and guided to release from their downward spiral when they don't get their own way. Early on in parenting, I learned the best way to do this is through distraction. By bringing their attention away from the continued negative reaction and finding something that made them happy, I was able to show them that they have the ability to pull themselves away from misery and back into happiness. This has allowed more times of peace in our household.

An eye-opening outlook in Positive Psychology for me was the concept that stress isn't totally bad. When we exercise and work our bodies we are stressing it out. However, the thing that allows this stress to not become detrimental to us is the ability to allow for a rest period. Achieving requires some ability to push past old norms. But this also needs to be balanced with time-outs. Finding what works for you as far as timeouts is a beautiful thing to learn about oneself. For my oldest daughter, painting is her choice of time out. For my youngest daughter, bath time with toys is what recharges her. And for me, being in a yoga class where someone else guides a flowing class is my opportunity to reset. So many times for me as a mom and business owner, I wait too long for that self-care. I expect myself to go constantly without hitting my recharge button. Resiliency doesn't ask that we go without stopping towards growth. It also doesn't ask us to get into Self Care obsession. It asks instead that we push past internal resistance and take a moderate amount of time to reset so that when the next challenge comes we can show up as our Best Self. A plant or tree doesn't grow to be resilient without the proper soil, water, and sun or too much either. In the same way, we need to fuel and nurture ourselves by providing self-care.

As my girls grow up I hope for them to hold the ability to be determined, strong, and self-sufficient while being able to flow without attachment to their heart's desires. This is a life lesson that serves our children as well as ourselves. There is a balance between being determined and focused on a path forward and backing off in the times that path no longer serves us. Resilience is not a task that we have to do, it is something that we get to do. The more we explore resiliency the more tools and tactics we learn to grow it. Finding this resiliency with love and compassion for ourselves as well as others through a non-harming, non-attached state is where true happiness lives.

Dawn Stidd | Rocky Point, New York

https://www.dawnstidd.com

Dawn began studying yoga in 2004 while studying music performance at Boston Conservatory. After receiving a BM in Music Performance and an MS in Music Education, Dawn went on to receive her 200 hour yoga certification at Kripalu Center for Yoga and Health.

In 2013 Dawn traveled to India to obtain her 500hr certification in Advanced Vinyasa Yoga. Always eager to learn more, she also obtained Certifications in Kids Yoga, SUP Yoga and 75 hours advanced training from Laughing Lotus.

In 2015, Dawn acquired a Certificate in Positive Psychology which she uses to bring smiles and tips on happiness in each of her classes. Dawn's classes are centered around challenging the body and mind. While physically challenging, she emphasizes the importance of finding the balance between honoring the body and finding new limits every practice.

Her classes will always bring you something you can take off your mat and into your life to live with more happiness and peace. With over 10 years of teaching experience, she will be sure to bring something new to you each class as you travel through the journey of yoga!

Dawn is now teaching between Vermont and New York and is available for Yoga Classes, one - on - one sessions and coachings along with Workshops and Teacher Trainings.

Courage

-James Dipisa

*I learned that courage was not the absence of
fear but the triumph over it.*
                        - Nelson Mandella

*Courage is the most important of all virtues because
without courage you can't practice any other Virtue
consistently.*
                        - Maya Angelou

One of the criticisms of positive psychology is that it is all
happy faces, and butterflies, and unicorns.

Courage is one of positive psychology's principal character
traits. Courage happens. And has always happened.

I happened to read an article in the Spring 2021 issue of Alpinist that described some of the first mountain climbers. The author, Katie Ives, wrote about Egeria who according to contemporary records was the first person to climb Mount Sinai. Egeria accomplished this feat in the 4th century CE. In the 7th century CE, the monk Valerius attributed Egeria's ascents to "God's help", but also to "her unconquerable bravery ..."

My job in this chapter is to talk to you about what to do when courage is the necessary virtue.

Why me? You may ask. Well, I asked that too. It may be that my "qualifications" swayed the editor.

One of those qualifications is that I served two consecutive tours with the US Army in Vietnam. Quite a bit of courage was displayed by both sides in that sad, awful conflict. On the US side, 257 Medals of Honor were awarded for acts of supreme valor in Vietnam.

But also, according to statistics kept by the Veterans Administration (VA), 30% of Vietnam veterans returned home with diagnosable symptoms of Post Traumatic Stress. My understanding of PTS is that it is not a "disorder" but an understandable reaction to an intolerable situation. According to the VA, the symptoms of PTS and the rate of incidence have stayed approximately the same since they first began keeping statistics during WW I.

So, I came home and, thanks to the GI Bill, trained to be a psychologist. Naturally, being a Vietnam veteran, I got the hardest job (there are statistics on that too). My job was as the interviewer on a child sexual abuse investigation team. That's a whole bunch of kids who were set up to deal with intolerable memories for the rest of their lives.

Some years ago, some good doctors at the CDC and Kaiser Permanente asked a large number of patients about their childhood experiences. Specifically, they asked if the individuals, as children, had been the targets of abuse or witnessed other family members being abused. This was called the Adverse Childhood Experiences study. The results were that 50% of patients with a score of 4 out of 10 or higher on the ACE questionnaire reported significant learning or behavioral problems as adults.

You may be asking why I started this chapter with "war stories". Another Vietnam veteran, Tim O'Brien, in his book - *The Things They Carried*- explains why starting a conversation with "war stories" is important. O'Brien wrote:

> A true war story is never moral. It does not instruct, nor encourage virtue ... As a rule of thumb, you can tell a true war story by its allegiance to obscenity and evil.

All of the veterans and children of whom I speak experienced obscenity and evil.

And yet, I consider it the greatest privilege for me to speak for those veterans who can no longer speak for themselves. And for those children who had the courage to be the member of their respective families to speak the truth.

Because for those people touched by trauma – but not overwhelmed – there exists the possibility of Post Traumatic Growth. You can recognize a PTG survivor because,

1. They find benefits in their experience
2. They are successful in maintaining a future orientation
3. They have coherent narratives that transform their losses into positives.

PTG survivors start with a broken self-image. Let me explain. In western thought self-image can be defined as filling in the blank in the sentence stem: I am a _____. Here are three responses that indicate that you're in trouble.

> I can't _____ (do math).
> I am _____ (a bad girl).
> I am _____ (a killer).

The antidote to this disastrous response to stress is focusing on gratitude. That was as surprising to me as I imagine it is to you.

In the remarkable book, *The Book of Joy*, the authors, His Holiness the Dali Lama and Archbishop Desmond Tutu, define gratitude.

> *Gratitude is the recognition of all that holds us in the web of life and all that has made it possible to have the life that we have … Thanksgiving is a natural response to life …*

Trust me, it's not easy. You have to start small. Right now, I'm grateful for the sunlight streaming in the window as I type. But with strength and courage The Dali Lama and Archbishop Tutu – who both experienced terrible trauma – were able to write that thanksgiving is a natural response to life.

Getting in touch with that "web of life" may happen most directly and dramatically by being in the "natural world". As Barbara Kingsolver says,

> *People need wild places. Whether or not we think we do, we do. We need to be able to taste grace and know again that we desire it. We need to experience a landscape that is timeless, whose agenda moves at the pace of speciation and glaciers. To be surrounded by a singing, mating, howling commotion of other species, all of which love their lives as much as we do ours, and none of which could possibly care less about us in our place. It reminds us that our plans are small and somewhat absurd. It reminds us why, in the cases in which our plans might influence many future generations, we ought to choose carefully. It is important to know that we are a small, somewhat absurd part of the marvelous web of life. And, to be grateful that we have a place in that "singing, mating, howling, commotion."*

Finally, we are all fundamentally social creatures. But trauma devastates the social engagement system and the ability to function as a productive member of society. A substantial re-orienting is often necessary. This also requires great courage. The psychologist/philosopher Maria Sirois said:

> *Life will have its way with us … As we learn to forgive ourselves … we become a light that can offer that learning to others …*

One form of therapy that has been successful in people recovering from trauma is Eye Movement Desensitization and Reprocessing. According to Servan-Schreiber in *The Instinct to Heal*, the process of EMDR is:

1. Evoke the traumatic memory on emotional, cognitive, and physical levels,
2. Induce a Rapid Eye Movement (i.e., dream-like state) using bilateral stimulation,
3. With minimal verbal prompts assist the natural healing system of the mind **rewrites the story** (bolding mine). That is, develop a different perspective of the same memory.

It is important for the trauma survivor to re-orient their self-image by realizing that their behaviors were not evil or obscene. Their behaviors were what they had to do to survive. And, often included great courage and sacrifice so that others could also survive.

It takes work, and courage, and help, and gratitude, but we humans can recover from trauma and become inspirations for others. The Dali Lama and Archbishop Tutu defined the goal of surviving our struggles.

The goal is not just to create joy for ourselves but … to be a reservoir of joy, an oasis of peace, a pool of a serenity that can ripple out to all those around [us] … joy is, in fact, quite contagious. As is love, compassion, and generosity.

It is important to note that the behaviors of PTS survivors were once a rational response to an irrational situation. If you can fill in the "I am" blank, you can't make "killer" or "bad girl" go away. But, you can, with courage and practice, and effort, learn to breathe and say, "I am a peaceful and generous person".

After all, the Buddha may have said, "Everyone is entitled to lead a life of compassion and dignity".

I am grateful that survivors are strong and courageous. Veterans recover from their wounds. Small children told me horrible stories because someone in their family had to speak the truth.

Survivors have terrible scars because they did what they had to do to survive. They can recover and lead lives of compassion and dignity.

Not all of this re-ordering is the responsibility of the individual PTS survivor. Probably one of the hardest things about coming home from war is the change in behavioral expectations. The common expectations for soldiers are found in the unofficial Soldier's Code.

1. The mission always comes first.
2. I will never surrender
3. I will never leave a man behind, dead or alive.

One of the difficulties in coming home is learning that this level of commitment, honor, and courage are often held up for ridicule in our society. I think society can also change. We can honor the courage of the PTS survivors among us.

In closing, there are 58000+ names on a black wall in Washington, DC. One of those names is Michael D. O'Donnell. The following poem was found among Chief Warrant Officer O'Donnell's belongings after he was killed in action in Vietnam.

Letters from Pleiku

If you are able, save for them a place inside of you...
And save one backward glance when you are leaving
For the places they can no longer go ...
Be not ashamed to say you love them, though you
may or may not have always.
Take what they have left and what they have taught
you with their dying
And keep it with your own.
And in that time when men decide and feel safe to
call the war insane,
Take one moment to embrace those gentle heroes
you left behind.

And for those of us left behind the words of the narrator from the movie *Platoon*:

> *Those of us who did make it have an obligation to build again; to teach others what we know, and to try with what's left of our lives, to find goodness and meaning in this life.*

That is, those of us who survived must honor those who can no longer enjoy a lazy summer day with loved ones because they overcame fear, acted on their convictions, and, persisted toward their goals. We can only do that by refusing to shrink from threat, challenge, difficulty, or pain.

Courage the Character Strength

The research findings of the VIA Institute (based on hundreds of surveys over the last 25+ years) identified 8 character virtues. Each virtue consists of several character strengths.

The virtue of "courage" is defined as the quality that "helps you exercise your will and face adversity".

The four character strengths included in the virtue are:

1. Honesty. Defined as:
    a. speaking the truth;
    b. presenting one's self genuinely and sincerely;
    c. being without pretense; and,
    d. taking responsibility for one's feelings and actions.
2. Perseverance. Defined as: Finishing what one starts despite obstacles.
3. Bravery. Defined as: Not shrinking from threat, challenge, difficulty, or pain.
4. Zest. Defined as: Approaching life with excitement and energy.

Once, long ago, we had a president who wrote a book called Profiles in Courage about politicians who had spoken the truth as they knew it and did not shrink from threat.

That same president had also demonstrated great physical courage during WW II in saving the lives of all the sailors on his PT boat when it was sunk by enemy fire.

Of course, John Kennedy had character flaws – we all do – but, in times of stress and danger, he was able to activate the positive characteristics of his personality.

In researching this article, I found a definition that divides courage into six attributes.

1. Physical courage: bravery at the risk of bodily harm or death.
2. Social courage: risk of social embarrassment or exclusion.
3. Intellectual courage: willingness to engage with challenging ideas.
4. Moral courage: doing the right thing, particularly when risks involve shame, opposition, or the disapproval of others.
5. Emotional courage: feeling the full spectrum of positive emotions, at the risk of encountering negative ones.
6. Spiritual courage: fortifies us when we grapple with questions about faith, purpose, and meaning.

Surely, almost everyone will be confronted at some time in their life with a demand for courage in one or more of these six areas. So displaying courage, for all of us, boils down to answering yes to three statements:

1. I act on my convictions;
2. I am honest with myself and others;
3. I persist toward my goals.

Or, in the words of Mark Twain: "Courage is resistance to fear, mastery of fear-not absence of fear."

James J DiPisa, PhD | Massachuetts

Jim DiPisa has been a licensed psychologist for 40 years. He has worked in public schools in Connecticut and has been a faculty member for several universities.

Jim got his first training in Positive Psychology on the referral of his yoga instructor who is a graduate of Kirpalu's yoga instructor program.

Donna Martire Miller was a TA in Jim's positive psychology class where they discovered the happy coincidence that they lived in the same town.

Presently, Jim is retired and living in Massachusetts with his wife Liz.

Finding Positive Emotions in the Face of Challenge: Put on Those Cute Shoes and Do What You're Being Called to Do!

-Lisa Bailey Sullivan

1. I started writing this chapter on the anniversary of a life-changing moment.
2. I started writing this chapter soon after Meghan Markle held her all-telling interview with Oprah where she revealed her depression over not being able to be herself.

3. I started writing this chapter one year after the world was in lockdown due to a pandemic.
4. I started writing this chapter after a very rough day at work.

5. I started writing this chapter after just spending 15 minutes crying in the shower.

And I believe the crying in the shower was in large part due to due to items 1-4.

I take care of my family. I am there 24-7 for my kids. I am running my own business to spread hope, joy, and happiness to people. And I am the communications director for my beautiful little city. That's a lot.

And some days it just all feels like too much. Some days I just want to run away. Some days, I just want a good cry in the shower. Some days, I just want to be myself without having to slap a fake smile on my face like Meghan had to do.

I think we all have days where it all feels like too much, where we just want to run away. Sometimes finding the positive is really challenging. But I'm here to tell you it always gets better. The happier times come back.

All you need to do is start loving who you are right now.

When you start loving yourself, the positive emotions start to flow. And soon all that love and positivity leads you in the direction of your purpose. You're ready to put on some cute shoes, step out in that new direction, and set the world on fire.

But how do you begin to love yourself?

Let's Start at the Very Beginning… or at Least 4 Years Ago

Let's start with that anniversary of a life-changing moment. Four years ago (that now feels like eons ago in a corporate galaxy far, far away), I was a corporate marketing exec. I worked for a great company that paid me a lot of money to do things I loved to do. I was able to support and care for my family with a job that allowed my husband to be a stay-at-home dad for our wonderful two kids. The company even allowed me to become certified in Positive Psychology and create happiness workshops for the company.

Then my world fell apart and my safety net dropped away: My company was purchased by a private equity firm and I was laid off. I went from a six figure salary to zero, with a husband who hadn't worked in years, with a son in college and a daughter in middle school.

I went from a relatively easy-going life to a sheer panic about how I was going to bring in a paycheck and take care of my family. My life was eat, pray, panic.

Through the panic, I took each day as it came. I picked myself up each day and did whatever I could to breathe each day and move on, often using the same tools of positive psychology that I taught in my happiness workshops.

It was also during this time that I decided to do something totally out of my comfort zone. I became a certified teacher in Let Your Yoga Dance®, which is a fun practice that combines yoga and dancing moves with music, focusing on each chakra energy center of your body.

I'd never taken yoga before, I was (am) extremely out of shape, and was something that my introverted self felt extremely uncomfortable doing. This was way beyond my comfort zone.

But this practice helped me go inside and love myself for who I was, not what I thought others wanted me to be. It added fun into a life that hadn't had fun in a long time and healing to my mind and spirit. It helped me tap into what was important to me.

I took this practice (woo-woo) and my training in positive psychology (science) and combined them to create a women's retreat for those going through what I went through. I took everything I knew to start helping women be all they can be. I started helping women find ways to feel safe and tap into their power, courage, self-love, and joy. And I started helping companies tap into their happiness through on-site workshops and virtual workshops during the pandemic.

I want to share some of the things that helped me do just that. These are a few of my key philosophies on life. Like my retreats, they are a little bit of science and a little bit of woo-woo, that combine for a whole lot of happiness for me, and I know will help you when you're seeking that unshakable happiness during those times when you just want to run away.

Here are my simple practices that help me feel happier, help me with my purpose, and make me want to put on those cute shoes and chance the world:

- Be Open to Everything and Attached to Nothing!
- Always Remember That What Anyone Thinks of Me is None of My Business!
- Stop Comparing!

- Find that Benefit!
- Forgive myself!

Be Open to Everything and Attached to Nothing

When you're at the place where you want to run away, a shift in how you look at things can help. A simple shift in thought can make the bad good. When you embrace that life has ups and downs, you look for more things to bring you the ups and you suddenly become open to new things.

When I went through training to become a Let Your Yoga Dance teacher, I was in the biggest change and challenge of my life. It was right after being laid off. I felt lost, unwanted, and was suffocating from fear. But I decided to do the training because I wanted to do something far outside of my comfort zone and completely outside the corporate-world-zone.

I was expecting to feel uncomfortable, and it didn't disappoint. I asked myself often, "What the hell am I doing here?" The first night, I wanted to run. I packed my bag and was almost out the door.

I decided to stay. That decision to stay was a pivotal one for me.

I talked to myself a lot that night. The one thing that got me to stay was a quote I told myself, a quote I heard years ago: Lisa, be open to everything and attached to nothing.

That quote gives me peace. It helps me let go of any expectations.

So, I let go of what I was expecting to come out of the training and just became open to wherever it took me. What I met were many other women going through challenges. They didn't have the challenges of being laid off with no money, but their challenges brought the same feelings: feelings of fear, feelings of being lost, feelings of being not enough. I discovered a beautiful group of women who came through their challenges by stepping out of their comfort zones, too.

I let go of expectations, became open to everything, and had one of the most amazing times in my life. And Let Your Yoga Dance became one of the two pillars of my women's retreats, retreats that would not have happened if I hadn't been open to new experiences.

Be open to everything and attached to nothing. It will bring joy and new experiences into your life.

What Anyone Thinks of Me is None of My Business

One of the most important things you need to become happier in life is to finally embrace, once and for all, the practice of not giving care to what anyone thinks of you.

This is also the critical key to embracing your true power and, in turn, tapping into that unshakable happiness that's inside you. Because when you stop caring what others think, you start becoming the person YOU love, not the person you think others will love. It is the moment you become the real you.

This is NOT an easy thing to accomplish. You'll ask yourself these questions often:

- Is this okay to do?
- What will people think of me?
- Will it make her/him angry?
- What if they don't like me?

• What if I hurt her feelings?

But I guarantee if you try to follow this tenet, your life will soar. At my retreats, whenever I share the importance of not giving a "flip" what others think, the reactions from the women are overwhelming. It's as if their entire lives they've been caring too much about the feelings and opinions of others rather than their own and they finally feel free. They explode into a catharsis of reaction when I bring it up.

And I love it.

I don't love that it's happened to them. I love that they've had it. Their mantra is "ENOUGH" and it's wonderful to hear.

The reality is no matter WHAT you do, someone is not going to like it. You cannot control the thoughts and feelings of others. You can't make everyone like you. You can only control your own thoughts and feelings about something. Care only about what you think about yourself. What anyone else thinks about you is none of your business.

When you live your life based on what others are going to think, you're living their lives, not yours.

I'm not saying it's time for you to become a raging honey badger. I'm a huge believer in the power of kindness. But I'm also a huge believer in embracing your true self and loving every bit of it. I'm a huge believer in being the real you.

So, the next time you find yourself wondering, "Is she going to get mad at me?" or "What if I do this and they don't like me?" stop and repeat this a few times: What anyone thinks of me is none of my business.

Stop Comparing!

The sister to "what anyone thinks of me is none of my business" is "stop comparing."

Until you stop comparing yourself to others and caring what others think about you, you're never going to be who YOU truly were meant to be or find true happiness.

Comparing yourself to others takes away your happiness.

Here's just a sample of the voices in my head:

- She's putting on a great event, why can't I?
- She wrote a book. Why is her story better than mine?
- She's such a great writer, why can't I write like that?
- She's getting these speaking engagements. Why can't I? God, she's a great speaker. I'll never be able to motivate an audience like that.
- She's so funny! Why am I so boring?

All of this is usually based on fear. For me, it is the fear of not being enough and not having enough. If I can't be enough, if I can't be as successful as those women I'm comparing myself to, then I won't have enough to take care of my family.

It wasn't until I stopped trying to be what everyone else was and when I stopped comparing myself to others, did the fear of not being enough go away, too.

Comparing can turn into a vicious cycle: I want to be great like others, yet I'm really wanting to be my own great self, but I don't feel like my own great self is enough, so I want to be great like others. WTH?

If you're comparing yourself, stop. I know it's easier said than done. It took me a lot of meditating and soul searching and a lot of loving-kindness meditation. And I still on occasion compare myself, but at least I catch it when I do and that helps me stop.

And I also permit myself to be human when I fall back on comparing. I'm not perfect. Neither are those I'm comparing myself to.

Find that Benefit!

You've probably heard about the importance of gratitude in your life. There's been so much research done that clearly shows that writing down what you're grateful for can increase your levels of happiness.

But writing down what I'm grateful for has been a struggle for me. It's not fun for me. I feel like it's an "assignment" and I've been done with school for (um) decades. I often buy gratitude journals with good intentions. I start writing down what I'm grateful for but then I get bored quickly. If you looked in my home office, you'd find at least 10 gratitude journals that have maybe 4-5 entries in them.

Writing down my gratitudes is obviously not for me.

But here's a practice that has helped me more than expressing gratitude. I discovered the benefit of being a benefit finder. Being a benefit finder is like gratitude on steroids for me. It's a powerful practice that also helps you feel a little more of your own power. Being a benefit finder means you find something "good" in anything "bad" that's happened in your life.

This is not always easy. Sometimes it takes a while to find the benefit in the middle of a challenge. But when you start to practice it, it becomes easier.

When I got laid off, I immediately found some benefits in it. It took a while for the benefits to sink in, but I was able to find them.

- It helped me realize I didn't want to work in the corporate world anymore, I needed a break. I was a VP of marketing during the day, but a mystic at night. Being a mystic was now more important to me.
- I was grateful to the company because I discovered positive psychology because of them. Ironically, if I hadn't been so unhappy, I never would have realized the importance of happiness in a company. Because of my experiences there, I found that one of the things that lit me up was helping others find ways to become a little happier using the science of happiness. Being laid off gave me the push to pursue something that really touched my heart.
- If I hadn't been laid off, I might not have started my own company helping women and companies through my retreats and workshops.
- If I hadn't been laid off, I wouldn't have met many of the amazing women I've had a chance to meet over the past couple of years.
- If I hadn't been laid off, I wouldn't be writing a chapter in this book!

No matter what you are going through, you CAN find one good thing from it. There's always a nugget of a benefit in there somewhere. And when you find that nugget, you're taking back your power to live the life you want and you're tapping into that unshakable happiness deep inside you.

Forgive Yourself!

If you are older than 4, you know the importance of loving yourself. My god, we hear it all the time. Social media is filled with "loving yourself" motivational memes ...

- "You need to love yourself."
- "You can't love someone else without loving yourself first."
- "Love yourself first and everything else falls into line."
- "Loving yourself starts with liking yourself, which starts with respecting yourself, which starts with thinking of yourself in positive ways."
- "If you don't love yourself, nobody else is going to love you."
- "Be gentle with yourself, learn to love yourself, to forgive yourself, for only as we have the right attitude toward ourselves can we have the right attitude."

Loving yourself can be hard. We've been ingrained to spend our days taking care of others more than ourselves. We see images all over social media and other media telling us how to look great, how to age gracefully.

Phooey.

I'm here to tell you that you don't need to listen to anyone or be anything. If you don't love yourself right now, that's okay. It will come.

But you do need to forgive yourself. When you forgive yourself, self-love and happiness come flowing in.

- Forgive yourself for all the things you've said to yourself over the years.
- Forgive yourself if you haven't treated your body the way you "should" have treated it.
- Forgive yourself if you feel you haven't been the best friend to you or others.
- Forgive yourself if you feel like you've spent too much money on stuff you don't need.
- Forgive yourself for all the energy you've wasted over the years not loving yourself.
- Forgive yourself for everything.

When you forgive yourself, you let go of the negative feelings in your life, like shame and anger and replace them with gratitude and power. You let go of competition and comparing yourself to others and replace them with the knowledge that there's always enough. You accept yourself and all your strengths AND weaknesses and a sense of peace comes over you.

It all Adds Up to Loving Yourself and Unshakable Happiness!

Once you begin to forgive yourself, you can start to show gratitude for everything you've done well in your life. The more you acknowledge the good, the more your self-love will grow.

Loving yourself doesn't take a monumental shift. It's one small act at a time.

A small act of being open to everything and attached to nothing. A small act of not caring what others think about you. A small act of not comparing your beautiful life to others. A small act of finding the good in anything bad. The small act of forgiving yourself.

These little acts help you find your positive emotions in the face of challenge. All these little acts add up to loving yourself a little more each day.

And when you start loving yourself, you start finding ways to love and help others. You find that unshakable happiness inside. And best of all, you don't want to run away anymore. All you want to do is put on those cute shoes and start setting the world on fire.

Lisa Bailey Sullivan | Dripping Springs, Texas

https://www.lisabaileysullivan.com

"Put on some cute shoes, take a big breath, and set out to do what you're being called to do."

Lisa Bailey Sullivan is a wife, mom, recovering marketing exec, and the C-3PO (Chief Compassion, Courage & Positivity Officer) of her crazy-happy life. As a happiness activist, she's motivated to create positive change in the world. She's particularly passionate about helping women unapologetically play big and have fun, embrace their true selves, and do what they're being called to do – no more delays!

Drawing from the science of positive psychology, her more than two decades of marketing leadership experience, and a little woo-woo, Lisa offers simple, tested actions that can help reduce stress and anxiety and cultivate a lasting sense of wellbeing, at work and in life. She is certified in positive psychology through The Wholebeing Institute and a graduate of the Happiness Studies Academy. She is trained in Google's Search Inside Yourself Program and a certified Let Your Yoga Dance® teacher. She is the founder of Camp Atta Girl!™, an empowering retreat that helps women rediscover their voice, power, self-love, and joy. She is the author of "Atta Girl! The Art of Tapping into Your Power and Moxie and Living Fearlessly Happy (in the middle of a sh*tshow!)" And she owns some cute shoes.

Learn more and purchase her book at lisabaileysullivan.com and campattagirl.com.

She put on some cute shoes, took a big breath, and set out to do what she was being called to do.

Building Social Capital

-Phoebe Atkinson

When we ask, miracles can happen.
                                    –Wayne Baker

"Social capital" is a term coined by Wayne Baker, one of the world's foremost experts on building and strengthening connections. Baker, who serves as faculty director of the Center for Positive Organizational Scholarship at the University of Michigan, defines social capital as "how willing people are to help others in their social network." This concept relates to reciprocity in general, which is the "exchange of resources between two people."

During this past year Wholebeing Institute has been building its social capital in a variety of ways. One example of this is a program launched during the pandemic called The Positivity Hour.

Seeking Positive Solutions

> *Faced with uncertainty, it is common for people to seek positive solutions*
>
> *- Soklaridis, et al, 2020*

In 2020 Barbara Fredrickson was invited to speak by her colleague Jane Dutton at a summit entitled 'Unlocking resources for Recovery, Renewal and Resilience.'
Dr. Fredrickson emphasized the need to be intentional about developing resources such as compassion, courage, resilience, hope and self-care.

Shortly before this summit in March 2020, when the reality of COVID-19 was just beginning to sink in, the JCC Manhattan and the Wholebeing Institute had already joined together in a groundbreaking effort to forge connections and to share skills for navigating life in a crisis. In 52 weeks of free, lunch-time Positivity Hours, Megan McDonough and Phoebe Atkinson of the Wholebeing Institute and CIWPP alum Caroline Kohles of the JCC introduced faculty and alumni from the Wholebeing Institute who offered understanding, concrete help, and practical skills drawing from the field of applied positive psychology.

Just as the Positivity Hour was marking its one-year anniversary, an article appeared in the 2021 edition of the *Journal of Positive Psychology*. A dream team of positive psychologists, many of whom have been faculty or guest speakers for Wholebeing Institute, came together to share their findings about "the role that positive psychology factors can play in buffering against mental illness, bolstering mental health during COVID-19 and building positive processes and capacities that may help to strengthen future mental health."

The paper considered how three processes (buffer, bolster, build) can be generated through nine positive psychology topics: meaning, coping, self-compassion, courage, gratitude, character strengths, positive emotions, positive interpersonal processes, and high-quality connections.

The nine topics highlighted in the article have enriched the discussion around positive psychology and its impact on well being.

For instance, speaking on positive emotions and positive interpersonal processes, new data presented by Fredrickson in the 2021 *JOPP* article discusses the impact of positive emotions on mental health. Fredrickson has proposed that positive emotions and positivity resonance are especially important in the midst of a pandemic. When we build in durable resources (friendship, resilience) we are more likely to get into these moments again. The application means we intentionally prioritize our positivity - and invest in upward spiral practices - injecting more positive moments into each day.

Fredrickson's research has shown that positive emotions can coexist with negative emotions. Citing her findings on the positive emotion of hope, she explains that hope is the only positive emotion that is activated under dire circumstances. Hope in the literature is described as "fearing the worst" (not denying the circumstances) and "yearning for better and thinking better is possible." This vital resource which is activated in adversity helps us mobilize as we imagine a positive future. Consequently, she says, we become more planful. "Hope unleashes innovation and effort and resourcefulness and doggedness," says Fredrickson.

When we set out to collaborate and create a series offering applied positive psychology we did not know what it would mean. The topics in the 2021 article served as a kind of exclamation mark – a validation of the Positivity Hour offerings - as the nine areas described in the *JOPP* 2021 paper corresponded directly with the wide variety of applied positive psychology topics faculty, friends, and alumni of the many WBI programs presented throughout the pandemic.

What we did know when we started our collaboration was that there was a need for people to learn about resilience. We felt sure we could tap into the deep social capital embedded within Wholebeing Institute and inferred that many people would be willing to contribute.

Many of the authors in this book have been featured guests on the Positivity Hour and have given freely of their knowledge and talent to serve the greater good. Each of their singular voices have been an active ingredient throughout the pandemic. Our presenters have served up daily doses of applied practices which have nourished individual and collective wellbeing.

Series participants have shown up consistently with eagerness and openness to learn and engage with the material. We have witnessed the broaden and build effect within our community. The broadening has happened as participants have increased their intellectual resources and many have told us about how they have built psychological resources such as resilience and self-efficacy and have described increased social resources. This build effect is felt in the widening circles of connections that have been made within the learning community that has grown exponentially both in live attendance as well as reflected in those who listen to the recordings found at our WBI repository.

A central feature of students who have graduated Wholebeing Institute courses is that they embody a deep sense of gratitude and a commitment to serve the work forward. The series has been a wonderful opportunity for them to offer support to the greater good.

Reciprocity according to Wayne Baker, means "I help you and you help someone else, and maybe that person will end up helping me (or someone else) sometime in the future." Baker's research has shown that when reciprocity is widespread in organizations, it improves productivity, promotes learning, and builds a climate of trust.

In 2020 Dr. Fredrickson advised that in order to address the challenges of the pandemic – individuals and organizations would need to generate resources and build alliances and teams. The Positivity Hour continues to answer this charge.

It stands as a testimony of the ever-expanding social capital woven throughout Wholebeing Institute.

Dr. Baker's research shows that asking and getting is much easier than we think, and he encourages us all to consider that this is even more true in a suddenly virtual world. All you have to do is ask! As a result of us asking ourselves how we could help and asking others to collaborate and serve – we have been able to co-create upward and outward spirals that have generated virtuous circles of reciprocity and giving.

References

Follow this link for archive recordings of Positivity Hour:
https://wholebeinginstitute.com/category/blog/jcc/]

2021 JOPP article PP in a Pandemic

[https://www.tandfonline.com/doi/full/10.1080/17439760.202
1.1871945]

Soklaridis, S. , Lin, E. , Lalani, Y. , Rodak, T. , & Sockalingam, S. (2020, April). "Mental health interventions and supports during COVID-19 and other medical pandemics: A rapid systematic review of the evidence." *General Hospital Psychiatry* , 66, 133–146

Phoebe Atkinson, LCSW-R | New York, New York

Phoebe Atkinson is a licensed clinical social worker, certified coach, and board-certified trainer, educator, and practitioner in psychodrama, sociometry, and group psychotherapy.

She serves on the faculty for WBI's Certificate in Wholebeing Positive Psychology and has mentored WBI's teaching assistants.

She is also a graduate of the program. She is a core faculty member of WBI's Positive Psychology Coaching Certification program and teaches in the online Positive Psychology: Skill-Building Intensive course and Positive Psychology Coaching Mentorship.

In March 2020, Phoebe began curating the Positivity Hour featuring WBI alumni in partnership with the JCC Manhattan.

SECTION 3: LIVING WITH INTENTION

- DONNA MARTIRE MILLER

Joseph Bologna

Living with intention takes some practice. It takes introspection and closely examining your choices. Then taking action. This is a self-directed path that is individualized by and for you. Finding unshakable happiness is about developing a series of practices that enable us to engage in our lives as authentically as possible. The Buddhists call this living and behaving right-minded. In fact, most religions or wisdom traditions offer a map of virtuous intention to live in this way. Once we develop our *Ideal* self, we can then align our thoughts, words, and behaviors with what we value and begin to engage in life in this way. Today's studies in neuroscience show that our brains are not rigid structures. At any age we can change, evolve based on our intentions, actions, and how we experience life. We hold the potential to develop ourselves. It all begins with setting our intention towards a life worth living.

Along the way, we will encounter some obstacles. Knowing our choices and how to handle them is crucial. This section will read stories that address forgiveness, self-compassion, resiliency, flourishing, and growth mindsets. These can be very tender personal concepts; they all involve utilizing the character strengths of humility and bravery in some way. Dr. Loren Toussaint, an expert in forgiveness studies, explains that when we feel hurt, one of the last things we want to do is to think of the other person or situation and empathize with them. It can seem easier to take the position of being righteous, holding fast to our own moral superiority over the other involved.

Yet, all of us are faced with needing to forgive or want to be forgiven at some point in our lives. Even more importantly, according to science, holding on to unforgiveness activates the stress response of the sympathetic nervous system. According to Elaine O'Brian, Ph.D., this actually accelerates the aging process of our cells! It can also reduce the health benefits of engaging in positive activities like loving social connections, gratitude, awe, and experiencing meaning and purpose. Unforgiveness increases the stress response in our body every time we reminisce about the situation. Our ability to feel peaceful and to relax is impaired. Learning to forgive stimulates hope, wellbeing, and peace. It offers resolution and relief in families and relationships. Realizing that the intention of the other probably has more factors involved and is a bit different than what our thoughts and feelings have told us about the situation.

To move forward, we can begin to forgive…in some cases, it can be dangerous to forgive and forget, and I am not suggesting that at all, especially if that would put you in harm's way. However, if we can forgive, we can begin to live in balance again.

One of the most popular models of forgiveness used today is the REACH model by Everett Worthington.

R = Recall the hurt. Start the healing process for yourself by facing the pain and deciding to let go of the past without retribution.

E = Empathize. Write a note to the one who hurt you saying everything from your heart. Then write back to yourself, imagining what the other would say as to why they hurt you. In this way, you may develop compassion which is healing.

A = Altruistic gift. Maybe because of your *Ideal* self-belief, spirituality, or virtues, you can give forgiveness as a gift and experience gratitude for doing so.

C = Commit. Once I attended a religious retreat, I went to a confession. I went back as far as I could remember trying to humbly admit my regrets. The confessor said after a while, "haven't you ever confessed these things before?" I said, well, yes, and he then said, when you are forgiven, it is forgotten … why do you keep reminding people?" I laughed and understood about committing to permanently letting things go.

H = Hold onto forgiveness. Forgiveness takes courage. It is a heroic thing to do. It is a strength and an accomplishment. Taking action to forgive is proven to help us have a more positive attitude and further develop our personality attributes such as love, compassion, and gratitude.

When we can forgive ourselves and others, we no longer see ourselves as the victim of something painful. Instead, we can step forward into a life appreciating what is meaningful to us, with improved mental and physical health and peace, unshakable and in control of our own wellbeing.

Meet Nancy, Erin, Slava, Christine, and JoAnne. Enjoy their stories of resiliency and flourishing!

To Give Completely

-Nancy Polsky

Now, this is supposed to be a chapter on forgiveness. It is. It's not a prescribed set of steps to forgive. It's a story of how leaning into your strengths – possibly in new ways – opens a path to a forgiving heart. What I learned was that when I am present with gratitude and love, my heart opens wide and forgiveness comes.

What Do You Do With a Tender Heart?

The Latin root of the word forgive is to "give completely without reservation." So, what exactly are we giving completely?

I write this beside my ailing mother's hospital bed. She's on heavy narcotics that manage her pain, yet her mind keeps her prisoner to her suffering. A month in bed, and Mom is in steep decline. The doctor tells me that a bad fall at 85 years of age can be the start of the slide. An accountant by trade and a mathematician by design, Mom now has taken to compulsively counting in her final journey, dozing in and out of pain, relentlessly doing simple arithmetic. With eyes squeezed closed and face grimaced, she gets frustrated when she skips a number by mistake. Her despair is audible as the equations don't add up in her head, as if making mathematical sense might somehow be the elusive key to unlocking her suffering. "It's not working!" she cries out. Numbers are always dependable; Mom would tell me when I was a kid; they make sense, she'd always tell me: 2 always comes before 3, and 1+1 always equals 2.

So, what do you do when things don't always make sense, as numbers no longer do for Mom? What do you do when what worked before doesn't work now? What do you do when it makes no sense that those we love hurt us? We use all our strengths to learn to forgive.

> *You can't forgive without loving. And I don't mean sentimentality. I don't mean mush.*
> *I mean having enough courage to stand up and say, 'I forgive. I'm finished with it.'*
> - Maya Angelou

Anyone who knows Mom will tell you her life's journey has been filled with boundless love: of kindness, of compassion, of connection – for her family, her friends, for strangers. Mom's been the mom with whom our friends and cousins could let their hair down when they could not in their own homes. Mom was helping others less fortunate than herself before 'Social Justice Warriors' were a thing: teaching adults to read, singing to seniors in nursing homes, doing taxes pro bono for those in need.

She's been the neighbor keeping the community together through COVID, waving to passers-by from the safety of her socially distanced lawn chair each afternoon. This year, she's been baking cookies and bringing them to her pharmacist, calling him her 'COVID hero' as tears well up in her eyes. Her handyman tells me he's never had a customer as kind as Mom; he stops by just to chat even when nothing needs repair.

Her journey has also been one, in part, of grudges and hurts carried for decades, resentments even for those long gone. Bar mitzvah seating charts were complicated, as someone in the extended family was always not talking to someone else.

Mom's list of indignations was a metaphoric twist on Santa's Naughty list: my brothers and I joked which of our latest trespasses warranted a top spot on her proverbial Shit List. Mom regularly boycotted local restaurants due to perceived service slights – family lore claims Mom single-handedly took down one Burger King for bad service! (Even as I write this bedside, I'm trying to navigate her healthcare insurance: Mom tells me in a fog of pain she got mad at one insurer and now has another.)

I always said Mom's emotions run in her veins right under the surface of her skin; the slightest prick and they gush out. So what happens to such tenderheartedness in the face of life's hurts? What happens with our sadness and our hurt, our anger and our grief, when we feel so wholeheartedly but don't have effective tools to handle the inevitable injustices that life hands us? We armor up with unforgiveness.

What is Forgiveness?:

Recent theories about revenge and forgiveness claim that remembering others' trespasses has its roots in human evolution. Those who exacted vengeance or retaliation quickly signaled to the broader group that there would be a cost to the next trespass. Remembering past aggression – at least until retribution is enacted - served as a deterrent for the next harms. The fact that we're hard-wired to seek revenge, however, doesn't mean we always act on it: it seems that vengeance has short-term evolutionary benefits but that we also have a complex wiring for forgiving designed to engender group cooperation for long-haul survival.

> *Forgiveness is perhaps the most challenging of all the resources available to us – and the most transformational.*
>
> - Shauna Shapiro

So what exactly is forgiveness? We know it when we see (or give) it, and certainly, we feel it when we don't. Psychologists generally define forgiveness as a conscious choice to release all feelings of resentment or vengeance toward a person who harmed us or who we perceive to have harmed us. Forgiving does not mean condoning, forgetting, or not acknowledging said offenses. Though forgiveness may help repair a damaged relationship, it does not obligate us to reconcile with someone who harmed us, nor does it mean punishment should go unmeted. True forgiveness is uncoerced and voluntary. If you are not ready, you cannot forgive half-heartedly.

When we forgive, we let go of deeply held negative feelings that hold us stuck in painful hurt, corrosive anger, or blame; forgiving liberates our soul for inner healing. It is for this reason that forgiving is for the forgiver and not for the one who is forgiven. It is an internal process for the one who forgives and does not need to be an interpersonal process between forgiver and forgivee. We can forgive at any time, even after the person has passed from our life.

An unhealthy, mismanaged focus on the past offense keeps us from moving forward with greater well-being; forgiveness, then, empowers us to recognize the pain without letting it overwhelm or define us.

Yet, for most of us, forgiveness doesn't come naturally when we've been hurt; we hold grudges, we feel victim to the offense, we seek revenge, we get self-righteous. The good news is that with willingness and effort, we can develop our forgiveness to lead a healthier, more flourishing life.

The Origins and Physiology of Forgiving

> *All major religious traditions carry basically the same message; that is love, compassion, and forgiveness. The important thing is they should be part of our daily lives.*
>
> – Dalai Lama

While faith traditions have stressed forgiveness for millennia, the secular world has only recently begun to pay attention to the role forgiveness plays in our lives. Over the last 25 years, political scientists have come to cite South Africa's Truth and Reconciliation Commission as a successful model to move nations forward whereby victims are given the opportunity to put a voice to offenses, and those who harmed them can acknowledge wrongdoing and ask for forgiveness. Even if the offender never acknowledges wrongdoing, however, forgiving helps the forgiver shift away from an unhealthy, overwhelming focus on the past offense. Medical researchers have empirical evidence that forgiving positively impacts our physical well-being: it calms stress levels; lowers the risk of heart attack and sleep disorders; reduces pain and blood pressure; improves immune system function, and reduces anxiety and depression.

Brain scientists have found that the tendency to forgive is a trait linked with certain brain characteristics. Anatomical studies using functional magnetic resonance imaging suggest that people with more gray matter are more forgiving than others. However, biology is not necessarily destiny: other brain studies of metabolic activity show that we can alter – or train – ourselves towards more forgiveness with effortful practical activities. This is hopeful news because apparently, we need it: 62 percent of American adults say they need more forgiveness in their personal lives and a whopping 92 percent say we need it as a nation and across the globe.

In the last twenty years, the field of Positive Psychology has contributed tremendous research to our understanding of the emotional and psychological aspects of forgiveness, including what forgiveness is and how it leads to improved emotional well-being. Dr. Frederic Luskin, author of *Forgive for Good* and Co-Founder and Director of The Stanford University Forgiveness Project, has been leading the largest interpersonal forgiveness research ever conducted to reduce emotional and physical distress that comes from not forgiving. He describes a universal process that shifts us towards forgiveness regardless of the type of offense, its magnitude, and whether or not the perpetrator acknowledges wrongdoing. He developed a forgiveness-training program and works with a broad array of individuals: victims of heinous abuse and violence to those managing mundane hurts of everyday life. He writes:

> Forgiveness may be viewed as an... ability to see one's life through a positive or healing lens. It may be that all of us could benefit from training in managing life's inevitable hurts and using forgiveness to make peace with the past. In this way, forgiveness may be, as the religious traditions have been claiming all along, a rich path to greater peace and understanding that also has both psychosocial and physiological value.

Overcoming Reactionary Response with Strength Training

> Between stimulus and response, there is a space. In that space is our power to choose our response. In our response lies our growth and our freedom.
> - Dr. Viktor Frankl

We go through most of our days stimulated then responding, largely unaware and involuntarily. In moments of stress, anger, or hurt, our space gets narrow, so it is difficult to respond as our best self. Dangerously cut off in traffic? Profanity ensues. Teen caught smoking? I'm reminded of the 'Modern Family' episode when Claire and Phil discover their teen tried a cigarette and quickly regret their immediate response to 'cancel Christmas.' I too can struggle with my responses from a narrow space when I feel hurt by those I love. But over time, I have learned to widen that space through the effortful practice of a few strengths that help me better respond to life's painful stimuli more often than not. They include presence, gratitude, love, and, most recently, forgiveness.

Presence:

Twenty years ago, I was battling debilitating chronic disease when I was introduced to mindfulness meditation through Dr. Jon Kabat-Zinn (whom I once heard referred to as the "James Brown of mindfulness"). Jon's seminal Mindfulness-based Stress Reduction program (MBSR) led me to an a-ha moment: week after week I would crawl into class riddled with pain despite a plethora of medications on my countertop; one day I was able to fully focus all my attention on lifting my arms overhead as instructed by our teacher and, in doing so, I had the briefest cessation from the pain that had come to define me. I focused solely on the physical sensation, and in those thirty seconds, my mind was not filled with the thought of bodily pain. Through paying attention to the present moment – 'mindfulness' – I widened Frankl's space. I knew that if I have more present awareness, I'd have less suffering.

With new optimism, I became inspired to develop habits of body and mind to live a flourishing life; over the twenty years since, I have doggedly pursued widening the space through several habits that have fundamentally shifted my perspective and my health towards well-being and expansive quality of life. Bodily care (exercise, nutrition and mindfulness habits) has been transformational; so too have heart-based choices like gratitude and loving relationships.

This being human is a guest house. Every morning is a new arrival. A joy, a depression, a meanness, some momentary awareness comes as an unexpected visitor...Welcome and entertain them all. Treat each guest honorably. The dark thought, the shame, the malice, meet them at the door.... and invite them in. Be grateful for whoever comes because each has been sent as a guide from beyond.

– Rumi

This past summer tested me with illness yet again: as the COVID surge filled hospital beds, I lay in my bedroom running a high fever, laboring to breathe, my body aching, and my heart racing like a sprinter. For sixteen days, I was isolated in my room, the endless moment as my constant companion. I worked with what I knew to help me for the last two decades: presence, gratitude, and love.

My bodily pain was managed better when I could be present to it with equanimity: in the stillness, I noticed the sensations of my body – my heart pounding hard then returning to normal; my breath tight then fuller still; my armpit lymph nodes aching then not. I knew from experience that if I could do this with physical difficulties, I could do it with difficult emotions, too: anger at my failing body; fear that I would not recover, sadness my son was not with me. Being present to bodily pain and difficult emotions instead of running or distracting myself from them reminded me to greet them like guests, grateful for the guidance they would give me.

Gratitude:

I once attended a lecture by one of my heroes Maya Angelou: in her most delighting of voices, she proclaimed "an attitude of gratitude" had gotten her through some of life's unimaginable pains. I went home, promptly wrote that phrase on my kitchen chalkboard, and have been adjusting my attitude towards gratitude ever since.

Since Ms. Angelou shared her wisdom, each day before I open my eyes, from my bed, I think on whatever three gratitudes first pop into my head. It started out as a forced morning exercise much like a New Years Resolution forces you out of bed to get to the gym – but very quickly, it moved beyond formulaic activity to become a real attitude of gratitude. Now I experience my days with a greater savoring of life's marvels, big and small.

How grateful I am to have been practicing gratitude when I got sick in quarantine! In the stillness, I welcomed the sun shining through the window, trees moving in the wind outside, the soft mattress beneath me.

Positive psychologist Dr. Barbara Fredrickson's "Broaden and Build theory" helps explain how to move away from sheer survival mode by choosing more positive, thoughtful approaches – like present-awareness and gratitude – which build upon themselves in an upward spiral of better well-being. Practicing mindfulness and gratitudes during my illness allowed me to be present with the challenge and to cope with it much better. In Dr. Fredrickson's theory, both positive and negative emotions co-exist to help you to see the current situation as broader than your hardest moment. We are wonderful creatures with rich and complex lives filled with joys and difficulties: focusing only on what ails us robs us of the opportunity to savor it all.

Loving Connection:

Beyond present awareness and gratitude, love is the third strength upon which my healing stands. The Beatles may have simplified it a bit – "All you need is love" – however, undoubtedly, we do better, we are happier when we experience love and connection. Harvard University has conducted one of the longest-running studies on happiness that shows a strong link between happiness, life expectancy, and close relationships. Loving connection creates mental and emotional mood boosters while isolation is a mood buster, says Harvard's Dr. Robert Waldinger. Isolated in quarantine, I needed to connect deliberately with others through technology. Beyond my immediate family, even lifelong friends didn't know I was struggling because we all had become so separate during COVID lockdowns. I let a couple of close friends know and soon their regular texts and phone calls added warmth in the darkness; and when they broadcast to my wider community, get-well video texts and social media well-wishes from so many dear ones I'd met along my journey truly elevated me. I felt enveloped in love, and it helped me immeasurably in a time of need.

While presence, gratitude, and love were crucial to working through this challenging time, I'd be lying if I said there weren't occasional moments of great suffering. It wasn't the physical pain, the loneliness, or the fear from which I suffered most. It was an overwhelming helplessness in wanting my estranged son by my side, to rub my head, to stroke my hand. On the rare occasion that I became overwhelmed by a longing for his comfort that was not forthcoming, I suffered tremendously.

You Gotta Vary Your Workout: Developing Forgiveness Muscle

There is a crack in everything. That's how the light gets in.

– Leonard Cohen

Over the coming weeks, my cracked body began to recover, but it would be months before that of my fractured heart. Out of immediate physical danger, I could turn to hurt and righteous indignation; I soon found myself unforgiving toward my son in his continued estrangement. And that unforgiving made me miserable.

Not one to stay in misery too long, I pulled out my familiar bag of tricks – three gratitudes, phone-a-friend, a run on the beach – but this time, it was like Mom's futile counting from her hospital bed: my old reliable ways of coping no longer worked. Faced with the new challenge of my son's continued separation, I had to develop new ways of practicing presence, gratitude, and love. And so I phoned my teacher, Dr. Maria Sirois. Maria's brilliant work on resilience through adversity is matched only by her storytelling, authenticity, and humor. When we spoke, Maria did two things: first, she validated my difficulties – it sucks that your son wasn't there when you were sick – and then she did something else: she reminded me to intentionally pursue positive thoughts and actions. The genius of the AND. As Maria describes it, we must acknowledge the "swamp" of difficulty and actively add to the "pond" of happiness. We are both broken and whole, she says; we must find ways to hold the cracked pieces and still choose thoughts and actions that build us up.

Maria asks me my top character strengths. It's gratitude and love, I tell her, but they're not working, I say! Then try using them in different ways; Maria says I'm stuck in the LP record groove with the same three gratitudes. She suggests the simplest of tools, one I've suggested countless times in my own coaching work with business leaders: a 30-day challenge. I put a call out for co-challengers on social media, and four friends join me: each day, we text one thing we celebrate that day: the sun on our face, an early morning workout, a good night's sleep, a successful job interview, a warm cup of tea. I could have celebrated on my own and it would have been helpful but doing it with others lent accountability and a cheer squad and had the wonderful effect of reconnecting with old friends not otherwise in regular contact. Texting one another took exactly one minute, and the payoff was enormous.

So with my gratitude strength back on track, I also wanted to feel more loving connection. I was laid off due to COVID during this time and overnight went from days filled with Zoom meetings with cherished colleagues to silence. So I created a concurrent thirty day challenge just for myself: each day, I connected by phone or video with one dear-heart friend I hadn't spoken with in a while, one moment of connection in an otherwise pretty silent day. And the process of creating a list of 30 people I adore who adore me too was so elevating by itself!

And I kept a quick log of what I celebrated and who I spoke with each day; writing it down further savors the experiences. The key is that during those 30 days, I didn't sugarcoat that I was having a rough go of it with my health, job loss, my son: I simply added to Maria's pond celebrating small wins, connecting with loved ones, and writing it down.

> *Forgiveness is giving up all hope of having had a better past.*
>
> - Anne Lamont

With momentum building (Dr. Fredrickson's upward spiral!), I resumed my abandoned practice of the exquisite Lovingkindness meditation. I recalled how it had powerfully reset compassion for myself and others during the most rocky of relationship waters in my past; it did not disappoint this time too. With greater compassion for myself and my son, I was able to drop attachment to the past that did not happen in my illness and to a future dictated by my own expectations of how our relationship would be.

And so, with no expectation of a reply, I wrote my son a letter of love and gratitude. From an open and tender heart, I reminded him my love was immutable and told him I detached from an outcome of regular connection.

Two weeks later, he called.

A Journey of Forgiving

> *Forgiveness says you are given another chance to make a new beginning.*
>
> - Desmond Tutu

The pandemic gave us an opportunity to study together. Each Sunday this past fall, Mom and I gathered with my brothers on Zoom eagerly discussing Dr. Laurie Santos' popular online course, The Science of Well-Being. Mom came from that grin-and-bear-it generation that "didn't do" psychotherapy but really loved this idea of well-being, especially the character strengths. A modest person, Mom seemed to really identify with her essential strength of kindness, and she eagerly looked for new ways to brighten people's days. We discussed our strengths in overuse, how honesty in overdrive can lead to righteousness or unforgiveness. And as each week of study went by, there were fewer and fewer complaints about poor customer service and nobody on the Shit List for in as long a time as I can remember. Without a doubt, this was a peaceful time for Mom; she was happy, flourishing even. On Mom's last birthday, I remarked on how much she'd accomplished and seen in her life. "I'm just getting started!" she replied with a grin.

Just as we were finishing Dr. Santos' class, Mom took her fall. I visited with her day after day in her decline; not a thing was left unsaid in those long days. And just like that – with lovingkindness for himself, for me, for his grandmother - my son showed up to tag in bedside beside grandma.

Mom passed. And with it, so too did three generations of unforgiving.

Nancy Polsky | Fort Lauderdale
nmp2@yahoo.com

Nancy Polsky is a leadership coach, speaker and award-winning leader in corporate learning who specializes in expanding employee and organizational capabilities through leadership and talent development.

Nancy currently supports learning strategy for a global technology company, and recently led leadership development efforts for the largest privately held healthcare staffing company. Both companies are part of *Fortune's 100 Best Companies to Work For* ranked in part for their strong commitment to employee learning and development. Nancy has served on the advisory council for *Chief Learning Officer Learning in Practice* awards. She has been recognized as a leader in workforce development as part of the *Training Magazine's* lifetime achievement Top 125.

A health crisis 20 years ago led Nancy to discover the power of personal choice to move towards a happier life. Since then, wellness and mindfulness practices help Nancy maintain an active lifestyle as a busy mom, an avid runner, and a yogi.

She's most recently taken up bodysurfing on the beaches of Fort Lauderdale!

You Deserve the Space You Take Up in This World: Moving Beyond Inferiority through Self-Compassion

-Erin Crosby

Have you ever experienced that feeling when you walk into a room or talk to someone and you lose all sense of confidence you ever thought you had? I sure did. I always wanted to just shrink and have no one even look in my direction. This profound sense of inferiority dominated my life until I began my Certificate in Positive Psychology. I joined the program mainly for professional development. Being a clinical social worker, I thought it would help me gain more tools to help me in my work. Not surprisingly, it turned into one of the most powerful experiences of my life.

Inferiority, driven by constant self-criticism, caused me to live a life I desperately wanted out of. After finishing graduate school, I had settled into a life of perceived monotony that drove my feelings of inferiority every minute of the day. Somehow, I had created a working life that mirrored what I always told myself I deserved–a place where I was not valued and never felt like I belonged–but I was comfortable in it because I knew how to handle those feelings. One day, while driving home from work, I unexpectedly flew into a rage because another driver would not let me merge lanes. After screaming at them and hitting my steering wheel repeatedly, I began crying so intensely that I had to pull over. It was at that moment that I realized that something had to change, but I did not have any idea how to begin. A few months later a coworker shared a book about compassion and suddenly I felt like I had found a lifeline. That book spurred me to register for a conference on the topic that ultimately led me to the Wholebeing Institute.

My energy and focus had always been about finding ways to help others. Amid my despair, I could not find the reasons within me, to start the program for myself. That sense of inferiority and feeling of not deserving the good things I wanted in my life were deeply ingrained. I am so grateful I found a way to start.

Self-criticism often stems from times when we feel humiliated, inadequate, or like a failure. In my case, those emotions came from many years of being bullied for my weight. The cruel words from peers at school became a daily reminder of my inferiority and helped create my lack of self-worth. Each school year, there always seemed to be a group of kids who made it their mission to torment me; to try and make me feel worthless because I was overweight. I spent a long time wishing I had not let these kids affect me so much, but I was so very young. When you are that age, what your peers think means everything. What they say feels like the truth, with no exceptions. They said it, therefore it must be true. No one could convince me otherwise, or help me to not internalize what was being said to me. As a result, my life from about seven years old developed into a battle with my inner self-critic. My inner monologue would continuously tell me things like, "you are fat and ugly," "you don't deserve to have friends," and "nobody wants you here."

The most painful experience came in eighth grade when I was thirteen years old. A group of three girls decided that I looked like a buffalo. For that whole year, they followed me around the school yelling "buffalo" for everyone to hear. That time was one of the most powerful reinforcements of shame about myself and my body that I have ever experienced. Fast forward a few years and we all grew up a bit. I excelled academically, lost weight, and the bullying stopped. However, the damage was done. They had taught me everything I needed to continue for myself what they had started. I had turned into my own bully.

Their hurtful words shaped my image of myself and contributed to me becoming people-pleasing, perfectionistic, and risk-averse, to name but a few exhausting character traits. However, there is a silver lining to the shame I experienced. That same shame also caused me to become empathetic, giving, and caring to nearly everyone I meet. Furthermore, it led me into my profession, and despite its challenges, is exactly where I want to be.

I tell you about this experience because we all have stories of difficult times that have shaped our lives. We all learn how to treat ourselves through how we are treated and what happens to us. Worst of all, we do not learn to meet this struggle with compassion – most of us meet it with more cruelty. Years of hearing those words left their mark. Therapy helped me to understand and find the purpose in the experience, but no matter what I tried, I could never alter the negative voice in my mind criticizing my every move or action; reminding me that I was never good enough to be among the company I was in. I felt inferior to everyone. My self-critic spoke up for anything and everything. Those words formed the core of a cruel, running inner monologue. Though my weight fluctuated, and no matter what I looked like or what I accomplished, the voice never gave me a moment of peace. "You are disgusting," repeated in my mind. Through the study of self-compassion, I started to realize that if I speak to myself as an enemy, I will never be able to create the life I want for myself. How could I possibly get to and maintain a healthy weight when I constantly tell myself I am revolting and an embarrassment? That I'm still that buffalo that used to be? How could I create the fulfilling work I want when I tell myself I am stupid and will always fail? It is hard to say here, but that was my experience, and I know it's the experience of so many others. That is why I am writing this, as scary as it may be.

Courage is not the lack of fear. It is acting in spite of it.
– Mark Twain

193

I first came across the concept of self-compassion in my Master of Social Work program, but the pace of my life took over and self-care was relegated to the back burner. When I think about it now, that should come as no surprise seeing as I was never used to taking care of myself. Self-cruelty was so normal that even something as important as self-compassion was not immediately integrated into my life. That all changed once I began my Certificate in Positive Psychology (CiPP) and read Self-Compassion by Kristin Neff, Ph.D. The idea resonated with me in a way I had never experienced before. Self-compassion encompasses many things, but the general idea is that you learn to be caring and understanding with yourself rather than harsh, critical, and judgmental. You also learn to understand that all humans are imperfect, mess up and fail, that that is okay and can connect us. Mindfulness is also a key component to recognizing when your self-critic is at work.

During my time in CiPP, I began putting this concept of self-compassion into practice in my life. One day, after about six months of practice, my self-critical brain was doing its thing on my way to work. Suddenly I just naturally and gently told myself, "you are okay." Let me tell you, I nearly fell over! I asked myself, "where in the world did that come from?!" I laughed at my reaction, and I think people on my train thought I was a bit off! It was so shocking to experience something so powerful AND be aware of it. Nothing like that had ever happened in my life before. It was a wholly new experience. Until that point, I can honestly say that I had no recollection of ever uttering a kind, encouraging, or compassionate thought so naturally to myself in my life. That was so exciting! That moment was the spark that began a gradual shift in my natural thoughts. Since then, the cruel voice has become less and less powerful. In all honesty, the voice refuses to go without a fight. It's still there at times and gets stronger when I feel overwhelmed, stressed or when I get sidetracked from my healthy habits. But I know my thoughts are just thoughts, not the truth as I once believed. While I may not currently look the way I would like to look, and I may not have created the life I want just yet–I believe I will get there when I am ready. I will not be the one to stand in my way any longer.

When you decided to pick up this book or any book about finding and creating happiness, what were your thoughts? Before I began studying and implementing the strategies of positive psychology, I was endlessly searching for the book that would "fix" me. I always believed there was a beginning, middle, and end to the process of being "fixed." When I decided to write this chapter, I knew I wanted to talk about this idea because I also believe self-criticism is a trap so many of us find ourselves in. It helps to sustain the inner critic's place in our life, which only perpetuates those feelings of inferiority. I used to believe that if I was not "perfect" at fixing myself then I might as well throw away any progress I had made and give up. There was no room for the ups and downs of daily life.

What I want you to know is that there is no day when you will feel fully "fixed." Create the healthiest habits you can create and make small changes. Eventually, those small changes will add up to the bigger changes you desire, and one day you will have a lifetime of healthy habits that help you to create the life you have been searching for. You will not need to feel "fixed" anymore because you will understand that perfection has no place in making changes and feeling better. Perfection isn't achievable. There will always be days and maybe even months where your old habits sneak in and you feel like you have failed. My inner critic is something I deal with nearly every day. The difference now is that most days I choose to use the strategies I learned through CiPP to meet those critical words with self-compassion rather than assume they must be true without hesitation.

When you make a choice, you change the future.
— Deepak Chopra

So how do I keep this peace I have with my inner critic? How do I stand up and walk tall when I feel like I don't belong or am unwanted? For me, the number one, first step, and most important factor was developing awareness of my thoughts through mindfulness. I knew from all that I had learned that I would not be able to challenge my self-criticism if I did not first know it was happening. Negative thoughts and self-criticism are most insidious when you're unaware they're happening. They do their damage bit by bit. To foster mindfulness, I placed Post-it® notes around my house with reminders of, "breathe," "you are not what you tell yourself," and as my title suggests, "you deserve the space you take up in this world." These negative thoughts often take years to develop, so remember, they will take time and help (even in Post-it® form!) to reverse.

Support was also a key factor for me as I worked to build my self-worth and challenge the negative thoughts. This was where the power of being in a group of people learning about positive psychology came into play for me. There was an energy and openness to others that grew out of being among people who were all seeking to make changes in their lives. It helped me to understand that I was not in this difficult place alone.

We settled in small groups of six and met all year long to support and learn from each other. These women accepted me for who I was without question or judgment. The support they gave me–and I hope what I gave them in return–is what I believe was the turning point in my healing. Finding these women has been a gift that I look on with immense gratitude. Even though we now often go for long periods without speaking, all I need to do is think of them, and that power they helped me find within comes right back to the surface and fills me with strength. My personal experience has shown me that one of the most important things you can do to help build and sustain the happiness you are looking for is to find a support system that cheers you on and builds you up.

Through the building of this awareness of my self-critical voice and leaning into the support I received from my group, I was able to slowly begin to see where I deserved to take care of myself. And while I sometimes need reminding, I have tried to develop my sense of personal boundaries as a way of taking care of myself and to help mitigate my self-critic. I know that voice emerges again during times of stress or when I am in new environments with new people, so I try to prepare myself to get ahead of the criticisms before these situations.

Here's an example. Starting new jobs has always been difficult for me. My self-criticism and feelings of inferiority often become so loud that I feel like I can do nothing but listen, and my people-pleasing tendencies come out strong. I want people to think I am smart, and I want to excel at what I do. I want to feel like I deserve to be there even though inside I am normally telling myself everyone else is smarter, better, and more important than me. Eventually, I realized that if I know this is what happens to me when I begin a new job, then why can't I take time beforehand to ensure I am doing everything I can to have compassion for myself in that situation? I try to be mindful of my self-talk and set aside time to preemptively think through what I might struggle with. That way I have words already in place to challenge any negativity at the moment. I make sure to plan time with my support system to get an outside perspective on what I am worried about. Lastly, I think through what expectations may be placed on me so I can prepare how to vocalize healthy boundaries while still getting the job done. In the end, I put myself back in control of a situation where I may feel like I have no control.

Work has played a big part in my healing in a different way. As a clinical social worker, I have worked in hospitals, community mental health, and inpatient/intensive outpatient programs. Until a few years ago, I spent my career in high-intensity, high-stress workplaces. When I decided to become a social worker, I believed my days would be spent in private practice helping people just as my remarkable therapist had helped me. I was naïve and did not research to understand that there is a whole, long process to making that happen! As a result, the burnout and stress I had explained earlier set in and I felt I had no way out but to spend my life working in places I did not want to be. Now I know that these jobs served a valuable purpose. In addition to all the experience and learning that took place, these jobs led me to CiPP. They have helped me discover how I want to use my career to help others in the way that brings me the most fulfillment.

While I have not been able to practically take the full-time leap into private practice, I understand now what I need to do and I have a plan! My goal is to build a therapy practice for women that allows them to feel empowered to be who they have always hoped they would be. Life has a way of taking us down paths that are different than we once imagined for ourselves, and it can often feel extremely overwhelming and difficult to get back on track. I understand this and hope to utilize the tool of self-compassion to help others build feelings of empowerment. I believe this is key to overcoming feelings of inferiority.

It is my hope that sharing my story will help you to begin your healing. I nearly decided not to take part in this project because I believed my experiences could never hold value while in the same space as these other amazing authors. I believed I was inferior and undeserving. When I realized I was limiting myself based on my old, self-defeating, critical thoughts, I decided to go for it. I literally laughed and said, "why not?!" while my dog stared at me in confusion! When that voice started telling me, "you can't do something like this," and "everyone else will be better than you," I took a deep breath, found the self-compassion, and said, "this scares me but I believe I can do what I set my mind to no matter how scared I might be." All our stories have value and the ability to help and connect us to others. I owed this to myself, and maybe most of all, to the little girl who was so sad and scared all those years ago, to be heard. We all deserve to be heard and stand tall in the space we take up in this world.

There's a difference between thinking you deserve to be happy and knowing that you are worthy of being happy. Your being alive makes worthiness your birthright. You alone are enough.

– Oprah Winfrey

Erin Crosby, LCSW | Northern Virginia

www.erincrosbylcsw.com

We all deserve to be heard and stand tall in the space we take up in this world.

– Erin Crosby

Erin resides in Northern Virginia where she works as a Licensed Clinical Social Worker specializing in helping women of all ages regain or develop their confidence and feel empowered in their lives. She earned a Master of Research in Psychology from the University of St Andrews in Scotland and a Master of Social Work from the University of Pennsylvania. Erin completed her Certificate in Positive Psychology from the Wholebeing Institute in 2017.

Saving Compassion

-Slava Madorsky

My breakdown might have happened during any of the obvious moments.

I remember, for instance, interviewing two young men– brothers–the younger of whom had lost all four of his limbs as a result of an explosion in Iraq. I was a refugee officer with the US government at the time. My job was to go where the refugees were and conduct thorough interviews that met a specific legal standard to determine whether they are eligible to enter the United States. This also meant that my job was to hear the most horrific details of what they suffered, and at times, what acts they had committed themselves that caused suffering to others. And I was good at my job. Good at asking

FINDING UNSHAKABLE HAPPINESS

the right questions, good at analyzing the answers and making decisions, and good at doing it all with flowing compassion.

During this particular interview, I spoke with the two brothers separately and asked why they wanted to go to the US. The older one spoke only of his desire to get his brother to safety and to a place where he could maybe get him some medical help. He said nothing of the danger to his own life or of the sheer exhaustion of being the sole provider of round-the-clock care to a quadruple amputee. The younger boy, when asked the same question, told me that he heard he could get a prosthetic arm in the US. Just one of his limbs was deemed eligible and he desperately wanted to try. The reason, he said, was so his brother could finally get some rest. Because when it gets really cold at night, he told me, he wants to be able to pull up his own blanket when it slips off. That way his brother doesn't have to worry about him freezing and can finally let himself sleep.

I don't think anyone would have been surprised if I broke down sobbing right after, if not during, that interview. It also would not have been unexpected after the three hours I spent with a former soldier who described to me in vivid detail the charred bodies of women and children that he saw following a massacre of a village that he helped perpetrate many years ago on orders from his commander. His own life was in danger now and he knew that had he lied about his past, he could get to safety in the US. But he couldn't keep living with a lie like that, couldn't live with the shame and guilt of it; and I could no more absolve him of it than I could admit him as a refugee. I could only listen, create a record, and stamp his case 'Denied'.

The breakdown might have happened any time during the years I spent overseas taking in thousands of stories of loss, fear, trauma, torture, and tragedy. Or perhaps even when my own life was put at risk by mortars, disease, violently unstable applicants, sudden border skirmishes, and credible terrorist threats. It would have made sense. And, under the circumstances, it might have even gone unnoticed.

But the way it finally did happen stood no chance of getting ignored. One day, about five years into my refugee career, when I was back home in DC for a short turnaround between trips, my dad took me to the ballet. There is nothing unusual about this in and of itself. As a child, my parents took me to the ballet–and theater in general–as often as it was possible to procure tickets. I grew up in the Soviet Union, where "procuring" was the name of the game, and it was not unusual in my family to put our procurement efforts toward cultural events. Going to the ballet was, in fact, so normal for me that I no longer have any recollection of what piece it was that my dad had taken me to see that one particular day. I just remember that it was at the Kennedy Center and I am about half sure that it was a Russian ballet company. What I recall with absolute clarity though, is that at some not-at-all dramatic or exceptionally moving point during the performance, tears started streaming down my face and there was little I could do to stem their flow. The more I tried to stop, the harder I cried. Tears became sobs and sobs made my whole body shake. My dad turned to look over at me and the concerned surprise on his face told me that, no, in fact, this was not a logical time or place to be having quite this many emotions. He tried to ask me what was wrong and to comfort me, but I had no answers, no power to stop crying, and no desire to leave the hall. I just stayed in that chair and let the tears run themselves out.

As the sobbing subsided and my body began to calm, I had to ask myself the obvious question–why? What caused this completely out-of-character full-body emotional meltdown? And when it came to me, still sitting there in that hall watching the dancers glide across the stage, the answer was the last thing I expected to hear. I realized at that moment that this was the first time in a long time that I was fully immersed in something truly beautiful for the sake of itself. I found myself in a world that was created to celebrate grace, talent, music, movement, emotion, and magic and it was a world the existence of which I had forgotten. After spending years submerged in a world of suffering, fear, and death, I forgot what it felt like to exist in a place of art and beauty–a world that had once been my normal. I cried not because I was overcome by the exquisiteness of the performance, but because this forgetting suddenly felt like a gut-wrenching loss and I was swallowed by self-pity and anger and an overwhelming sense of mourning something that I didn't know could die.

After "the ballet incident," as it came to be known, I understood that something very important had happened to me and I understood that there was something that I needed to do about the matter, but I didn't have the slightest clue as to where to begin. The next morning when I got to the office, I sat in front of my computer trying to figure out what to google. "Spontaneous ballet sobbing cures" didn't seem like it would do the trick. Sitting there, I began to wonder if maybe I am not the only one who experienced this sort of emotional episode and tried to recall whether I had heard anyone mention it before. We were a pretty tough bunch there, and most would not readily admit to such apparent weakness. Those who "couldn't hack it" simply left. The tough carried on without complaint. After all, what kind of monster would dare complain of some mild emotional discomfort when we were face-to-face each day with people who had experienced real suffering? And then I remembered something. A few years earlier, when I was just starting out, our management had brought in a psychologist to give our entire division a talk about the importance of self-care. These talks were organized for us from time to time, but they usually revolved around reminders to shower, exercise, and eat well. One time we even meditated for a few minutes as one big skeptical group of hardened legal professionals. These talks had little impact and were often the butt of more than a few jokes. And yet, sitting there pondering my predicament, I recalled something that the first psychologist said. He said people like us had to watch out for something called vicarious trauma and compassion fatigue. I had no memory of what that entailed, but I finally had some fodder for my googling.

There is a reason, it turns out, they call it compassion fatigue. It happens when we care about other people's pain and feel continually compelled to help them. Through continuous exposure to the trauma of others, we deplete our own psychological, physical, and spiritual resources, which in turn, if not addressed, leads to total burnout. It is a side effect of feeling compassion. A lot. Over and over. And the more of it you feel, the higher your risk.

Still a bit skeptical about the whole thing, I stumbled across a short self-assessment for identifying symptoms of vicarious trauma and compassion fatigue. I went down the list: numbing–check, detachment–check, bad decision making–check, blurring boundaries between work and life, social disconnection, startle effect, cynicism–check, check, check, check. There was no backing away from this now–the diagnosis was undeniable and I was not alone in sliding down this slope. I could suddenly see very clearly how little by little so many of us, most of us really, pushed pieces of our own lives out of the way to make space for the emotional toll of our work. Anything outside of work that elicited strong emotions had to go, be it sad movies, serious books, news updates, or complicated personal relationships. Nobody outside of our professional world–we thought–understood, or cared what we ranted about when we were back home, so in response we closed ranks and just shared with one another, which quickly turned to gallows humor and callous dismissal for the sake of self-preservation. For many, close relationships wore thin, and usual support networks stretched to the point of breaking. Long-term romantic relationships were severed and new, temporary, but urgently grasped-for ones popped up in their place. All sense of permanence disintegrated and all personal goals, hopes, and challenges were placed indefinitely on ice. Our compassion, our emotions, were reserved strictly for the confines of our interview rooms, and those were bound to run out at some point as well. This particular status quo stood no chance of being sustained and my wake-up call told me that, at least for me, the time to do something about it had come.

But what was I meant to do? Was I supposed to cut down on the amount of compassion I was feeling to avoid the fatigue it caused? Was I supposed to figure out how to regulate it? I went to debriefings and counseling sessions provided by my agency and read articles about dealing with stress, but the resources never seemed to be quite enough. Everyone spoke of how important self-care was for coping and healing, but nobody gave instructions for generating the strength to do it in the first place.

And then my millionth google search turned up something new. A class that promised things like creating positive emotions and building resilience for dealing with difficult ones. The name of the class–Positive Psychology–gave me pause. I mean, who wants to be told to be positive all the time, right? But on the other hand, there was a Harvard professor involved and it seemed like there were actual scientific studies that were being used. And finally, my decision was helped along by the fact that my own research was hitting a wall. Remarkably, the in-person immersive sessions were scheduled for the exact times when I was guaranteed to be stateside, so I took the year-long plunge in the hopes of finding answers.

I knew that I was in the right place on day one when I first heard the explanation of what Positive Psychology actually entails. "While traditional psychology looks at problems and how to fix them," explained Dr. Tal Ben-Shahar, the aforementioned man from Harvard–Positive Psychology looks at what's already working and how to make more of it. Oh, and by the way, it's badly named–he told us–it's not at all about being positive all the time because that would be crazy. The magic words had been spoken and I was all in.

Over the year that followed, a path toward healing unfolded before me. While the class offered insight on broad topics, the ones that called to me most were those that had the most direct impact on cultivating resilience while ameliorating trauma; and I was amazed to discover how many resources I already had at my disposal without realizing it, which is, I suppose, the entire m.o. of the field.

"We want to be who we are at our best in times of high stress," said Dr. Maria Sirois, a course instructor. In teaching us about the value of strengths-based work, she opened my eyes to the ways that, with a little attention, I could leverage the self-esteem that I draw from using my existing character strengths against the struggle or depletion I encounter, and in this way enhance my state of overall well-being. I began to see that my top strengths of fairness and perspective were the ones that made me good at my job and allowed me to continue to enjoy it even when it was difficult. I also understood that my strengths of honesty, humor, and forgiveness made me a good leader and teacher and supported my social bonds in tense and stressful times. Even without additional effort, awareness was beginning to create resilience.

I learned also that my natural inclination toward a benefit-finding mindset was a tremendous asset that I was already using to maintain a sense of purpose and optimism regardless of circumstances. John Milton, in Paradise Lost, wrote, "The mind is its own place, and in itself can make a heaven of hell, a hell of heaven." A fault-finding mindset creates a downward spiral in the mind and disempowers us in the process, while benefit-finding helps us to see and appreciate all the good that already exists around us and within us. A mindset can be changed by engaging in mindful awareness of the good around us and practicing gratitude, but this element, I realized, came easily to me because my personality was naturally primed for seeking out the bright side. But even so, in the practice of intentionally seeking out the good, I discovered something else: the integral importance of staying connected to meaning and purpose during times of stress. In recalling and focusing on the reasons I chose my line of work to begin with, I returned to a source of fulfillment, self-realization, and flow. I felt renewed energy for and commitment to my work, and a much-increased capacity for processing associated hardships. Friedrich Nietzsche captured this best, writing, "He who has a *why* to live for can bear almost any *how*."

And finally, and perhaps most significantly, I developed a profound awareness of and gratitude for the deep connections that I could always count on in my personal life–the life that continued to exist outside of work. Connection, after all, has a tremendous impact on our well-being, but in the years that I was traveling overseas and growing progressively more burnt out, I gradually started to take these relationships for granted. But now I was brought back to the fact that I was one of the lucky few at work who were locally based–I didn't uproot my life for my job and move to a new place only to be regularly sent even further away. When I returned from a trip, I was home. I was near my family and my friends. I could and did have a life that was entirely separate from work and not just that–I was surrounded by friends I have known and loved for over twenty years, friends who were there for me unconditionally, no matter how crazy I felt or how long I had been gone. My friends gave me the space to leave and come back, to change, and to be completely myself no matter what else was happening in our lives. They anchored me to love, safety, and certainty in a world that shifted, disintegrated, and caught fire all around me. The mere awareness of the significance of connections I already had in my life made me feel stronger, more capable of weathering any storm, and more emotionally equipped to continue my work.

I learned new skills and concepts as well of course–mindfulness, self-compassion, appreciative inquiry, post-traumatic growth–but being able to recognize the resources I already had in my arsenal, resources I didn't have to work to attain, was a game-changer. I went from being a lost and depleted burnout to a resilience ninja in the span of a year. At the same time at work, I shifted into a training position, which meant that I still traveled and conducted interviews, but now my primary focus was on training others. And this in turn meant I now had a platform for delivering these skills and resources to officers who were just about to begin experiencing the full force and impact of refugee work. I could tell them what to expect without sugarcoating and provide them with the resources they would need from the start so they can avoid the gradual and painful descent into second-hand trauma and burnout. A resilience-building class soon became a mandatory part of the training curriculum for new staff and each time I delivered the material and repeated the concepts, I was able to absorb them more and more myself and so the benefits continued to grow and build. For most brand-new officers, the material felt less relevant than the instruction they received on, say, legal analysis and national security, because they did not yet have first-hand exposure to the emotional and psychological strains of this kind of work, but I did notice that when I opened up the class to all–not only new–division staff, there was a lot of repeat business. After a few interviewing trips, officers began to reach back out for the resources they knew were there for them. Something, it seemed, was working, even if at times it was just the knowledge that someone cared, that someone was there to support them as the impact of their work inevitably began to take its toll. As a result, the desperate need for this resource was finally recognized and embraced by the decision-makers at the helm and new initiatives began to pop up throughout the agency, reaching more and more people, and in turn creating a more resilient workforce.

Compassion in this line of work is not optional. It is one of the key qualities of an effective refugee officer. It allows for the spirit of the law to coexist with the letter of the law. It mitigates guilt. It creates an open channel for the person on the other side of the desk to feel free to be truthful and to share their story. Compassion is imperative to have and at the same time, it is in tremendous danger of depletion when the trauma that accumulates in the process is not addressed. I have seen good officers resign after one or two years and I have seen officers become hardened and robotic as a measure of self-preservation. Neither is an optimal outcome. After five years of interviews, I found myself at a similar crossroads, but thanks to "the ballet incident" I had a third path open up in front of me. The lessons I learned along this path gave me another five years on the road, another five years of interviewing, helping, connecting, leading, and teaching. I got to leave on my own terms when I was ready to move on to new experiences and challenges. And I got to leave with my heart open and my compassion flowing freely toward myself and others.

To those who are on their journey of healing compassion fatigue and vicarious trauma, I say, find your strengths; embrace them and learn to lean on them in times of stress–

they will remind you of your power and lift you when you're facing a struggle. I say, find the silver lining and practice gratitude–because, in the words of Dr. Tal Ben-Shahar, "when we appreciate the good, the good appreciates." I say, reconnect to meaning and purpose–remember why you have chosen this path and all the good it has allowed you to create in this world; remember what makes your heart soar. And I say, connect to your loved ones, your community, your tribe, whatever that may look like for you–they will support and sustain you even when everything else feels impossible to manage; they will lift and strengthen you until you can face all the rest, and they will do it again and again in the same way that you have doubtless always done for them.

And if none of this works, well, at least now you know what to google!

Slava Madorsky | Baltimore, Maryland
www.GrowUnstuck.com

Slava Madorsky is the founder of Grow Unstuck, LLC, where she offers her services as a presenter, trainer, and certified life coach. Slava specializes in the positive psychology approach to wellbeing, specifically in areas of stress-management, burnout, vicarious trauma, goal achievement, and intuitive eating.

Before launching her business, Slava spent 10 years as an adjudicator, supervisor, and trainer in the refugee and asylum corps of the US Citizenship and Immigration Services, traveling to war zones and remote corners of the world to interview refugees seeking resettlement to the US and make decisions on their eligibility. Prior to that, she was a Holocaust educator at the Auschwitz Jewish Center in Poland and a genocide researcher in Rwanda.

Having experienced the draining emotional, mental, and physical demands of such work upon herself and her colleagues, Slava pursued psychology, health, and coaching coursework; and subsequently developed a program specifically designed to mitigate the effects of stress, vicarious trauma, and compassion fatigue, while promoting burnout prevention and recovery. As a form of emotional and physical self-care, Slava also specializes in helping individuals move away from a culture of dieting and toward embracing intuitive eating.

Since embarking on this path, she has worked with numerous groups and individuals to help them thrive and develop their confidence and effectiveness in challenging circumstances.

Slava holds a BA in English Literature from the University of Maryland, College Park; an MA in Coexistence and Conflict from Brandeis University; a Certification in Positive Psychology from the Whole Being Institute; and a Life Coaching Certification from the Life Coach Institute of Orange County. She is also pursuing certification as an Intuitive Eating Counselor, to be completed in October 2021. Slava speaks English and Russian fluently, and Polish on special occasions.

To learn more about the work of Grow Unstuck or to contact Slava directly, please visit www.GrowUnstuck.com.

Character Strengths ...
Those Superpowers ... What Are They?

- Christine R. Donnolo

What lies behind us and what lies before us are tiny matters compared to what lies within us.
                                    - Ralph Waldo Emerson

According to the VIA Institute of Character, "Character Strengths are the positive parts of your personality that impact how you think, feel and behave. Scientists have identified 24 character strengths that you can possess." To expand on this, the Positivity Project states, "It is a broad and complex family of thoughts, feelings, and behaviors that are recognized and encouraged across cultures for the values they cultivate in people and society. Character strengths are our superpowers. They are the sum of who we are. It is what is inside every one of us." We all have these qualities and the power within us to express them. However, we are all unique in how we use them. If it is "what is inside every one of us," let me share with you a few stories to describe how they enhance a person's life, the life of others, and strengthen one's sense of well-being and even relationships.

Superman, the Mad Scientist, a 1941 movie (based on Jerry Siegel's DC Comics character, Superman), opens with the planet Krypton about to explode. One of its leading scientists realizes this will happen and places his infant son in a rocket ship heading to earth. The rocket ship lands on planet earth, and the infant boy is found and placed in an orphanage. A thoughtful and loving couple living on a farm in Kansas adopts him. As the boy grows up, he and his parents realize he has superpowers. "Faster than a speeding bullet, more powerful than a locomotive, able to leap tall buildings in a single bound. The infant of Krypton is now the Man of Steel: Superman!" To best use his extraordinary powers in the never ending battle for truth and justice, Superman's parents recommend he leave home and expand his horizons by going to a metropolis. He does and assumes the disguise of Clark Kent, mild-mannered reporter for a great metropolitan newspaper. Superman realizes he has incredible abilities, which can be called character strengths, and he wants to use them to save people and make a difference in their lives. Have you ever read the comic series, watched the movie or TV show? Did you root for Clark Kent when he became Superman and rips open his shirt and dramatically reveals the famous "S" emblem, becoming the Man of Steel? It would be nice to have the strengths and personal superpowers of bravery, courage, kindness, love, fairness, leadership, humility, self-control, and the host of other powers the Man of Steel exhibits. Is it possible you have them but do not recognize them? Well, you do; we all have them. We may not appreciate or focus on them as Superman does, yet they are a part of you and me.

Let me share another story you may better relate to and be familiar with, *The Wonderful Wizard of Oz*, written in 1900 by L. Frank Baum. It became a movie in 1939. I bet you have at least seen the film since, according to the Library of Congress, it is the most watched film ever. The Library of Congress has declared it "America's greatest and best-loved homegrown fairytale." In this magical fairytale, L. Frank Baum captured the minds and hearts of children and adults for over a century.

The *Wizard of Oz* is a charming story of Dorothy and her dog, Toto, who live on a farm on the Kansas prairies with her Aunt Em and Uncle Henry. As the story unfolds, a cyclone is about to happen and Dorothy, along with Toto, try to find shelter. They are in her bedroom, where she falls on the bed and strange things happen. Dorothy falls into a dream state where she and Toto get swept up by the wind. When she wakes up, they are in the magical Land of Oz. Although Dorothy is frightened and extremely curious about the land, she realizes that Aunt Em is most likely looking for her and she wants to go back home. Amid this beautiful country, Dorothy sees the queerest looking people, called munchkins, which look nothing like the people back home. They tell her that the only way she can return home is to walk through the forest on the Yellow Brick Road to the Emerald City, where a powerful ruler called the Wizard of Oz lives. The munchkins tell Dorothy to ask the great and powerful Wizard of Oz to help her. In this enchanting land, she also meets up with a Good Witch called Glinda, whose strengths include kindness, love, and justice, she offers to help her return home. Glinda gifts Dorothy with a pair of ruby slippers to keep her safe and to help her return home to Kansas. Dorothy is a loving, curious, kind, fair, and courageous girl. She starts walking along the Yellow Brick Road, where she meets a TinMan looking for a heart, a Scarecrow who desires a brain, and a Cowardly Lion who craves courage to be brave. Dorothy has compassion for them and decides she is going to help them find what they want. L. Frank Baum wrote this story in the early 1900s. What he tapped into is the positive psychology of people, their strengths, and virtues, even though he was not a psychologist or social worker. He was a writer who wrote a fairy tale about a magical city and a Wizard.

I suspect, though, when you came across this story, you may have found a likeness in yourself in one or more of the unforgettable characters. I believe Baum and Siegel tapped into the relationship between the characters and how they use their character strengths and virtues. Like the characters, we all possess these traits. These strengths were gifted from birth and can help us throughout our lives, but we often do not always recognize them or use them to our advantage.

Interestingly, the concept of Positive Psychology was not voiced until 1998 when Marty Seligman, Ph.D., became president of the American Psychology Association and Positive Psychology. Before his presidency, most people in psychology, when dealing with people's issues, focused on past histories and unhappiness. Positive Psychology focuses on what makes life most worth living, and it builds on "the good life" instead of repairing the bad. Isn't that what the characters in The Wizard of Oz wanted? Isn't that what Superman possessed?

Is that something you want to enhance your life, the life of others, and strengthen your well-being and relationships?

When I first had the Wizard story read to me by my Mom, I was probably 4 or 5 and a little older when I got to see the movie. I was fascinated; it captured my imagination and curiosity and instilled a love of travel for far-off places. Yet I'm sure when I saw and read the story, there is no way in the world I ever thought about virtues and character strengths. It was just an incredible, captivating story about a girl, a dog, and some funny looking characters. When I watched the TV show, Superman, I was fascinated by this very handsome fellow who had superhuman strength, lightening speed, stamina, and was invulnerable. Yet, in the past few years, having studied Positive Psychology through the Wholebeing Institute, all that comes to mind is how insightful Siegel and Baum were. They wrote stories that shine a bright light on people's character strengths and virtues, yet the concept didn't develop until the late 1990s. In 2000, through the VIA Institute of Character, character strengths and virtues were formalized. When I think about the characters, I view these stories now based on a new light. I recognize the characters' strengths and use them to overcome insecurity, loneliness, and behavioral issues.

The VIA Institute of Character regards strengths as the backbone of the science of positive psychology. There are signature strengths that are more accessible and natural for an individual to express. Other lesser ones arise when needed in particular situations, and some don't come as easy for a person to use.

The framework has six categories of virtues and groups the twenty-four character strengths under them. Grouping the strengths under their Virtues we have:

1. **Wisdom** - (cognitive) – creativity, curiosity, judgment, love of learning, and perspective;
2. **Courage** - (emotional) – bravery, perseverance, honesty, and zest;
3. **Humanity** - (social & community) – love, kindness, and social intelligence;
4. **Justice** - (protective) – teamwork, fairness, and leadership;
5. **Temperance** - (protective) – forgiveness, humility, prudence, and self-regulation;
6. **Transcendence** - (spiritual) – appreciation of beauty & excellence, gratitude, hope, humor, and spirituality.

If you want to find out more about character strengths and virtues, you can check out the VIA website which is found at www.viacharacter.org and the survey. This instrument will help you recognize all of these characters and virtues in your life.

Let's review the character strengths and virtues and see how they apply to Superman, The Wizard of Oz, and our lives. Some of Superman's character strengths stand out, especially those that help individuals and himself. Undoubtedly, the virtue of courage is one. He exhibits the character strengths of bravery since he doesn't shrink from any threats or challenges. He shows no fears and speaks up on what's right and wrong. He is persistent in overcoming enormous challenges and obstacles throughout the story. In the movie, Superman says, "It's not about where you were born or the powers you have or what you wear on your chest; it's about what you do." The virtues of temperance and humanity are apparent in this statement.

Let's now focus on the characters in *The Wizard of Oz*. The Scarecrow - does he want a brain? Could it be that he wants wisdom? The Scarecrow is intuitive. He doesn't mind his legs, arms, and body stuffed with straw, yet he surely doesn't want people to call him a fool. He wants a brain for wisdom and his love of learning. In the book, he says, "How am I ever to know anything if my head is stuffed with straw instead of brain." Curiosity rings true based on the fact he keeps asking Dorothy questions when she says she is going to the Emerald City to ask the Great Oz to help her get back home. He wants to know "Where is the Emerald City" and Who is Oz? And what about the TinMan - he so wants a heart. The TinMan needs the heart to love and marry one of the munchkins girls. The girl lives with an old woman who doesn't want her to get married because she does all the cooking and cleaning. So the old woman goes to the Wicked Witch of the East to stop them from getting married. The Wicked Witch does help, and the TinMan no longer has the heart. He wants to get his heart back because when he had been in love with the girl, "He was the happiest man on earth, but now, how could he love her without a heart." Could the signature virtue of humanity and character strength of love – wanting to love and be loved; kindness – having compassion and nurturance; and social intelligence – having feelings of oneself and others be some more of the TinMan's characteristics?

I can relate to many of these character strengths in my life, especially the signature strength of the "love of learning." While at Kripalu Center for Yoga and Health in Massachusetts,

I saw a program offered through the WholeBeing Institute on Positive Psychology in a catalog. I was curious since how people figure things out and act always interested me. When I was a young girl, I always wanted to be around my relatives and friends. I was always eager to know what they had to say about various family members and friends. I grew up in an Italian family with my parents and my maternal grandmother. My grandmother's five children and families often came over for coffee and cake and from time to time for lunch and dinner. Chatting and food were indeed central in our home. I can't say they came daily, but it sure seemed that way. I can remember once saying to my Mom, "Do we always have to have company?" It was frustrating as a child always having to be on your best behavior and "good." I digress – the talk at the kitchen table was most of the time about what was happening with their children and the family.

There was lots of talking, but also lots of insights into the behavior of people. I devoured it all. I loved that time and the delicious treats that seemed always to be around when they came. I'm sure I developed the virtue of wisdom during these times, and they influenced my love of learning and being extremely curious about people and what made them tick. It gave me an excellent big picture perspective of the world. It also helped me with critical thinking and judgment, quickly figuring things out, and helping people. My familial background made me realize how important the virtue of humanity and character strength of kindness is to me in my daily life.

When I studied Yoga, what always interested me was the Yoga tradition's teachings. In the Yoga Sutra 1:2, Patanjali writes,

"Yoga is the complete mastery over the mind's roaming tendencies." He continues, "The mind is the repository of all our thoughts, feelings, and memories. It is the store-house of our likes and dislikes. We see the world, and ourselves, through the eye of our mind." I believe Positive Psychology helps one master his/her mind focusing on the positive, not the roaring tendencies and negative aspects of one's life. It seems to look at humanity as well as happiness and fulfillment. It is so intriguing that even as early as 600 BC, Lao Tzu, the founder of Taoism, stated that "The key to growth is the introduction of higher dimensions of consciousness into our awareness." He believed that knowing our true nature was key to our happiness. In 350 BC, Aristotle's theory of Eudaimonia (happiness) is the natural outcome of well-being, and unhappiness is due to dysfunction. As the centuries and years progress, numerous people in psychology, such as Maslow, Horney, Antonovsky, Langer, and many more published research on well-being and happiness. Again, isn't that what Dorothy, the Scarecrow, TinMan, and Lion wanted – a life of well-being and happiness?

Now let's focus on the Cowardly Lion. What are the virtues and character strengths that predominate in his life? The Lion indeed has courage on his mind. He knows how to roar to frighten people, but he is afraid of the forest animals. The Lion is unhappy and wants to go with Dorothy to the Emerald City. He feels he is not brave enough and views himself as a coward, making him unhappy. Yet, in actuality, he has courage, is honest, and persevering in overcoming any of the obstacles he comes across in the forest. For me, courage comes into writing this chapter. It takes perseverance and patience to put one's thoughts on paper. This chapter took many iterations, and I had to apply my lesser strengths to complete the project. Without paying attention and acknowledging these strengths, I doubt I could have written this chapter!

Like Anne Lamott, a national bestseller author writes in *Bird by Bird, Some Instructions on Writing and Life* that all good writers need to write "shitty first drafts … the first draft is a child's draft, where you let it all pour out and then let it romp all over the place". I can't tell you how many times I re-wrote a paragraph or line. Talk about being persistent. One other of my character strengths is bravery, such as facing challenges. William Zinsser, another best selling author, wrote in his book *Writing to Learn* that there are two fears the American education system seems to inflict on all of us in some form. "One is the fear of writing… and the other is the fear of a subject we don't think we have an aptitude for …" I must admit that I have had to grow my courage and strength of bravery to complete this work.

I could discuss the characters in the story and how they show up in my life, but I think you can now notice them in yourself and others. Each of the character strengths and virtues is part of a person's personality, and tapping into them, especially those that are our signature strengths, will benefit you and all the people in your life! They are our superpowers!

My hope is I've inspired you to take the VIA survey and look at your character strengths and virtues … those superpowers and how they can enhance your life. Let me leave you with a quote from Eleanor Roosevelt, "The purpose of life, after all, is to live it, to taste experience to the utmost, to reach out eagerly and without fear for a newer and richer experience."

Christine R Donnolo | Scranton, Pennsylvania

www.ChristineDonnolo.com

Christine R. Donnolo is the founder of Aging Well Coach, blending her professional business and educational experience with training, teaching, and coaching in wellness and Aging Well. She believes as we age, taking care of our bodies using holistic practices learned through yoga, Ayurveda, the Wholebeing Institute, healthy eating, and money management is an essential aspect of graceful aging and health.

Christine has a MA in Industrial/Organizational Psychology and a BBA in Marketing/Management. She holds certificates in RYT500-hour and 200-hour teacher training, Ayurveda Specialist; Wholebeing Positive Psychology; Two-year Acting program, and a Registered Financial Gerontologist. Christine lived in Bulgaria for four years. She was a two year, Peace Corps Business Development Specialist volunteer and then spent two years working as the University of Delaware's Director of the Business Development Center.

She has worked at Penn State, James Madison and Yale University, UN International School, and various other institutions as an administrator and adjunct professor in business and financial literacy trainer. For over ten years, Christine hosted a bi-weekly television show in Northeast PA on business and money matters. She lives in Scranton, PA, with her husband, Gene, and cat, Coco!

Planting Seeds of Positivity Internationally

- Joanne Travers

The best and most beautiful things in this world cannot be seen or even heard, but must be felt with the heart.

- Helen Keller

I had just finished a yoga teacher training at Kripalu, and after that last scrumptious lunch I walked down the hallway feeling wonderfully full of happiness and thinking I did not want to leave. I stopped to read a poster promoting Wholebeing Institute's Certificate in Positive Psychology (CiPP) and looked deeply at the smiling faces of Maria Sirois and Megan

McDonough, inspirational leaders of the organization. "That's a reason to stay!"

When I googled Positive Psychology, it was perfectly aligned with how I worked with schools and families of children with hearing loss in developing countries. Grateful for how another door opened its welcoming wing, I enrolled in CiPP.

I had started an international charitable organization, Partners for A Greater Voice, in 2001. It was inspired by my two children, born with hearing loss and other disabilities. I passionately juggled their communication and development with my determination to provide informational and relational supports in aural education to families and schools coping with childhood hearing loss. My enthusiasm came with suitcases full of education materials, hearing devices, and training manuals on every mission I traveled. Beyond the transfer of knowledge and donations, initiatives bloomed into therapy programs, parental support, and starting a school.

CiPP combined with my yoga experience transformed my inner world. Being optimistic and forward thinking were ideals I always carried within me. After all, the motto of my non-profit is "Make the World a Bigger Place for A Child with Hearing Loss" and a common catchphrase in the industry is "Dreams Made Real." The scope of positive psychology and the CiPP coursework renewed my purpose and spirit. I learned how self-compassion would guide me onto new pastures, and how positive psychology could transform my non-profit after fifteen years of humanitarian service to practitioners and families who embraced aural deaf education.

Planting positive psychology seeds in places I had worked became a renewed focus of my international work. A new paradigm for coaching caregivers would instill compassion for self, and a more holistic approach would enable the greatest potential of caregivers. I wanted to make the task of helping children with disabilities less of a burden and more of a joyful and engaging journey.

The parents I work with faced harsh stigma, guilt, abuse, isolation and limited resources. Teachers face a myriad of trauma that children experience, from hunger and poor health to abuse and neglect. Many parents are abandoned by their own families, asked to live in a backyard shed or find new housing. All because their children are deaf. Some parents do not know how to read. Many have no emotional support system either, nor the wherewithal to find supports and disability services. Teachers also struggle to make a living. They are paid very low wages and have limited training. The teachers we encounter starve for knowledge in aural education and effective ways to coach and empower caregivers of the children who are learning how to communicate.

Helping practitioners become compassionate coaches of caregivers became an important component of our training programs. With volunteers I recruited, we wanted to help hearing health practitioners (teachers and audiologists) recognize the value of positive psychology tools and how to shift the paradigm of traditional support. Rather than coach caregivers on the 'how tos' and 'to dos', positive interventions that work from the inside out would balance the process and make the journey a happier, confident one.

Within a year of completing Certificate in Positive Psychology (CiPP) I launched a week-long mission to the Dominican Republic with Neal, a volunteer and director on my board. We traveled to four regions of the Dominican Republic, locations we had worked in for over fifteen years. Our workshops and coaching aimed to lift up over two-hundred people using strengths-based storytelling and active listening. We talked about hope and possibility to shift limiting beliefs. We helped people identify their personal resources such as spirituality, social supports, and state of mind. As I watched the smiling faces elevate the room, an atmosphere of shame and stress dissolved. Positive energy filled the room as families came together in recognition of each other's abilities and capabilities.

Our missions planted the seeds of psychological well-being, and I envisioned a wave of encouraging interventions pour into the communities we worked in. We would water the gardens of homes, schools, and therapy rooms. We would water the minds and hearts of capable careers of children with hearing loss. Then we would watch them grow into a tapestry of positivity and color.

Learning the science of happiness and ways to flourish seeped into my life like wildflowers in a meadow as well. Knowledge was my sun and the rain nurtured my love of learning. My self-compassion continued to grow as mother, wife, friend, and consultant. My relationship with husband Paul improved. My friend Katy told me how I had become more attentive and sensitive. I listened better. I was happier, wiser, and stronger. Self-compassion wove its ways into my heart as a yoga teacher and graduate of CiPP. At my best self, the weight of work and family demands were lifted from my shoulders.

In truth, I witnessed how positivity ebbs and flows, moving like the shadows of the sun across a landscape. I have grown to appreciate the impermanence of life and the joyful moments that feed a heavy heart.

In 2008, I consulted a start-up parent organization based in Mumbai called VConnect. The first parent meeting I facilitated welcomed seventy families around a conference table. Located in a school for the deaf near a busy intersection in Khar-West Mumbai when the temperatures were so hot we had to keep the lights off, the group shared intimate moments that connected us as one tribe. It was the first time a group of families in this region of India had gotten together to talk about deafness, their emotions, and things they faced with their children at home and in school. It was the inspiration for getting together again; to remain tethered to possibility and potential.

VConnect grew to a few hundred families in the following years, and in 2017 the two founders were ready for more in-country support. As their partner, and with global funding, I embarked on a plane to India two years after graduating from CiPP and conducted a parent leadership conference in three locations: Pune, Mumbai, Ahmedabad. In total there were over two-hundred parents who attended.

The conferences began with my story. I told them what I felt the day my daughter was diagnosed with severe hearing loss; heat rose from the earth into my feet and this felt like lava filling up my legs, my heart, and throat and drying my tearing eyes. That frightful day I froze. It was with compassion for myself and connection to other parents that allowed my heart to open to possibility, my body to move. I envisioned my best self, my determination to advocate for their needs, and my innate strengths of perseverance, forgiveness and love of learning that helped me to help my children. As a result, they thrive as independent adults now.

Conferences were key to connecting parents, but also an important opportunity for informational and emotional supports. We practiced mindful moments of silence. We engaged in active listening where small groups could privately share their personal challenges. I encouraged growth mindsets by weaving in positive outcomes of children and success stories that I had heard from other parents. I wanted them to believe in themselves. Building their self-esteem meant we needed to explore their beliefs and values. "Write down the vision you have for your child. Where do you want your child to be in twenty years?" Parents had never been asked these questions. "Write down three great characteristics of your spouse. Now write down three skills you believe your child to have." We explored beliefs, leadership skills, and character strengths. To empower parents, helping them recognize the good in the mist of challenging situations was vital. I could see positivity growing throughout the day of workshops and presentations. Two certified, master clinicians of Character Strengths told me afterwards, "Brilliant! The people of Pune have such low self-esteem and the progression of positivity was terrific!"

I was grateful for being welcomed by so many people and sharing my understanding of positive psychology with partners and affiliates of VConnect. I also met with practitioners at AURED, the therapy center where I first met with parents in 2008. Over thirty teachers and a few audiologists gathered one afternoon to learn about holistic techniques that would motivate parents to support their children's learning and communication. Far too many teachers felt that parents relied on them for the outcomes of their children. "What motivates parents? Do you allow time for caregivers to explore their personal resources? Do you ask parents how they feel?" We discussed ways to nurture caregivers' personal power and discover a sense of success and joy. We talked about character strengths and innate potential. We talked about ways to intrinsically motivate caregivers, and how identifying, exploring and applying character strengths can be a tool to engage parents further. Being empathetic and compassionate with caregivers was necessary to balance the informational and technical supports many practitioners focused on. And it was important to use positive strategies that helped caregivers acknowledge and overcome difficult situations.

The VConnect advisory and board saw possibility through a new lens because of those initial leadership conferences and meetings we had with their partners in Mumbai. We had many conversations during the hours of driving through traffic to and from locations we visited. I loved acknowledging their strengths of curiosity, perseverance, teamwork, and kindness!

I returned to India in 2018 to plant more seeds of positivity. Parents closely tied to the VConnect mission and who ran circles of parent groups in their communities participated in an extended weekend immersion I planned. A grant paid for a retreat center in Alibaug, a boat ride from the Gateway to

India, and all related expenses for everyone. Fifteen parents, referred to as leaders of VConnect, came from different locations and Caste systems. Many of these parents had never left their children and communities. It was the first time they got together as one group. I was a root connecting their many branches.

That was my thirty-fourth international mission. I was prepared as always, with education materials including a self-published workbook designed for the immersion. I facilitated exercises, group work and shared intimate conversations. I offered yoga and meditation early in the morning. I wanted them to reflect within themselves before coming up with projects that would help others in their parent group.

The first day focused on character strengths and leadership skills. We reviewed leadership styles and participants picked one or two they connected with. After taking VIA Survey, everyone picked two top strengths and used post-its. We tacked everyone's strengths and leadership skills (with no associated names) on a flip chart to see the collective display of VConnect strengths! (There was one man who was illiterate, and we helped him take the VIA online aurally in his language; his top strength was leadership!) For two days, we reviewed concepts and delved into other activities. After working through many exercises and conversations, the last day was reserved for innovation.

I wish I recorded the final day of presentations. Set outside on a veranda landscaped with flowering vines, hibiscus and lotus flowers, banyan trees and plumeria, the VConnect group percolated with excitement under the shade. I asked each parent leader to choose a positive psychology topic, one that resonated with them and one that they felt comfortable weaving into their own parent centered initiatives. Based on what they experienced, they created projects to implement in their home communities. I encouraged ways to hone-in on attainable goals. Hands flew, laughter resounded, and they gave each other supportive feedback. Communicating in positive ways with parents, fostering mindfulness, and unlimiting beliefs would proliferate in local parent circles. From this extended weekend, there were a dozen programs that emerged, many of which included personal growth and development and ways to enable parents more effectively.

From that initial meeting in 2007 to the intensive in 2018, a garden of positive psychology has grown, and parent leaders have come together to collaborate and support the expansion of their network. I am amazed at the leadership of VConnect, the team of parent leaders working in their communities to improve the lives of families coping with their children's hearing challenges. Supporting parents in novel ways has spread like sunshine over colorful villages crowded with family businesses, traffic, housing and people. Life is busy in India and working in low economic communities is challenging. Parent leaders of VConnect are applying their strengths of compassion, and positive psychology roots have sprouted. Their perseverance, kindness, love, leadership, and zest has helped the parenting road easier to travel. Parents have found ways to support and inspire each other. Last year, mental health has become a pillar of the VConnect organization. They have been working toward more projects that include content we have shared with them.

In late 2018, I met Devangi Dalal at an annual Coalition for Global Hearing Health conference in Arizona. Devangi founded Josh Foundation in Mumbai, India and had received numerous awards and recognition for her work in audiology. She is a wonderfully positive person to be with, radiating with love, kindness, and spirituality. We talked about ways to coach and empower caregivers using positive interventions described in my book.

Devangi wrote to me in March of 2021, "I take inspiration from Joanne and her book, and I add love, compassion, strength and spirituality to my day-to-day life and writing to spread positivity and to make a change in the world." She began posting her wisdom and blogging every week in 2019, and then compiled fifty articles in a book called, *Spreading Positivity*. The virtual book launch occurred on her 50th birthday, and there were over one hundred on the call. As Devangi's guest, she asked me to comment on her book:

> *Devangi iterates our innate potential to thrive, regardless of disability, by grounded us in words of wisdom and positivity. She beautifully weaves ancient philosophy with present day stories of persons with hearing loss, composing essays on compassion, happiness, and consciousness. Reading Devangi's blogs reminds us of our responsibility to be kind, to draw upon virtues granted to us at birth, and to do so by being present to the human, day to day experience. Spreading positivity in our world, and within the deaf and hard of hearing community especially, cannot be expressed enough.*

Helping caregivers of children with hearing loss overcome personal challenges requires taking actionable and compassionate steps. Our humanitarian missions to India have flourished on their own accord. With open hearts, truth, kindness, gratitude and innate gifts of character, we spread positivity to others. VConnect has turned hope into action. They have turned shame into growth mindsets. They have continued to foster strengths in parents that help them navigate the many challenges they face.

Devangi has continued to blog and share positivity. Stepping over weeds and stones in a lush garden has moved her and VConnect onto grassier fields where feelings of confidence and success are flourishing.

I received a message from VConnect in early February of 2021. The message read, "Dear Joanne, you have been our biggest inspiration and support. We want to invite you to our virtual Annual Day. We'd truly be happy if you'd log in for an hour." The live event took place February 20th, 2021 and showcased VConnect's success and children's talent! Children from age four to nineteen jubilantly shared what makes them happy: artwork, singing, poetry, gymnastics, music, dancing, Rubik's cube puzzles! The voices of deaf children were clear and radiant; their confidence enabled by the power of positive parenting.

The success of these children exemplifies the success of parenting. Children are happy and their parents must be proud! VConnect loves their work, and they now inspire over 1500 parents supporting the development and success of children's hearing loss and mainstream education.

Seeing others thrive helps me to see my own happiness and gratitude more clearly, beginning with those immersion days of CiPP. I reflect my fellow 'CiPPsters', the joy, kindness, love, compassion, optimism, character strengths they all share. It is an inspiration to know that so many wonderful people share a belief in positivity as a science and the way to change the world. As a yoga teacher, I naturally weave Positive Psychology into my yoga classes. I use character strengths as a theme in many of my classes. I sit in meditation with affirmations. I happily talk with friends and family about their character strengths and suggest they take the VIA Institute's online survey. Positive psychology is a journey, and my learning continues as I flourish along its supportive and nurturing path.

The journey of happiness for me is an ongoing state of awareness and being. Life has its challenges and when these are present, I remind myself of life's precious gifts. I remind myself of my strengths of kindness, perseverance, forgiveness,

curiosity and creativity to share with the world. I remind myself of the many challenges people face in developing countries and the hard work it takes to plant seeds of positivity. I find joy in sharing my knowledge with others, guiding yoga classes, and being present to life's beauty and wonder. In other words, I sow the seeds of a creative and beautiful life.

Joanne N Travers | Ipswich, Massachusetts

www.greatervoice.com

Joanne has embraced hope and optimism for the inclusion of aural deaf and hard of hearing children throughout the world. Inspired by her children who were born with hearing loss and other disabilities, she established a parent network in her home state of Massachusetts that connected hundreds of families who coped with mainstream education, technology supports, and child development. Her positive outlook and perseverance led her to incorporate an international charity called Partners for A Greater Voice that has served practitioners and caregivers in developing countries since 2001. Joanne has completed thirty-four humanitarian missions in the Dominican Republic, Honduras, and India in partnership with over seventy volunteers. Her organization has provided technical training, school services, and positive parenting supports.

The Wholebeing Institute's Certificate in Positive Psychology opened Joanne's eyes to humanistic ways to help people thrive. Studying and practicing Positive Psychology transformed her mission work and inspired new ways to inform and support caregivers. Based on her international experience and CiPP, she published a book called *Coaching and Empowering Caregivers of Children with Hearing Loss, An Approach to Foster Well-being.* A grant allowed her to mail over one-hundred free copies to practitioners in over thirty countries. For more information go to:

http://www.greatervoice.com.

Joanne holds a Master's degree in International Management and a certification in Positive Psychology from Wholebeing Institute. She is also a nationally certified ski instructor and yoga teacher. She is writing a memoir called *Mission Passion.*

SECTION 4: ENGAGING IN LIFE

- DONNA MARTIRE MILLER

Hoi An, Vietnam Graduation

Where your attention goes, the energy follows! Flourishing in life.

Many things in our life and society compete for our attention. At times, it can be easier to focus on distractions than what our intention to focus on is. Research in the science of happiness shows us how important it is to shift our attention to what really matters to us. Paying attention is a way to take control of our thoughts, word, and actions.

What is it that moves you forward? What is it that lights you up when you see or do it? Do you believe you are capable of what you desire? Do you believe you can live an inspired, happier life? If we have higher self-esteem and a natural growth mindset, we can answer these questions with optimism. If we feel like our life has been handed to us, fixed as it is, and there is no possibility for change, it might be harder to answer these questions with any conviction. This would be considered a fixed mindset. Our thoughts are not just thoughts. They are a force that determines what we believe about a situation, how we feel, and how we act or react.

Meditation and mindfulness give us the tools to control our inner critic or thoughts of the worst-case scenario. John Kabat Zinn teaches that mindfulness is the practice of purposely bringing one's attention in the present moment without judgment, a skill developed in meditation. These practices are known to expose what really matters to us. Our truth rises up and positively affects our mood, increases our positive emotions, and decreases anxiety and negative emotional reactivity. Research also shows us the health benefits of engaging in meditation and mindfulness daily. Our heart, blood pressure, T-cells, cancer, and Alzheimer's are some of the health disparities that mindfulness and meditation positively affect. Also, those fighting addictions use these tools to control cravings and recidivism.

Once we have our thoughts moving in the right direction, making the mind-body connection becomes imperative. The brain and thoughts are proven to influence the body and its functions. Today you can read articles everywhere about the newer discoveries in science that demonstrate how the health of the mind affects the health of the body. Mind-body medicine works with practices that can improve health, such as relaxation, meditation, yoga, and Let Your Yoga Dance! Meditation, prayer, mindfulness, and movement are keys to our well-being. It helps us pay attention to what brings us meaning and helps us live a healthy, flourishing life gaining peace for our body, mind, and soul.

This section will introduce Cate, Megha, Natalie, Andrea, and Lori as they share their inspiring stories of acquired joy!

Repurpose Your Purpose

- Cate Conti

The purpose of life is to discover your gift; the work of life is to develop it, and the meaning of life is to give your gift away.

- David Viscott

Part 1: FALLING OFF THE CLIFF:

Have you ever wondered why you're here, what's your Grand Purpose in Life? For years my greatest fear was that I would find myself on my deathbed and have to admit that I'd wasted my only Life because I didn't know my Purpose. My lack of direction wasn't for lack of trying. Even as a kid, in Catholic school, I prayed along with everyone else to discover my vocation. I envied people like my older brother who knew exactly what he wanted to do by age fourteen - save lives as an emergency room doctor! I was vaguely aware that I wanted to do something different- Explore the world or be an artist or a writer. Unfortunately, those pursuits weren't deemed entirely appropriate, and I was left aimless. Still, I had to make a living so I became an Interior Designer. It wasn't a bad fit since it took advantage of my spatial, artistic, and interpersonal skills, but something was still missing. I knew that having a Purpose, which uses your strengths and passions, can energize your whole life and infuse it with Meaning. It was that sense of *meaning* I was missing.

I was able to shelve my low-grade malaise for years at a time because I assumed I'd eventually have a family of my own. Raising those kids to thrive and be happy would give me the sense of purpose that I craved.

But alas, it was not meant to be. Relationship trouble ensued (was I too independent?) and one short year after finally marrying my "Now and Forever Husband," in a romantic Italian wedding, I learned I was never going to be able to have kids of my own. It was like falling off a cliff- or like that awful feeling when you think there's ONE MORE STEP at the bottom of the stairs -the phantom step- and you go plummeting off into space. The vision I'd based my whole life on was an illusion. But, if I wasn't meant to have kids of my own, what was I meant to do?

I'm embarrassed to admit that it took me almost a DECADE to recover from WISHING THINGS WERE DIFFERENT (which I now know is one of the root causes of suffering!) I still gratefully hosted my various nieces and nephews on weekends, and persevered in a tricky relationship with my stepdaughter, but slowly sunk into a low-grade functional sort of depression. Even as I put on a cheerful face, I began studiously avoiding my clients' kids because it generated too many painful conversations.

And then the economy crashed, and I got sick with a mysterious ailment. I'd been bitten by a tick carrying Lyme's Disease, but without the tell-tale bull's-eye, I grew sicker and sicker and sicker. By the time I convinced the doctor to test me, I was chronically fatigued, barely sleeping, and the antibiotics couldn't touch it.

My Life was now officially a wreck. My work didn't satisfy, my marriage was strained, I was exhausted, medical science had failed me, and my dream of having a family of my own was in tatters. Not to be melodramatic, but there were times during this stretch when continuing to breathe felt like too much effort.

Part 2: THE LONG HARD SLOG:

Of course, it's often when we've hit rock bottom-and I certainly thought I had- that we're compelled to do the hard work required to claw back from the pit. I read everything I could get my hands on, started doing yoga every day, and joined group meditations. It was during a spiritual retreat that I heard the voice (of God!?) say, "I GAVE YOU A BRAIN, NOW USE IT!" The message was so unlike my way of phrasing that I had to laugh out loud right there, laying on the floor, in the middle of meditation. But wherever it came from, the message gave me the impetus to keep searching outside the box. A Homeopath helped me slowly recover physically, and the Yoga I was now doing faithfully helped so much that I thought maybe that's what I should be doing. So, I enrolled in Yoga Teaching Training, but halfway through had another Eureka moment. After class one night a fellow student asked me why I wanted to be a Yoga Instructor. I surprised myself by blurting out that I already knew I didn't! I explained that there wasn't enough talking involved! (where did that come from?) Instead, I said, I wanted to grow joy by exchanging ideas, encouraging people, and inspiring them! Without missing a beat, she said, "Oh, then you should be one of those Club Ladies." A Club Lady? What's a Club Lady? I asked, and she explained, "Oh you know, one of those Ladies who go around giving speeches on various topics at different clubs." I was rendered speechless. I didn't know what to do with that information because I was terrified of public speaking, but it was like the proverbial light bulb went off over my head. Her comment felt so prescient that I wrote down every word she said.

Part 3: SERENDIPITY STRIKES:

And then serendipity struck. While browsing a catalog from Kripalu Center for Yoga and Health, I spied a course description that would change my life forever. It was a year-long Certificate Course in Positive Psychology led by Whole Being Institute and Dr. Tal Ben-Shahar (who'd taught it at Harvard!) Marie Sirois Ph.D., and Megan McDonough.

The course, focusing on Human Flourishing, promised to be EXACTLY what I needed, but would I DARE sign up? I hesitated because my freelance business wasn't thriving, but the feeling that this was my destiny was so strong that by week's end I'd plunked down the deposit. I rode that high for about a month, but then, on the first get acquainted conference call doubt reared its ugly head. I felt so inadequate compared to everyone else who I imagined were all already professionals in the field. Who did I think I was? (And yes, I now know that comparison is the second most common cause of suffering.) I chickened out and canceled my registration.

Anxiety suffused my soul. I worried that if I passed up this opportunity- because I felt unworthy- I would hate myself. Wracked by indecision I made a deal with the Universe. If I could suddenly earn the balance of tuition, I'd re-enroll! Do YOU make pacts with God? I know it's not the approved method of communicating with the Creator, but it worked! That very week a client handed me a check and I called to re-enroll. Whew! That decision turned out to be the best I've EVER made because it helped everything else make sense. I learned dozens of tools that can be practiced regularly to uplift the spirit, build resilience, and find our niche. I even learned to appreciate the good already in my life- which is one of the first keys to happiness. As Tal Ben-Shahar has said, "When you appreciate the good, the good appreciates!" Being happier doesn't mean we won't face challenges or be disappointed, and it doesn't mean we have to smile all the time. Unshakable Happiness means practicing in the good times so we can bounce back more quickly in times of adversity. We learn to celebrate what we have, accept what can't be changed, and do the work to change what we can.

I experienced an upward spiral that I'm thrilled to say hasn't quit in the eight years since. In fact, I've recently had surgery and radiation for breast cancer -yes, *cancer*- for me the scariest word in the English language! And I admit I've been anxious and terrified on and off for months, but thanks to Positive

Psychology and the knowledge of my purpose in life, I've been able to re-establish my balance more quickly. I take it one step, one day at a time. I'm ALIVE! and will never again waste a decade in mourning!

Part 4: REPURPOSING MY PURPOSE:

The two most important gifts I derived from the Positive Psychology course were the clarity I achieved about my Purpose, and finding the Way-Power to get there. I already had an idea about my new Purpose -to Inspire and Encourage people -but I nailed it down using Tal Ben-Shahar's MPS Process described in his book *Happier*. He instructs us to ask three crucial questions- "What gives me meaning?" "What gives me pleasure?" and "What are my strengths?" (See Resources for a bibliography and link to the VIA STRENGTHS TEST.) As the MPS Process directs, I then noted the overlap in the lists and represented my findings Venn Diagram style (remember these from high school?)

Our True Purpose lies in the roles and activities that appear on all three lists and at the very center of the diagram. It's the intersection between what we love to do, what we're good at, and what makes us feel that life has meaning. Ben-Shahar is careful to point out that this work doesn't have to be something we do for money. Our Purpose can be a hobby, volunteer work, or a role you fill in family or society. Maybe your Super-Power is that you're almost always cheerful and your zest and positivity spills out over everyone you meet each day. Not brain surgery perhaps, but potentially just as important. When I did this exercise, my intersections were Curiosity, Love of Learning, and ZEST (my three greatest Strengths,) and Teaching, Writing, Encouraging, Inspiring, Art, and Interacting with Kids. I remembered that the gal in yoga class had said I should be a "Club Lady" -and realized that by writing, giving speeches, and leading seminars I'd be able to exercise my Zest and Love of Learning and then share what I've learned with others. But what to do? I was afraid of public speaking!

Yet again, coincidence struck, and in one month's time I happened upon three separate references to Toastmasters. I'd never heard of Toastmasters and thought it was a Breakfast Club! After the third mention, I decided I'd better check it out. Turns out, it's an International Speaking and Leadership Development Organization-not a Breakfast Club! I found a group near me and then procrastinated for two months before attending my first meeting as a guest. Of course, I wanted to skulk quietly in the back of the room remaining incognito, but Toastmasters are a generous, gregarious bunch; they immediately took me under their wing, and I've never looked back. Joining Toastmasters was the second-best decision of my life because it gave me WAY-POWER -a framework within which I could make steady progress in my goals.

Part 5: WAY-POWER: MY FABULOUS FUTURE AND THE STEPS TO GET THERE:

Just knowing what I wanted to do wasn't enough. Like you, I've had plenty of Inspiration in my day and have pursued very few ideas after the first blush of excitement wore off. I needed a way to lock in what I'd discovered and then Make it Happen in the Real World.

First, I created a statement of my ULTIMATE PURPOSE. Businesses call this a Mission Statement and it outlines the Vision and Goals of the company. I worked on my statement for months until I felt it reflected who I am and who I wanted to be.

Here's my MISSION STATEMENT: My Purpose is to Reflect God's Love as much as possible, and to Encourage and INSPIRE those I meet to greater Joy, Fulfillment, and Well-Being in a way that Grows Joy in my own life too!

Of course, I don't always live up to this lofty goal, but I try! Next, I harnessed the power of a practice we learned in the course. I journaled the story of MY FABULOUS FUTURE and THE STEPS TO GET THERE. The idea is to write, in as much detail as possible, what life and the world will look like when everything you hope for comes true. What will you see in the morning when you awaken? Where will you be? Who will you be with? What work will you be doing? I repeated this exercise many times to refine and reinforce it- and I never fail to feel uplifted by my Vision. Just doing this exercise increased my confidence, energy, and self-efficacy (the belief that I could do it!) You can also illustrate your Vision by cutting out photos or drawing pictures of places, objects, and people doing all the things you will be doing. This is commonly called a Vision Board and you can make it even more vivid by pasting your own face onto the bodies depicted. Most importantly, have FUN with it! I know I did.

Next, following Tal's advice, I outlined all the small steps I'd need to become a confident writer, teacher, and public speaker- like writing and delivering my very first speech, and then later, delivering a speech outside the protective environment of Toastmasters. Breaking down the steps is crucial because otherwise the big audacious goal can seem overwhelming and we're likely to give up. Listing the small steps gives us the Way-Power to focus on just one or two sub-goals at a time, and then celebrate when we achieve them! Also, each year, instead of making just one New Year's Resolution, I create a grid of thirty different sub-goals that I can work on throughout the year. Some are very small, others are larger and potentially carry over from the previous year, and some- like my health and relationship goals- appear every year because without your Health, and Love, everything else is much more difficult. Having a selection of goals also means that if I get stuck on one, I can work on a different goal until Inspiration strikes again -which it always does if you're open to it!

Part 6: LIFE MAP:

The fourth, and crucial practice for me was to put all this information together in one place for daily and weekly review. I call it my LIFE MAP. I typed up my STATEMENT OF PURPOSE, THE STORY OF MY FABULOUS FUTURE, and THE STEPS TO GET

THERE, and then pasted them all into a pamphlet I created of construction paper. To this day, I still revise my booklet periodically and keep it on my bedside table for Inspiration!

Part 7: UNSHAKABLE HAPPINESS:

Knowing my Purpose and the Steps to Get There has made all the difference in my Life, and I guarantee it will in your Life too! I no longer fear arriving on my deathbed having to admit that I've wasted my Life. I'm happy in a contented way, and my life is full of meaning and purpose. I've achieved many of my Goals, and for each one completed a new even more audacious goal happily takes its place! Meanwhile, I've learned to be patient and listen with kindness. I've also spoken to groups of Girl Scouts, given presentations in corporate environments, taught courses in Positive Psychology, led Vision Board workshops, mentored others on their Paths, written a BLOG on Happiness, and was even a Guest Speaker on a Radio Show! Whew! Each of these efforts required energy, attention, and time, but because I know I'm fulfilling my Purpose they leave me energized and uplifted (which is how you know it's your true Purpose!) I've even found new energy in my design work. I now realize that by creating aesthetically beautiful and harmoniously functioning spaces I help- mainly moms- stay sane while trying to raise their own families! How's that for Appreciating the Good! By discovering and fulfilling my Purpose I've become a better version of myself and know that I'm doing my part to make my corner of the world just a little bit brighter. And that, my friends, is the Grand Purpose of Life!

With Love, Cate Conti

Cate Conti | Solebury, Pennsylvania

Cate Conti is a Health and Happiness Advocate. Her work helps people make changes in their lives to be Healthier, Happier, and More Fulfilled ON PURPOSE, and her design work helps them stay sane!

Cate's also a Curious Explorer who Loves to Learn, Grow, and Pass On what she's Learned. Cate used to worry that this "dabbling" made her a dilettante, but in fact, it's her SUPER-POWER and provides the SPICE that makes Life FUN! As a "Spicy Lifer," Cate wears many hats: she's an Artist, Designer, Traveler, Writer, Storyteller, Public Speaker, Teacher, Mentor, Student of Positive Psychology, and Compulsive Reader. Cate also loves Hiking, Biking, Yoga, Dance, and anything you can do in or around the Sea.

Cate is a graduate of WholeBeing Institute's "Certificate in Positive Psychology Course" - a year-long training in Evidence-Based Research and High-Performance Outcomes of Positive Psychology. https://wholebeinginstitute.com/ She holds additional certifications in Positive Psychology Coaching and Teaching for Transformations. Cate also graduated from Jefferson University's Mind-Body Stress Reduction Program (MBSR,) and the University of Pennsylvania's Resilience Skills in the Time of Uncertainty. Finally, Cate is certified to teach Art and Yoga. Currently, Cate gives speeches and leads Seminars on Positive Psychology, Finding Purpose, Facing Fear, and Speaking With Courage.

Since 2014 Cate has been deeply involved in Toastmasters International, a professional speaking and leadership Development Organization. She has held various officer and directorship positions and has earned the DTM- which is the organization's highest designation.

RELEVANT BOOK LIST in reverse order of publication date:

1. *The Great Work of Your Life*- Stephen Cope 2012
2. *Flourish*- Martin Seligman 2011
3. *HAPPIER*- Tal Ben-Shahar, Ph.D. 2007 (MPS Process described on pgs 103-104)
4. *The Power of Story*- Jim Loehr 2007
5. *The Power of Full Engagement*- Jim Loehr and Tony Schwartz 2003
6. *Finding Flow*- Muhaly Czikszentmihalyi 1997
7. *Man's Search for Meaning*- Victor Frankl 1959

STRENGTHS TESTS:

1. VIA Strengths: http://www.viacharacter.org/
2. University of Pennsylvania Authentic Happiness Strengths Test: www.authentichappiness.org
3. Strengths Finder (Gallup Poll): https://www.gallupstrengthscenter.com/?utm_source=googadwords&utm_medium=web&utm_campaign=newhomepage&gclid=CjwKEAjw0-epBRDOp7f7lOG0zl4SJABxJg9qh3uCN27WutRefMJSTw7pbAedg4DRxNvJxJUUu1yV9RoCKMHw_wcB

The Transformative Wisdom of Let Your Yoga Dance, Embodying Positive Psychology

- Megha Nancy Buttenhiem

Twenty-five years ago, I created a transformational movement practice called Let Your Yoga Dance. Tagline: *Where Joy and Fun Meet Deep and Sacred.* The Mission of Let Your Yoga Dance is: *to spread joy and consciousness throughout the world by transmitting body health, brain health, heart health, and soul health to all populations.* Having lived in a yoga ashram for twelve years, and having been a professional actor for a decade before that, I chose to bring together all the elements I loved in this world: user-friendly dance, moving gentle yoga, theatre, music, Mother Earth, moving meditation, dance prayer, qigong, and the chakras (the body's energy centers). I named the practice Let Your Yoga Dance because I wanted everybody – and every body – to feel free, safe, brave, infinitely joyous, and self-expressed. I wanted my students to know that Everyone is a Dancer. The words Let, and Your were equally important to me as Yoga and Dance.

Two and a half decades later, there are Let Your Yoga Dance instructors teaching in many countries around the world, Donna Martire Miller being one of them.

Although I could tell you now about many aspects of the Let Your Yoga Dance world community and the practice itself, I am particularly interested in demonstrating two things:

1. The ways that the Chakras provide a roadmap for consciousness within this yoga dancing practice.
2. The ways that Let Your Yoga Dance together with Positive Psychology offer a path to health, happiness, and congruent living.

Let Your Yoga Dance and the Chakras

The word *chakra* means "wheel." In yogic anatomy, the chakras represent the seven energy centers of the body, spinning currents related to the different elements. Although visible to the naked eye, the chakras are said to reside within and around the physical body, flowing upward from the base of the spine to the crown of the head. They are spinning vortices of energy-based around and radiating out from the curves of the spinal column. I will list the seven energy centers and show how they weave their way through a Let Your Yoga Dance class.

Chakra 1 relates to the earth and solid matter, to alignment, safety, and security. **Location:** Base of the spine, the tailbone. In the Let Your Yoga Dance practice, the feet and legs are included as the root within this chakra. In Chakra 1, we warm up the body, preparing for the Dance of Yoga.

Chakra 2 relates to water; birth, sensuality, sexuality, pleasure. **Location:** Sacrum, womb, genitals. This chakra reminds us that we are watery, fluid beings. The dance during this chakra is also fluid and watery, with the focus on the hips and sacral region. This area can be fraught with a lot of self-judgment. Bringing fun blues music into the mix can help people slowly start to open and explore a place in the body and mind that may have been off-limits.

Chakra 3 relates to fire: strength, power, authority, aggression, and resilience. **Location:** Solar plexus. This chakra is crucial when we need a boost of power and well-being in our lives. When we dance our yoga in the third chakra, we build power and intensity. Our body heats up. We move the feet. We might punch and stomp, moving into dynamic dancing Warriors. In the third chakra, the music might be filled with drums of passion. The energy in motion in Chakra 3 helps us release old emotions and limiting beliefs. When we dance in our power center, the solar plexus, we discover a new sense of strength and resilience, which in turn facilitates the creation of fresh, empowering emotions. This newfound energy is then free to blast upward from the solar plexus right into the heart, the fourth chakra.

Chakra 4 relates to air, representing the heart of devotion and compassion. **Location:** Heart. This fourth chakra is the bridge between the first three (lower) chakras and the next three (higher) chakras. Here we dance lyrically with love songs to remind ourselves that LOVE is the great healer. Love is ultimately the only way our Mother Earth and her inhabitants can thrive and grow. I love playing beautiful love songs in Chakra 4. It is glorious to see people smiling and falling in love with themselves and one another. Positive Psychologist Barbara Fredrickson has let her yoga dance with us; she enjoys the practice. In Chakra 4, her great research on broadening and building positivity resonance comes to life as together we create micro – and macro - moments of love and compassion, which then weave into the rest of one's day, week, or even month! Barbara's book *Love 2.0* is a must read.

Chakra 5 relates to space either; it represents sound and truth, self-expression, communication, joy, and creativity. **Location:** Throat. Here we dance more wildly. We sing our most delicious song, moving fast and furious around the room (going at our own pace, of course). If you are chair-bound, no problem! Engage your upper body and use your vocal cords. Sing your heart out. Express yourself with freedom. Go for joy!

Chakra 6 relates to light and inner seeing, representing intuition. **Location:** the point between the eyebrows at the center of the forehead. This is potentially the sweetest, the deepest part of the Let Your Yoga Dance experience. As our energy moves upward to the place between the eyebrows–the third-eye center–we dance away from extroverted wildness and turn our attention inward. We look within to our quiet, intuitive self, and with this third, internal-seeking eye, we dance inside ourselves. This part of the class combines dancing yoga cool-down with Dance Prayer. Creating Dance

Prayers and helping others discover their own moving prayers has been one of the highlights of my life.

Chakra 7 relates to thought, wisdom, and unity. **Location:** Crown of the head. Relaxation and meditation bring us to stillness and peace, silent wisdom. We take rest. We feel the lingering effect of the dance of yoga while receiving the brilliance of the body's inner wisdom. In yoga, Savasana, the final resting pose, is said to be the most important of all yoga postures, as it promotes receptivity and deep relaxation. As students take rest, they receive an opportunity to simply be. Just be. Tal Ben-Shahar teaches the importance of "Permission to be Human." I also like to teach the importance of "Permission to Be." Our culture has become deeply exhausted, stressed, worried, and frightened. Research shows that taking rest through relaxing and meditating is not a luxury; it's a necessity. In Let Your Yoga Dance, after relaxing in the 7th Chakra, we conclude the class with a meditation and often a poem, perhaps by Mary Oliver, John O'Donahue, David Whyte, Wendell Barry, or other great poetical exemplars. By now, the class is complete; all the chakras, these magnificent centers of energy, have been danced, opened, and balanced.

My fellow Let Your Yoga Dance instructors and practitioners agree that these chakras truly do provide a roadmap for a healthy, joyous, conscious life. Look at the seven elements. If you study each one and live fully into each of the chakras, your life might just feel more whole. The chakras miss nothing. For over two and a half decades, I have been exploring and teaching these chakras through the body with Let Your Yoga Dance. I learn something new every class I teach and take. And all of us instructors agree that if we start teaching the class while in a foul mood or deep in rage or grief, we end up in sheer unabashed joy–every time.

The Chakras, the Granddaddy of Positive Psychology – Abraham Maslow – and his Hierarchy of Needs

In 2011, I joined the faculty of the newly formed Wholebeing Institute under the aegis of Megan McDonough and Dr. Tal Ben-Shahar. Tal was a great Let Your Yoga Dance enthusiast himself and had taken the first module of my training. Although my practice was based in the chakras, I wanted to make sure that the students in the certificate program in Wholebeing Positive Psychology would learn how to bring all these teachings into their bodies, rather than just their heads. I strongly believed (and still do!) that the body is more than something to keep the head portable, but our culture has been snail-like in understanding this truth. I wrote a book with Tal's prodding, *Expanding Joy, Let Your Yoga Dance, Embodying Psychology*. *Expanding Joy* was and still is the first book ever written about embodied positive psychology. Although Tal was initially unsure about my intention to bring the energy centers into positive psychology due to a lack of academic research on the chakras, I knew that even though my work was based on the Chakras, I need not mention them. I could focus outwardly on dancing with the positive psychology character strengths and the Wholebeing Institute SPIRE model.

A few years later, I was delighted to learn that Positive Psychologist and Psychodramatist, Dan Tomasulo, was also interested in the chakras. He was intrigued by how these seven energy centers blended beautifully with Abraham Maslow's five Hierarchy of Needs. In a clear chart, Dan mapped out the similarities. He gave me permission to include his chart in my book. Observing these two models placed side-by-side was fascinating. Dan said that whether knowledge of the chakras influenced Maslow's thinking or not, in the end, both the Hierarchy of Needs and the Chakras point to human beings striving for higher levels of creativity, health, and self-fulfillment. Blocks at lower levels impede this growth; the tendency toward this higher level is natural, even essential. Please see the table on the next page.

Although the chakras have yet to make their way into the scientific research lexicon, that does not mean they have no value. They're simply way ahead of their time (just like Let Your Yoga Dance)! In yogic anatomy, the body's energy centers have been studied and honored for thousands of years. The chakras are also a part of the physical body. Many models of consciousness out there are simply mental constructs. But the chakras are alive and well within us. These chakras REALLY pack a punch. Over the decades, hundreds of people have come up to me in tears after class. They struggle for words that often sound like this: "Thank you so much! I don't even know why I am crying so hard! I am actually happy! I have never felt this kind of JOY! All I can do is cry right now! This class was worth 10 years of therapy! I didn't know I had a body until now! May I have a hug?" Many of the writers in this very book have shared these words with me. I think It is my job to help people laugh, help people cry, help people truly experience their bodies, and understand the fifth layer of the yogic multidimensional self: ANANDA: Bliss. We have a blissful self that is hugely untapped in this culture. Let Your Yoga Dance can help us discover and/or rediscover that bliss.

Maslow's Hierachy of Needs	Chakras
Self-Actualization (morality, creativity, spontaneity, problem- solving, lack of prejudice, acceptance of facts)	**Seventh Chakra:** understanding, self-knowledge, and higher consciousness **Sixth Chakra:** Imagination, awareness, self-reflection, and intuition **Fifth Chakra:** self-expression and a deeper connection to others
Love and Belonging (family, friendship, sexual intimacy)	**Fourth Chakra:** love, self-acceptance, perspective, compassion
Esteem (confidence, achievement, respect of others, respect by others)	**Third Chakra:** esteem position, strength, and status
Safety and Security (of body, resources, family, health, employment, and property)	**Second Chakra:** family, creation, belonging
Physiological Needs (breathing, food, water, air, sex, sleep, homeostasis, excretion)	**First Chakra:** Life, survival, safety

Although Let Your Yoga Dance is a joy-based practice, and Positive Psychology is the science of happiness and resilience, we don't want to put band-aids over pain. Dancing through the chakras gives us permission to feel our feelings fully, be they ecstatic or sad, lonely or enraged. The chakras help us to *feel*. Let Your Yoga Dance targets these chakras so that everything that has been pushed aside, suppressed, forgotten will come out to be healed. I like to call this: "Healing through Joy." Although we can certainly do the practice alone in our homes (I do all the time), it is particularly sweet to be in the company of others – in person or on Zoom. Why? Because believe it or not, we fall in love with ourselves and with one another. Dancing together in a field of loving kindness, compassion, and care can only bring us into our own hearts. As Barbara Fredrickson reminds us, this love has a ripple effect that dances out into the rest of our day – and longer. My students with Parkinson's often say that Let Your Yoga Dance has a similar effect to their Parkinson's drugs – but the only side effect is joy.

I would like to end with a powerful practice from the Let Your Yoga Dance tradition, borrowed from one of the ancient Buddhist Brahma Vihara teachings. It is METTA, lovingkindness. Barbara Fredrickson's research on this practice (which she calls LKM: loving kindness meditation) is vast. If you are struggling with depression, Metta will be very helpful. My favorite meditation teacher and beloved mentor, Sylvia Boorstein, created a lovely metta resolve (a limerick!) many years ago. I asked her permission to change the third line of the resolve to suit my needs. She loves the line and is now using it herself! Here you are: From Sylvia to me, from me to you:

May you be protected and safe
May you feel protected and pleased
May your body, mind spirit be lived in Grace

May your life unfold smoothly with ease
Many blessings,

Megha

Megha Nancy Buttenheim | Sarasota, FL/Pittsfield, MA
www.meghanancybuttenheim.com

Megha Nancy Buttenheim is CJO (Chief JOY Officer) and Founding Director of Let Your Yoga Dance ® LLC. She is on the faculty with the Wholebeing Institute. She has been teaching with the Wholebeing Institute since its inception in 2011, creating an embodied joy-based curriculum to bring positive psychology teaching tenets into the body. Until its closing due to Covid 19, Megha was a senior faculty member and teacher trainer at Kripalu from 1985-2020, training thousands of people in yoga, holistic health, and moving meditation, along with her own signature training: Let Your Yoga Dance Teacher Training. She teaches zoom classes in Let Your Yoga Dance for all populations, including the elderly and people with Parkinson's. Megha also teaches gentle yoga and qigong. Her credo: Everyone is a Dancer.

Megha is the author of:

- Book: *Expanding Joy ~ Let Your Yoga Dance, Embodying Positive Psychology*
- DVD/MP4: *Let Your Yoga Dance – with Megha*
- MP4: Moving With Your Strengths, a series of mini health videos Megha filmed to welcome all 24 positive psychology character strengths into the body, using yoga, qigong, relaxation, meditation, and Let Your Yoga Dance.

All these products - and more - can be accessed on Megha's online store: https://store.letyouryogadance.com/

The Gift of a Grateful Heart
- Natalie Hoerner

My journey to the Certification in Positive Psychology and a gratitude practice began upon reading a 2010 article in *The Buffalo Newspaper* titled "Gratitude Reveals Great Wealth." It revealed how practicing gratitude in the good times and bad can change your life. That article propelled me into the ride of a lifetime, and I became compelled to create a gratitude journal. I had always been a collector of poems and quotes; everywhere I went, I would jot them down and carefully tuck them away (before cell phones). As I pondered the creation of this journal, I asked everyone I came in contact with if they knew how I might do it.

I wanted to create a one-of-a-kind gift for family and friends that contained all the things that touched my heart over the years, a living legacy, so to speak. I found a local artist, willing to take this project on with me. We worked for a year putting all the finishing details into place. The journal was hand-bound with a cover made of baby's breath on handmade Italian paper, and it was presented in a beautiful box that could also store the recipient's own treasures. It was so unique and beautiful that many who received it didn't want to write in it!

Phase two of the little journal that could began by finding another author to chat with and seek guidance about the publishing process in order to bring the journal to an audience beyond my close family and friends. A friend put me in touch with a woman who helped me understand how to get my journal into print. During our conversation over coffee, she reiterated the need for me to visit a yoga and meditation center in the Berkshires (Western Massachusetts), called Kripalu, whose values aligned closely with the work I was doing with my journal.

In June 2013, I took my first class at Kripalu that focused on thriving in midlife. At the end of this memorable week, I found out about the Certificate in Positive Psychology course and was intrigued. However, I had reservations about the yearlong commitment involved. Ultimately, I was encouraged by one of the facilitators and signed up. It was the best thing I ever did for myself, my family, my friends, and my life as the course material studies different practices which all contribute to living happier and healthier of which gratitude is a strong proponent.

Gratitude has always been a part of my makeup for as long as I can remember despite growing up in an environment in which negativity was abundant. Whenever given something, especially as a little girl, I always cherished the gesture and tried never to take anything for granted. As I embarked on my Certificate in Positive Psychology journey, I took the VIA (Values in Action) Character Strengths Assessment. I soon recognized my top strengths of gratitude and love of learning, unfolding. The course presentation, exercises, teamwork, and accountability partner system instilled in me the necessary tools and support needed to thrive. The course was everything and more to me because it gave me the intellectual background, science, and practices needed to grow my beloved gratitude practice.

One of my key takeaways was learning about neuroplasticity which is the scientific idea of the rewiring that takes place in the brain through tiny changes reinforced over time. These small changes are often referred to as "kaizen" changes. Kaizen is a Japanese term used to describe continuous improvement through tiny positive changes that can lead to significant transformations over time. It was with this practice of instilling daily pauses for presence, even just for a few minutes, that I learned Dr. Tal Ben-Shahar's lesson in real-time.

What we appreciate, appreciates.

At the beginning and end of my day, I stopped all that I was doing to "pause" and focus on the five senses: sight, sound, taste, smell, and touch. The goal of this grounding exercise is to create the space in which we can become centered and present to the only moment we have, the now. As a result, I found the more I paused to observe the good around me, the more I found. Over time, this habit created new neural pathways in my brain that helped reinforce a new positive perspective significantly different from the perspective I learned in childhood.

The good news is you can start rewiring your brain by picking a tiny (kaizen) change, too! Here are a few small habits you could start with: looking for one thing a day to be grateful for; pausing in the morning before looking at your phone/devices; putting your phone/devices in another room away from where you sleep; turning off notifications except those deemed necessary. Once you take the first step of developing an initial habit, you can proceed with "habit stacking" or adding a new habit onto your current practice. To make things easier on yourself, you may want to start with something you already do, such as brushing your teeth (considered a keystone habit as you can easily add habits on to it). While engaging with this daily habit, you can make a concerted effort to practice gratitude or meditate on your breath as you brush. The list goes on and on. Anything you already do, you can stack a new habit onto it. Remember:

A journey of a thousand miles begins with a single step.
-Lao Tzu

As I transformed through my gratitude practice and positive psychology, I experienced in my life the heart of the original newspaper article: "Even in difficult times, we can find something to be grateful for." When my beloved aunt suddenly was hospitalized, diagnosed with cancer, and passed away within a week, I saw firsthand the power of gratitude amidst grief. As difficult as it was for me each day, my heart was grateful for the six days in the hospital that I got to spend with her in the present moment. The sadness and difficulty of the situation were constant; however, by continuing my gratitude practice during this time, I was able to hold both the sad feelings as well as the joy of gratitude. This balance is a key tool to helping us be more resilient in the face of adversity.

When you change the way you look at things or experience that internal shift like I did in difficult times, you change as does the world around you and how you interact with it. I am excited to share that not only have I benefited from this practice, but I have witnessed firsthand the positive impact it has had on the lives of those around me as well. A friend asked me to teach her how to practice gratitude after struggling to create the habit on her own. We sat for coffee and talked about one small task she could do. She decided to write three to five things for which she was grateful each night. About five months after diligently practicing gratitude and reporting back to me, she had a bad fall while walking her dog. When she told me about her accident, I empathized with the seriousness of the situation thinking I was going to be mostly supportive. However, I was pleasantly surprised to hear her perspective, which highlighted all the good things that had come out of her fall! As she continued on and on, I saw how the practice of gratitude had changed her brain so that even with the difficult, she found the good. Gratitude is such a simple concept, yet it can produce profound results.

Gratitude is a state of being grateful; this is the epitome of my journey. Again, I started slowly, looking for three to five things daily to be grateful for just like I encouraged my friend who had the accident. Today, my practice continues and starts in the morning before my feet hit the ground. I open my heart to give thanks for whatever comes to mind first: my breath, bed, good night's sleep, health, family, etc. I embrace all of it, and I set an intention for the day to practice gratitude through being present and savoring the extraordinary in the ordinary. Some of my favorite ways to do this are spending time outside in my yard looking to nature and allowing my senses to ground and center me in the present moment.

To live in the present moment is a miracle.
- Thich Nhat Hahn

If you're like me, you may find it helpful to have a reminder bracelet or alarm on your phone to prompt you to stop, look and listen. When I engage in that pause, I sometimes like to take photos especially when outside to later remember the moment and try to access those feelings. It might be the fine details of a flower, mini pinecones budding, or sparkling spider webs. I am seeing everything in the world with fresh eyes. As I do, I notice even more. For what we practice grows stronger. The world springs to life as we open our eyes and really see. How many times do we walk while so deep in thought that we never hear the birds chirping?

At night before bed, I recall the day. I savor those encounters with loved ones, friends, and the beauty of nature from my photos and write in my gratitude journal about all I was grateful for that day. With that, I am off to a good night's sleep. Remembering and bringing these positive things to mind helps us sleep better, which is another one of the many benefits of gratitude.

As a way to help my local community and beyond during the trying time of COVID and lockdowns, I started a gratitude postcard campaign. I knew that writing a gratitude letter was a powerful practice supported by Martin Seligman, the father of positive psychology's research. A gratitude letter is believed to be one of the most powerful gratitude interventions. It increases happiness, optimism, determination, and improves sleep and immune function. The effects of doing this just once can last for weeks. With that in mind, I set out to send three free postcards to anyone who signed up. It was a way to send positivity into a world in desperate need of connection and hope. It was a win-win for the giver and receiver. Many tears were shed after gratitude was expressed. Visit my website https://nataliehoerner.com/postcards to get yours!

Lastly, the SPIRE Whole-Person Well-Being model developed by the Wholebeing Institute, which I learned in my Positive Psychology course, looks at the spiritual, physical, intellectual, relational, and emotional components of an individual. By practicing gratitude every area of the SPIRE model is elevated. I've seen it firsthand in my own life, and I am happier and healthier than I have ever been. I am much more present in the moment, my relationships have greatly improved, and I am much more resilient. All these benefits and so many more. Just by simply being grateful.

I would like to practice my own gratitude here by recalling the faculty, staff, and fellow students who supported me through my Certification in Positive Psychology journey. It is a community based in the principles of positive psychology,

FINDING UNSHAKABLE HAPPINESS

brought about by love and connection in service to the greater good. My greatest gift is my accountability group called the Aspire Sisters, which still serves as a sounding board for all of our celebrations as well as our heartaches and everything in between. You name it, we come together, especially through COVID with Sunday morning Zoom calls. Whoever can attend does, and we all leave better for it.

> *Listen to your sisters' stories, for they house the echoes of answers to questions you have yet to ask . . .*
>
> *- Baraja Elihu*

We tend to look outside of ourselves for help or to be rescued, but the Certificate in Positive Psychology course teaches us that "no one is coming," and we cannot change others, only ourselves. Therefore, this process of doing the internal work is truly and solely an "inside job." Upon realizing that my happiness was my responsibility, I was empowered to continue my kaizen changes with gratitude being the driving force. This sustained me over time to witness the positive domino effect of the changes I had hoped for and those I never imagined. In 2016, I launched Gifts of Gratitude, LLC, a small business with a mission to empower all people to learn, live, and lead from a place of heart-inspired wholeness. I have learned and now live differently, which allows me to lead from an inspired heart in all its wholeness. A quote from Parker Palmer really captures the essence of the wholeness.

> *Wholeness does not mean perfection; it means embracing brokenness as an integral part of life.*
>
> *- Parker Palmer*

My passion is to help others transform their lives using the tools I've acquired from the Certification in Positive Psychology course, and those I've implemented in my own life and as a Positive Psychology Coach. I now host Meet-up groups, speak to organizations, give podcast interviews, lead workshops/retreats, and work with children in schools. I believe so much in the transformational power of this work that my once reserved shy self cannot help but speak up. This is not just a movement of the self it is a movement beyond the self in service of the greater good. As we, the tiny ripples move out and become agents of change, we create a tidal wave of positivity, light, and happiness out into the world.

My mentor in one of my courses was an editor. As I gifted her a gratitude journal, she was the catalyst for version number three. Somehow, this journal is meant to be the thread I tether. It propels me on to the next iteration of my journey, as we all know about the best-laid plans. God is laughing, and so am I. I know there is a plan for me. The lessons I have learned have been challenging, but they made me who I am today, and I wouldn't be the same without them.

The story above is beautiful, however it is only part of the story. I knew I wasn't happy in my life despite having what most people aspire to. I was married, had three beautiful children, a big house in the suburbs, and all the amenities that went with it. I kept thinking I should be happy. I was trying to convince myself, but I wasn't. Something was terribly wrong. I had lost myself. I had everything and nothing. All that I valued seemed elusive. From the outside, my life looked perfect, and on the inside, I was dying. Gratitude found me and saved me;

it led me to a place where I am no longer waiting for others to make me happy.

Through positive psychology and gratitude, I found myself again and my passion, my purpose, and my joy. To find yourself, heal and serve, you need to reveal your great wealth below the surface of your shiny exterior. To show the vulnerability, the cracks, the pain to give the world the unique gifts that are you. The world and each person you encounter on their journey will benefit from you letting your inner brilliance shine. In so doing, you influence and inspire others to be their authentic self. For we can not just talk about this we must truly live from this place of broken wholeness.

> *There is a crack in everything, that's how the light gets in.*
>
> -Leonard Cohen

This light I believe is the divine within us. Our true humanity, our true selves, the selves we were born to be. The joy of my journey is sharing it with each of you. I hope that I plant the seeds of inspiration that leads you to reveal your greatest wealth, and that is YOU!

Natalie Hoerner | Orchard Park, New York
https://nataliehoerner.com

Natalie Hoerner is a Positive Psychology Coach and the founder of Gifts of Gratitude, LLC.

She is certified in Positive Psychology, the study of what makes people happy, through the Wholebeing Institute. She is licensed in facilitating the Inspire Your Ideal Workshop.

She also received training at the Sedona Women's Institute to facilitate workshops and retreats for women.

Natalie's mission is to help others live happier, more meaningful lives through the power of gratitude. She hopes her efforts will serve as a beacon of light, hope, love and peace in the world.

Visit Gifts-of-Gratitude.com for gratitude journals, notecards, free postcards, or to learn about Natalie's workshops.

Recovering My Senses: My Journey to Freedom, Fun, Fitness & Unshakeable Happiness

- Andrea Cashman

We do not have to create who we are; indeed, we have been created in utter perfection. We just need to discover what about our life is not who we are, and let it go.

– Alan Cohen

My name is Andrea, a person in the process of discovering who she was created to be. I am empowered by unshakable happiness through my practices and the support of my community. I am gratefully recovering from addiction and despair, which diminished my true self. I'd love to share my experience, strength, and hope with you; here is my story.

Have you ever seen a tumbleweed? An iconic image of western movies, it was a common sight in my home state of California. This is what I felt like as I was growing up, rolling without roots, moving from one new home to another.

My parents met and married in Minnesota after the end of WWII. In order to stay gainfully employed, my dad accepted promotions that moved us all around the country. The average length of stay in each home was 4.5 years - just enough time to get settled, make some friends, then say goodbye. Homes in California, Michigan, Long Island, and Connecticut rounded out my journey through childhood. At the time, I convinced myself that it was an adventure, not realizing how shallow my root system was becoming from constant adaptation.

Most summers, I was away from the home du jour, with my mother at the wheel; we drove across the country at least five times to visit family. She was brave and resilient back then - no cell phones, no air conditioning in the car, so we drove through the desert at night. No cassette players or FM radio, we sang songs, fought with our siblings, and tried to enjoy the view. Most of the time, I just retreated into daydreams - being in my own head was all the company I thought I needed.

My mother adjusted to every move with seeming grace, her smile lit up the room. She entertained my dad's clients and colleagues and did her best to develop new friendships in each community. Their cocktail and dinner parties were sumptuous; my younger brother and I would play servants with white towels over our arms (then go sneak a sip of the punch). I do remember her staring sadly out the window when we lived in Michigan, missing the view of the California mountains. But, then she put the smile back on her face - and shut the sadness away. We were taught, "If you don't have something nice to say, don't say anything at all."

Starting at a young age, I always felt like a stranger in a strange land and didn't expect to stay long enough to change that. When we lived in New York, my mom warned me not to pick up the accent, as I was a Californian! In high school, I made friends but moved from one group to another ... never feeling like I quite fit in (I didn't expect to stay too long anyway). This was the 1970's, the age of Woodstock, rebellion, and I jumped right into the hippie lifestyle.

My dad let us stay in New York just long enough for me to graduate high school, then we pulled up stakes and moved on to CT. My father was eventually laid off from his job, so I had to quit my first college after sophomore year. I went to work at a local women's health studio, teaching fitness and coaching for weight loss. I enjoyed the work, promoted to assistant manager within a year, but I had high hopes for a life of adventure and success, so I didn't plan to stay for long.

When I turned 21, I moved back to California to pursue my dreams of freedom. I landed a job as a fitness instructor and Yoga teacher at the famous La Costa resort, now the home to Deepak Chopra's Center for Wellbeing. My Yoga studies drew me into a spiritual inquiry. Unfortunately, the southern California partying life led me astray from good intentions. At the resort, I made friends with a guest who became a friend and a benefactor. She offered me a scholarship to study abroad with Boise State University's Basque Studies program - I was off again!

I spent a year studying in north-western Spain, the Basque country. This is where I learned to hold my liquor (or so I thought). In Basque, the word for a pub crawl is Txikiteo - we would enjoy small drinks in every bar on the street (and there were quite a few in the little village of Oñate in the Pyrenees). At lunch and dinner, it was customary to have a carafe of wine on each table in the residence hall cafeteria! For the Basque people who were raised in this tradition, it was not such a temptation, but for the young Americans, it would prove to be a little too alluring. It took me decades to realize how much I wasted that year away in a bottle and how I let down my benefactor. I started my academic year with A's and ended with in-completes, avoiding class and responsibility.

Returning to Idaho to finish my schooling at BSU, my benefactor wouldn't return my calls, and I had no clue why. I got a job at European Health Spa to help pay the bills and stay in shape. It was fun living in Big Sky country, hiking, skiing, rafting the rivers, camping - and lots of drinking. I found myself embroiled in a toxic relationship with a troubled young man who wanted to control me while I wanted to heal him. I knew it wasn't good for me, but I struggled through, trying to make the best of life, with my smile in place just as mom taught me.

It took eight years to get through college, but who was counting? I somehow managed to earn a Bachelors' Degree in Business and set my sights on the corporate world and a new home. Graduating in 1982, during the "me-decade," I returned to CT and started up the ladder to success. Power suits with huge shoulder pads, big hair, and an attitude; I was ready to take the world by storm.

By the time I had reached adulthood, I believed my life had been blessed: with good health, good education, well-traveled - I had life by the tail, and I lived it to the max.

I was making money, traveling, partying - and spiritually running on empty.

At a beach party, I met a CT native who had never lived farther than 20 miles from his parents' home. We were both on the fast track, loved to dance, travel, ski, and drink; over time, we grew more serious, and he proposed. I broached the subject of moving out of state for a change of pace; I couldn't imagine staying in one state forever; it seemed so claustrophobic. Not realizing it at the time, I chose to align with a man who would tie me down to one place until I could grow my own roots.

Fast forward ten years: my career was put on the back burner after the kids came along; I couldn't believe how much my heart expanded with their presence in my life. Somehow this independent career woman took the step into the background; being a mother seemed the most important role at the time - and the work/family juggle of two wage earners was a continuous struggle.

I had no idea what I was getting into. Being a full-time mom is the hardest job of all; no lunch breaks, happy hours with colleagues, no promotions. Sometimes it seemed my life was doing laundry, washing dishes, and resolving sibling squabbles. Don't get me wrong, there was also tons of creativity, playtime, and unfathomable love - but being a homemaker had never been a life goal, and - at times, I felt totally trapped.

Marriage is not easy; it seemed that my husband had reverted to the 1950s, expecting food to be on the table when he got home and enjoy his time away for sports and partying with his buddies whenever he could. Even after I returned to work, I couldn't count on him to be supportive in the home. Our relationship began to crumble - after putting the kids to bed, I would stay up alone with a cocktail, hating my life. I really didn't know how to set my boundaries or ask for what I needed to be happy, so I wallowed in misery by myself, eating and drinking the troubles away. During the day, I kept a smile on my face and didn't share my despair with my family … I felt stuck and ashamed.

After some huge fights, I finally got the strength to get him out of the house. He realized that he had to make a change or lose everything - and he got help. He quit drinking, found support, and started to turn around his life. It took quite a long time for me to trust in the progress he had made, but we started to rebuild our relationship.

$$\text{Trust} = \frac{\text{Time}}{\text{Consistency}}$$

- J.Pacheco

Still, I felt discouraged and dissatisfied with my life, seeing no apparent solutions to my struggles. At the time, I was more than 40 pounds over my current weight, but that wasn't the only issue. I was completely stressed out from being part of the "sandwich generation" - caring for my pre-adolescent children and ailing parents; and not caring for myself at all. I was in deep pain from what I thought was arthritis, which had incapacitated my mother in her so-called golden years. My responsibilities weighed me down; like many others in my situation, I turned to the wine bottle for release from the pain.

I began to grow aware that the temporary dulling of the senses through alcohol didn't make anything easier; indeed, it made life much more difficult. However, the idea of giving up mommy's little helper seemed insurmountable. I thought: I can't quit drinking and do everything else I have to do; it's just too much! So, I stumbled along through life ... working full-time, doctor appointments with parents, keeping them company, and at the same time trying to be the best mom I thought I should be. At night, after the kids were in bed, I filled up my glass and ruminated on how hard life was - poor, poor, pitiful me. Feeling numb and helpless - this is my life?

How did I get here?? On the surface, life was good: two amazing daughters, a husband, a nice home. My parents were ailing, but they were loving, grateful, and had the resources to stay in an assisted living residence. What right did I have to feel unhappy? I berated myself daily: you're not good enough, you're fat, you're ungrateful, you don't deserve a good life - my stinkin' thinkin' was dragging me down into the ditch!

> *Suffering is the sandpaper of our life. It does its work of shaping us. Suffering is part of our training program for becoming wise.*
> - Ram Dass

When did I begin to see the light at the end of the long, dark tunnel? It was 2004, watching the Summer Olympics; I was struck with amazement at the talent, strength, and resilience of the athletes. How do they do that?!?! Then, I saw some of their backstories about their preparation ... the answer? Good coaches, support structure, and lots of practice. The innate talent of individuals can only take them so far. To thrive is a team effort.

Just about this time was when my parents' health began to fail. I had siblings nearby, but they were dealing with their own health struggles - so most of the parental care was left to me. The emotional drain of watching once-vibrant people deteriorate physically and mentally was so distressing, combined with all the responsibilities I felt ready to shatter into pieces - once again, I quit the workforce to become a caregiver.

Eventually, my parent's illnesses progressed to the point that I needed to be stronger, more present, and sober to get to the hospital at a moment's notice.

I remembered my thoughts about the Olympic athletes, and it inspired me to get support and practice taking care of myself. I needed the strength to take care of the others in my life, so I found a personal trainer. Then I returned to Yoga, taking classes regularly, finding that I could leave my worries on the mat, and my body and mind responded with renewed energy. My attitude was gradually shifting from dejection to positivity; I felt I could make even better choices for myself. On Easter Sunday of 2005, I chose to allow for my own resurrection and let go of the drink.

After my parents' passing, I realized how Yoga had saved me; the movement and breath released whatever stress I brought into the studio. I decided to become certified as a Yoga Instructor to share the benefits with others.

On one of my jaunts with colleagues in training, I went to Kripalu Center for Yoga and Health in the Berkshires. There I was introduced to Let Your Yoga Dance and its creator, Megha Nancy Buttenheim. This is a practice that combines the breath and movement of Yoga with free-flowing, non-performance dance. The modality is based on the Yogic philosophy of the Chakras or energy centers of the body. The music choices move you through the chakras, freeing the blockages resulting from trauma and disconnect. Further, the tenets of Positive Psychology are wound into the teaching, leading to empowerment and joy.

Through education and practice, I began to realize the parts of me that had blocked painful energy that needed to flow in order to heal. First and foremost, the Root Chakra or "Muladhara" that governs safety and community needed to be cleared. To truly embrace my authentic self, to stay sober - I had to feel at home in my own body and learn comfort in my own space. In my meditation and movement, I stay focused on the energy that supports me most in life.

Nothing worthwhile is easy; my journey has been rocky - with fits and starts. I had always been an independent person, moving all over the country as I was growing up. This was challenging to long-term friendships and trust. So, learning to stay put in a program, rely on others for help, and not run away was my task. The spiritual grounding of Yoga and Meditation and especially the grace of Let Your Yoga Dance has given me the tools I need to stay on my path.

Recovery, Discovery, Growth, and Gratitude have become mantras for me. Each challenge brings an opportunity to learn and change; each day is another day to live life fully with unshakable happiness. Namaste and Hakuna Matata.

Andrea Cashman | Milford, Connecticut
https://andreacashmanyoga.com

Andrea Cashman, 500hr Kripalu Certified Yoga Teacher is passionate about helping her students discover the physical, emotional and spiritual balance of Yoga and Meditation while maintaining a light-hearted and safe environment.

Andrea began teaching Yoga in her early 20's at LaCosta Spa in southern California (now the home of The Chopra Center). She then spent 25 years traveling, raising a family, working in corporate and education careers. She returned to Yoga for support as she cared for her aging parents - that healing experience inspired her to come back to her roots. She enjoys learning and sharing that knowledge with her students.

Her classes offer a full range of Yoga, from Core Strength Vinyasa to Gentle Yoga; and a variety of Meditation techniques to appeal to the different learning styles of her students. Andrea works at Studios, Schools, Senior Centers, Corporations as well as offering private classes, retreats and workshops.

Her specialty programs include Let Your Yoga Dance!® in high energy and gentle format. A fusion of user friendly dance steps with yoga to the beat of world music, and Yoga for 12 Step Recovery - Y12SR® .

What Matters Most

- Lori Tuominen

One of the founders of the field of Positive Psychology, the late Christopher Peterson, defined positive psychology this way: *"Other people matter."* It sounds so simple and yet it's so profound. People want to be seen, heard, and valued. In other words, they want to know that they matter.

Several years ago, I read a parable that captures the essence of relationships through the means of fault-finding versus benefit-finding, a concept I learned from Tal Ben-Shahar when I took the Certificate in Positive Psychology through the Wholebeing Institute and the Kripalu Center for Yoga & Health. What are you looking for? If you're looking for faults or problems, surely that is what you'll find. If you're looking for the positive or the silver lining, that is what you'll find.

I have searched for the source of this story so I could give proper credit where credit is due, but I have been unsuccessful. The parable is this:

> *A man was looking for a new town in which to live. He came to the city gates of one town, where there was an old man sitting. The visitor asked the old man, "I am looking for a new place to live. What are the people of this town like?"*
>
> *The old man replied, "What are the people like in the town where you live?"*
>
> *The visitor responded, "Oh, they are horrible. They are rude and uncaring, and you cannot trust them in the least. I cannot wait to get away from them." The old man said, "Well, keep looking because you will find the same type of people here in this town."*
>
> *A short while later, a woman came to the city gates, also looking for a new place to live. She asked the same question to the old man. Again, he asked her, "What are the people like in the town where you live?"*
>
> *She replied, "Oh, they're WONDERFUL! They're friendly and caring, they are helpful and loving... I will miss them very much."*
>
> *The old man smiled and replied, "Welcome! You will enjoy living here. The people of this town are very much the same as in the town where you live."*

What we focus on grows. If we focus on the negative, we see more of the negative; if we focus on the positive, we see more of that. So many of us excel at looking for–and finding–the negative! It's human nature to have, what Rick Hanson refers to as "a negativity bias;" it's what has kept humans safe for thousands of years. Hanson often says, *"Negative thoughts stick to us like Velcro while positive thoughts roll off us like Teflon."* What are the people like in the town where you live?

In his book *7 Habits of Highly Effective People*, Stephen Covey wrote Habit 1 as "Be proactive." He shared the following story: A man came up to him after a presentation and said he didn't love his wife anymore. Covey told him, "Love her. If the feeling isn't there, that's a good reason to love her." The guy asked how do you love when you don't love? Covey responded, "My friend, love is a verb. Love – the feeling – is a fruit of love, the verb. So love her. Serve her. Sacrifice. Listen to her. Empathize. Appreciate. Affirm her. Are you willing to do that?"

Covey goes on to say that reactive people make love a feeling. "Proactive people make love a verb. Love is something you do; the sacrifices you make, the giving of self, like a mother bringing a newborn into the world. If you want to study love, study those who sacrifice for others, even for people who offend or do not love you in return. If you are a parent, look at the love you have for the children you sacrificed for. Love is a value that is actualized through loving actions. Proactive people subordinate feelings to values. Love, the feeling, can be recaptured."

I love this. *"Reactive people make love a feeling; proactive people make love a verb."* Love is the action of showing others that you care about them. Love, the feeling, follows love, the verb.

FINDING UNSHAKABLE HAPPINESS

Over the years, when I've lost people I love, I am heartbroken. I know they can never be replaced, and I always miss them in some way. I know I am a better person for having had them in my life, even though they are no longer in mine. This is not only referring to people who have died, but also to people who are no longer in my life for whatever reason. Perhaps they've moved; perhaps *I've* moved (like when I was 9), or perhaps one or both of us have *moved on*. Perhaps the interests of one us have changed and so we just grew apart. Or perhaps I never knew why they left; they just … left.

Back in the early '90s, I got a job at a psychiatric hospital on the South Shore of Boston. I started the same day as Claire, (name changed to protect privacy) a single woman, recent college grad, about my age. She and I hit it off right away, and our colleagues thought we had known each other for years; that we had taken the job so we could work together. For the next year and a half, we often worked the same evening shift. We worked the same weekends. We saw each other outside of work. We talked daily on the phone. She was my best friend and it was reciprocated. However, after that year and a half, my husband took a job in a different part of the state and we moved.

At first, Claire and I kept in touch. She drove west to spend a weekend with us; I drove to stay with her near Boston. But somewhere along the way, we lost touch. I would send her Christmas cards and would hope to hear back from her, but after a while, I didn't hear from her anymore so I quit trying. I tried to call her but her number changed. She just … disappeared. I was so sad because I had felt so close to her. I wondered what had happened to her? I wondered what I had done for her to end the relationship so abruptly? In 2001, after the tragedies on September 11th, I decided to send Christmas cards to people who had been important to me in my lifetime and tell them how much they meant to me and that I love and miss them. Many people wrote back, including Claire! I guess 9/11 had affected others to evaluate what was most important in their lives as well. I thought that perhaps Claire's and my friendship would rekindle, but alas, this wasn't to be.

Years later, I ran into her while standing in line for the restroom at a women's conference in Boston. "Claire?" I asked, to which she responded, "Lori? Is that you?" and gave me a big hug. She was as happy to see me as I was to see her! I cannot even begin to tell you how happy this made me, because I knew it was genuine. She asked how my family was and I told her the kids are all grown; even our youngest, who was born the day after my last shift at the hospital. Claire said she had gotten married. I asked her if they had any kids and she said, "Sadly, no." Oh, how I wish I had asked that question differently! "Tell me about your husband." or "How is your family?" If I had asked this instead, would things have turned out differently?

We exchanged emails, gave each other another hug, and went on our way. I didn't see her the rest of the day, nor have I seen her since. Seeing her that day was such a gift; it proved to me that she still loved me, I could feel it. And maybe she couldn't remain friends with me because it was too painful, or maybe I had done something to offend her and she hadn't forgiven me. To this day I have no idea why the friendship ended. But I can tell you that seeing her that day, after a 20-year hiatus, showed me there was still love between us, and that was enough.

I did email her after that, once, although I never heard back from her and I never saw her again. However, seeing her that one additional time allowed me to tell her that I love her and miss her, and she'll always be dear to my heart; and then I was able to let her go.

Ed Diener and Martin Seligman's research has shown that *the number one predictor of happiness is our positive relationships with other people; people we care about and who care about us in return.* This is not only in romantic relationships but in all relationships. I know that with my friend Claire, the happiness was there while the love was reciprocated. When it was no longer returned, things changed. Happiness turned to heartbreak and then, after two decades and one more visit, to acceptance. Sometimes it takes a while.

In various parts throughout my life, I have wondered whether or not relationships with others were enough. Is it "noble" enough of a purpose to have relationships be an important part of one's life, perhaps even *the* most important part of one's life? I wasn't sure until I had an interaction with a friend, and she shared a perspective I had never considered before.

A few years ago, my friend Stephanie (name changed to protect privacy) and I were talking about our moms, who had both died a year or two before this conversation. I shared with her that I was at a crossroads around the time my mom had died; our youngest daughter had just graduated from high school and I was in a transition of sorts into finding/creating/doing work that was more meaningful to me than the work I had been doing. Not the work of being a mom, but rather, the work of having a secondary income or a "fine … for now" job. I kept trying to figure out a lofty, worthy goal to make my career move toward; something that had great meaning and purpose; something I really enjoyed doing; something that I could be remembered for; something to which I could "leave a legacy," so to speak. I was tired of running away from jobs that held no meaning to me and wanting to run toward something that had meaning and purpose. I wanted something that lit me up!

Up until that point, I had been "just" a mom. I had put being a mom as my top priority; I had not been career-oriented in the least. Oh, I still worked outside the home, but they weren't jobs that held great meaning to me. Being a mom is what had great meaning to me; the jobs I was doing while our kids were growing up were simply a form of income for our family. And now our youngest had just graduated and my role as a mom was shifting and changing. It was time to figure out what was next in my life.

Stephanie had told me, years ago, the amazing story of her mother, Irene (name changed to protect privacy) as a young child in a country being occupied by the Nazis just before the Second World War; a story that read like a spy novel. Irene's mother had died when she was very young; Irene's father worked for the government. When the Nazis rose to power, Irene's father went to work in another country as part of a government in exile. The plan was to work abroad, waiting for the war to end, when the government would be able to be reinstated at home. Irene was about 14 years old at the time. She stayed with a nanny in their home country. Also during that time, she became a messenger and courier for the resistance movement; she was alone, she didn't have family that she lived with or was close to, and no one would suspect her, a mere child, in this dangerous role. Just as important in her mind was that if something were to happen to her, there would be little family affected by it; no mother, no siblings, no cousins, and her only living relative, her father, was living and working in another country.

Irene's father had come up with a plan, should they ever need it, that would provide a way for Irene to know it was time for her to leave their home. At any point, when she would hear their designated code word, she would know it was time for her to get out of the country immediately because her life was in danger.

One night, Irene was at the movie theater with friends when a strange event took place. A woman showed up and began walking back and forth in front of the screen, saying one word over and over. It took Irene a moment to realize that it was her nanny, repeating the designated code word. The time had come for Irene to leave the country and go to her father in his adoptive city hundreds of miles away. Irene left the theater immediately and never went to her home again; not even to pack any clothes or possessions. She followed the plan she and her father had devised and got out of the country as soon as possible, saving her life in the process. They never returned to their country again.

Fast-forward to the discussion Stephanie and I were having after both of us lost our moms. I was sharing with her the story of my mom getting ready to move in 2001 from southern to northern Minnesota, and how what should have been a simple 15-minute errand took two and a half hours! I teased Mom that she was like the mayor of the town; everyone wanted to come and say goodbye to her and tell her how much they were going to miss her; from the drugstore clerk to the pharmacist and the shoppers in the store; even people who saw her on the street came over to chat with her.

Couple that with the number of people who came to visit my mom after her stroke; first in the Intensive Care Unit (ICU) and eventually in hospice. Or the people who wrote to us on the CaringBridge site we had set up; sharing memories of her positive influence in their lives, the lives of her students, colleagues, friends, nieces, and nephews ... for making them laugh, for listening to them, or helping them through a rough time. I was so touched by the number of people who reached out. I'd had no idea that my mom had affected people in the way that they were sharing she had (well, maybe I had a little bit of an idea; I *did* run errands with her as she was moving, and it took way longer than it should have!). Even her primary care doctor came to visit her in the ICU and said, "We had a lot of fun together. We laughed ... a lot." Whose doctor says this about a patient coming in for a physical?!

As she was dying, I thought about my mom and what she offered the world during her lifetime. Non-judgment. Adaptability. Kindness. Humor. Love. A caring nature. A good listener. Positivity. Love. Fun. Friendly competition (she loved games and she loved to WIN games!). Spontaneity. Laughter. Spunk. She was willing to go along with almost anything, even if she couldn't keep up (she'd bring a book with her and wait ...). She was also a good friend. A good mom. A good gramma. A good listener. An adventurer. A role model for incorporating healthy living after many years of not so much (she quit smoking after she had a heart attack and walked daily afterward). Many people said that she could light up a room simply by walking into it. The skeptic in me thought, "Yes, but is *this enough*? It's not saving the world, it's not curing cancer, and it's on a very small, micro-level ..."

I asked Stephanie, "It was lovely to see how many lives my mom touched, *but is it enough*? Is this a noble enough existence? Does it serve a big enough purpose? Does it leave enough of a legacy? In other words ... does it *really* matter?"

Stephanie got quiet and, while I don't remember exactly what she said, it was along the lines of this: "Lori, my mother was proud of the work she did when she was a teenager, being a messenger and courier for the resistance movement at the start of the war. She felt like that was her legacy. And yet, she died a miserable woman. My mom had what she would consider a purpose in life, at least in her early life, and yet she didn't have any close friends. She and my father stayed married even though they didn't get along all that well, and she was resentful that the early, exciting part of her life was over. She didn't want us to videotape her sharing the stories of her youth because she was a vain, bitter woman who wanted to be remembered only for her war stories, her bravery, and the beauty of her youth; she did not celebrate the fact that she had lived to be an old woman. Which is the better existence? My mom, living a life of purpose in her early years but not having any lasting, close relationships? Or yours, living what seems like a normal, some may even say mundane life, but having loads of family and friends who would miss her when she was gone?"

I've thought of this conversation many times since then, especially in the context of Chris Peterson's words, "Other people matter." This, I think, is what he meant by those words. It's connecting with others in a positive manner, letting them know that they matter to you. Feeling the love shared between you, knowing that you care and are there for them and that it's reciprocated. This is what makes life worth living. And I believe that being present–fully present–with the people I love is the key to their knowing–*really knowing*–that they're loved.

And then I think about the ripple effect; that if one person lives like this, and improves the world for their family and friends, and then their family and friends carry on the work, or light, or whatever you want to call it … that *is* the work. That *is* the purpose, both in my life and in the world. Being authentic to who I am and sharing my gifts with others, all the while acknowledging and validating others for what they bring to the world, too. This is what makes the world a better place. As Edith Wharton said, *"There are two ways of spreading light: to be the candle or the mirror that reflects it."*

The night our granddaughter was born, there was a time that our son was alone with his newborn. The birth hadn't gone as planned, and our daughter-in-law ended up having a C-section. Because of this, our son had time alone with his new baby daughter immediately after her birth … and he called us. We shared a really special time with him, even though we were 1,300 miles apart. The next day, after being a dad for less than 24 hours, Dan said the most profound thing I've ever heard him say, which was, "We don't even know what we cared about before yesterday."

That's it.

This is what matters most.

Lori Tuominen | Superior, Wisconsin
https://lorituominen.com

Lori Tuominen loves to learn, laugh, and connect with others. This isn't all that surprising since curiosity, humor, and love are her top VIA strengths.

She is currently the Program Manager for the Pruitt Center for Mindfulness and Well-Being at the University of Wisconsin-Superior, where she teaches Mindfulness-Based Stress Reduction and other proactive/preventative ('upstream') methods of improving mental health and well-being.

Lori completed the Certificate in Positive Psychology in 2014 and stayed on as a teaching assistant for the next four classes, where she received a priceless education and was lucky enough to work alongside of (and continue to learn from) her teachers, mentors, colleagues, and friends Tal Ben-Shahar, Megan McDonough, Maria Sirois, and Phoebe Atkinson (in addition to all her TA friends and CiPP students).

She is a credentialed coach with the International Coach Federation, has a master's degree in Positive Organization Development and Change, has a certificate as an End-of-Life Doula, and is author of the Nautilus Silver award-winning picture book, available on Amazon, *Ways to Be from A to Z* (that one of her daughters illustrated), a multi-cultural alphabet book about positive ways of being.

Lori and her husband, Mark, have four grown kids, three daughter/sons-in-law, and four grandkids.

SECTION 5: FULL HEARTED APPRECIATION
- DONNA MARTIRE MILLER

Sandra Martire & Friend

Beauty and Love are as body and soul:
Inexhaustible mine, and diamond-beyond-price.
I loved his beauty and Love flamed from me:
I grew beautiful, Love whispered my name.

- Jalal-ud-Din Rumi

What would happen if we stopped taking things for granted in our life? What if from the moment we awake in the morning until we close our eyes, we intentionally focus on what went well with our day, what delighted us, what tasted yummy, what in nature outdoors surprised us, where did we feel loved, and by whom? Where did we find an opportunity to share our joys, love, and strengths to support another? Shifting our focus from our problems (although they may hurt and are present) to what is going well with us creates more positive emotion. In the science of happiness, we do not ignore what feels painful or needs to be addressed otherwise. We name it, feel it and then utilize our strengths to better cope. This effort results in becoming more grateful for what we do have. Gratitude is essential to becoming happier.

Robert Emmons explains in his book, *Gratitude Works* that he is confident that learning to have an attitude of gratitude helps in any situation. It helps build positive emotions in the giver and the receiver (releasing all the juicy, happy hormones in our brains and bodies). More importantly, he shows how we have the most to gain by having a grateful perspective on life under crisis conditions. He says:

> *In the face of demoralization, gratitude has the power to energize. In the face of brokenness, gratitude has the power to heal. In the face of despair, gratitude has the power to bring hope. In other words, gratitude can help us cope with hard times.*

In a crisis or a sad situation, this will not come naturally, and I am not suggesting that it is an easy thing to do. However, being grateful produces better mental health. Suppose we shift our attention away from toxic emotions such as hate, resentment, jealousy, bitterness, revenge, or inadequacy.

Contrasting our perspective also helps us shift our mindset to more positive emotions. Then our focus can shift to what we have learned and how we grew. Looking to see where you are now will give you evidence that you have something to be grateful for. In this way, people begin to see the blessings in their lives. It replaces the rumination of painful or adverse life experiences with what you feel compassionate about and are grateful for. Discovering ways to be grateful in our thoughts, words, actions, and beliefs about ourselves and the life we have been given creates a psychological immune system that can catch us before we travel in a downward spiral. It is proven to develop resiliency and prevent the damage that stress can have on our minds and bodies. Life is filled with many forms of suffering. No amount of positive thinking exercises can change this. Our ability to cope with difficulties and become resilient starts when we plant the seeds of gratitude in the fertile soil of hope, faith, love, and charity. Meet Amy, Linda, Wendy, and Samantha as they share their stories of gratitude, thriving, and resiliency.

Filtering our life experiences with gratefulness does not mean ignoring negativity. It means realizing our power to transform the bad, sad, and the ugly into an opportunity to learn and grow. To transcend and rise to being our best self.

When you appreciate the good, the good appreciates.
                                                    - Tal Ben-Shahar.

Learning How to Rise and Thrive When Life Gets Turned Upside Down
- Amy Rogers

"You're so resilient." She is one of the lead singers in my personal "choir" of cheerleaders and supporters. She has seen me through ten years that have included my husband walking out, my divorce, rebuilding my life, taking on the care and eventually the death of my elderly father, a resulting and painful family rift, a significant health crisis of my own, and job insecurity that threatened to pull down my entire rebuild. She has walked with me at each juncture, talked with me, laughed, and cried with me.

I love her dearly, but all I wanted to do was slap her. Her comments were made from a place of respect, admiration, and affection after years of watching me get up off the ground, dust myself off and put one foot in front of the other. I was exhausted by the effort, bewildered by the way life seemed to keep kicking me into the dirt. I wouldn't have to be so damned resilient if things could just be normal. When I wondered, was my life going to calm down?

I was raised with the impression that my life would be linear. High school, college, job, marriage, children, family, professional apex, retirement. This was the prescribed order, the stages my life would track so that I could always know that I was "on track." A straight line.

If you want to make God laugh, tell him your plans. That was the lesson I learned in 2011. In the span of 18 months, I had moved my family to a new town, my four- and six-year-olds had started new schools and daycare routine, I took on a new high-profile professional position, and my husband had quit his job and been out of work for nearly a year. And then, he left me.

This is what Bruce Feiler, Best Selling *New York Times* author, calls a "lifequake." It can happen when life throws you a giant curveball that totally upends your life. More often than not, however, it occurs when several more minor transitions pile up all at once. Pulling up roots and moving my young family to a new community, at the same time starting a challenging new job, all while supporting my husband's professional ennui and taking on the role of family provider so he could find himself... I was already in the middle of a lifequake. It was a balancing act that I was just getting the hang of when he dropped the bomb: "I'm moving out."

His book *Life is in the Transitions* is a chronicle of Feiler's Life Story Project. Thrown by unexpected disruptors in his own life that diverted the path he had understood his life to be on, Feiler set out to learn more about how the expectations we have of a linear life influence our ability to adapt to change. Knowing that things don't always go as planned, why do we buy into the myth that we will have one job, one marriage, one home, and one overarching story plot to our entire lives? Feiler spent over a year traveling around the country, interviewing hundreds of people about their life stories and heard about every kind of life transition you can imagine. Lost jobs, lost children, lost homes; new opportunities, new relationships; spiritual awakenings, loss of faith; diagnoses and cures. Some 6,000 pages of life stories later, he identified 52 different types of twists, turns, and breeches in the expected that redirect us off our planned life path. He wrote his book in service of debunking the myth of the linear life to encourage us to embrace transition as an inevitable part of every life.

Feiler's research tells us that the average person can expect to face as many as three dozen disruptors in their lifetime; on average, they will come along every 12-18 months. Every now and then, we are hit by one or more interruptions that rise to the level of a lifequake, the collision of forces that can cause devastating damage, and aftershocks that continue for years.

The average person can expect to experience three to five genuine lifequakes throughout their life, and they can last as long as five years before we feel solid ground under our feet once again.

At the time of my husband's pronouncement, I knew we were navigating many of the challenges that come with having a young family and growing careers. It was tough sledding, but I had faith that we would get back on track. I had spent years waiting for "just this next thing" to pass before our marriage and family trajectory could really take off. Once the kids get a bit older and more manageable, I thought. Or once we settle in the new town. Once he quits the job he hates. Once he gets a new job he loves. It always seemed that true happiness was just around the corner; if only we could muddle through this one next transition. Real-life, I thought, would be the thing that came after whatever mountain was in front of me at the time. But lifequakes don't pass so quickly, and this time there was no waiting for it to pass for real life to begin. This was real life. Very real. I was 42 and suddenly alone with two small children to raise and provide for.

In hindsight, I can now see that I walked through those early days living by the "fake it 'til you make it" mantra. It has its place; don't underestimate its usefulness in the height of crisis. It got me out of bed every day. It gave me the strength to take care of my kids and soothe their hurt little souls. It helped me muscle through each day at work while keeping up some semblance of competence. I may have collapsed every night after the kids went to bed, retreating under my own covers by 8:00pm to hide from the world until I fell asleep. Still, I got through each day and started over again the next morning.

Competence breeds confidence. If I did it yesterday, I can do it today. The positive feedback loop this provides to allow you to put one foot in front of the other in moments of true crisis is a resource that can help you through the early days when you are struggling to incorporate your new circumstances into your understanding of your life. Ultimately, however, I knew I needed better tools to not simply survive but to learn to thrive in the long term.

I began by reaching for self-help books – everything from the insightful to the insane. I started paying attention to the people who surrounded me, what was going on in their lives, and what they were putting out in the world as a result of that experience. A colleague introduced me to the study of positive psychology, and I was enthralled. This exploration tapped into my natural propensity toward learning. What I learned has equipped me with skills and resources I have returned to time and again as life has continued to remind me who is boss.

We are shaped by our thoughts; we become what we think.

- Buddha

Have you ever gone for a walk on the beach right at the tideline when the water is ebbing? You can watch the waves recede and carve little rivulets in the sand. Each subsequent wave that comes up on shore finds those grooves, and the water follows those pathways as it once again ebbs, carving them deeper and deeper with each wave. Hours later, the sand bears marks of these pathways. Any remaining streams find their way to them and use them to ease their path back to the ocean.

It turns out, this is the same way our brains develop patterns of thinking. The messages we hear and internalize when we are young begin carving a route, a pathway that eases the journey. These neural pathways are helpful when we are learning to ride a bike, and it gets easier each time, or when we practice the piano until our fingers find the keys without our having to consciously think about every strike. Those well-worn paths get deeper and make things become easier over time. It is a brilliant system, except when it is not. When those grooves trap us in our worst thought patterns, we are flooded with deceptive brain messages. These are the ones that reinforce our worst thoughts about ourselves and our potential, about our fears and insecurities. They are built deep into our brains in neural pathways that keep us stuck.

We all suffer from deceptive brain messages. They are thinking errors that tell us the world is black and white. The ones that personalize everything or convince us we must be perfect to be worthy or loved. They lead us to diminish our positive experiences and dwell on the negative. We catastrophize and "should all over ourselves." Each time we allow our thoughts to travel one of these well-worn paths, we carve the groove deeper and give it more and more power over our happiness and self-determination.

My thinking errors were carved deep over the years of my own life experiences. Growing up with parents in an unhappy marriage who "didn't believe in divorce" and considered it selfish and ruinous, I knew for sure that conflict in a marriage is destructive. Therefore, a marriage without conflict must be a good marriage. My job as a wife and mother was to put the value of the family and everyone else's happiness above all else. Divorce destroyed a family, and children were irreparably damaged by it. Divorce was a failure. As unhappy as they were in their 60+ years of marriage, even my parents had managed to stick it out. I couldn't even keep my family together long enough to get my kids through elementary school. Clearly, I was a failure.

Deep, deep in those grooves was a fundamental sense of being unworthy. Life had taught me I was unworthy of a happy home life when I was young, and now I had proven I was unworthy of a happy home life as an adult. It hit me in waves of nausea when I crumpled in tears on the kitchen floor after the kids had gone to bed. It made my cheeks flush scarlet when I had to explain my marriage was ending to a friend or acquaintance. It caused my hands to shake when I filled out medical forms at the doctor's office and got stuck on the line that asked for my emergency contact person. I didn't have anyone's name to put on the forms – clearly, I was unworthy of even that. Whatever the input that came at me through the course of my day, my brain would find the well-worth path to what I understood to be my basic truth about myself.

You fill a bucket drop by drop. You clear your mind thought by thought. You heal yourself moment by moment.
- Lisa Wimberger

While the brain loves its habits, it can learn new ones. The scientific term is neuroplasticity, the ability of our brain to be rewired and reshaped. There are tools and techniques that are proven to help create intentional thought patterns that support the development of new pathways that lead to healthier brain messages. I will share a few here, but the most important thing to understand is that it is work. Knowledge and awareness are the first steps, but they are not the cure. Retraining your brain takes intention, commitment, and time. And, I hate to say it, setbacks and recommitment. But each time you coax a thought or a response through a new channel, you carve it just a bit deeper. Eventually, the new groove becomes the better-worn path, an express lane for healthier thought patterns that are more likely to lead to wellbeing and flourishing.

We are all a collection of the experiences we have and the stories we tell ourselves about them. Imagine you strike up a conversation with a fellow passenger on a transcontinental flight. You find them engaging, and conversation flows easily. The hours of the flight whisk by as you tell a complete stranger the story of your life. Take a moment and think about the major milestones you might be likely to share, the turning points, the inflections. What moments and anecdotes are you likely to land on to share in a bit more depth?

Still relatively new to my town and community when my husband left, I had a lot of practice telling my story to new people. I got it down to the point that I could rattle it off, dodging in and out of the anecdotes that add flavor to the timeline on how I ended up here, now, in this conversation. When it came to explaining my separation and divorce, I always boiled it down to a simple narrative: my husband left me.

It is factually true. He did. But it was a far more loaded and meaningful way to frame my story than I realized in the moment of telling it. In the throes of my lifequake, in my pain of feeling unworthy of love, I needed to be clear that I would never have broken up my children's family. I needed to let it be known that I was not selfish, that nothing was more important to me than my children having a happy childhood. I needed to paint a picture in which I understood that marriages have ups and downs; they are work, and commitment means something, even if my erstwhile husband missed this lesson in the book of "how to be a good husband and father."

It was not until I began to better understand the power that these stories we tell ourselves have over us that I started to see that in the way I was framing my story, I was a victim. I might be telling myself I owned the moral high ground; however, I was actually disempowering and defeating myself. Until I could change this narrative, I would never be in charge of my own life and happiness.

Transition is coming; be prepared.
- Bruce Feiler

Whether you are currently experiencing a singular transition or you are navigating a lifequake that seems to be shaking the very ground underneath your feet, you can start to retrain your brain today. Perhaps you are in one of those fleeting stages where everything seems to be going swimmingly. Lucky you. Start today planning for the next disruptor coming your way because I promise you it is. If you follow Feiler's data and do the math, you will learn that we will each spend nearly half of our lives experiencing and responding to one of these episodes. Instead of dreading or hiding from them, instead of wishing away the experiences that frame nearly half your life, why not embrace them as an opportunity? As confusing and confounding as they can be, transitions provide us with a remarkable platform from which to grow if we are willing to do the work.

Consider: who are you in your story? Are you the hero? The victim? The martyr? The bystander? Chances are, you are some version of each of these in the various stories about your life. And chances are equally good that there is a central narrative that all of your stories share. My victimhood went back a lot farther than my marriage. I grew up in a household of discord and chaos. I was an easy target for mean girls, and I let them teach me that I was not ever going to be one of the cool kids. My college boyfriend, I had explained for years, "broke my heart." It wasn't until I began to understand my narrative's role in my self-image and self-worth that I began to question that version of my story. He did, in fact, break my heart, as first loves often do. But he also taught me what it had felt like to be genuinely loved and the importance of being true to oneself – why was that never part of my retelling?

Once you have identified the way you frame your stories, your well-worn neural pathways that are limiting your resilience, and your ability to emerge from transition stronger and bounce forward, you have an opportunity to rewrite them. Identifying those patterns takes intentional effort and a bit of detached curiosity. After realizing how I was framing the story of my divorce, I started employing exercises to help me gain awareness, reframe my story, and find hope for a better outcome.

For me, one of the simplest and most effective ways to rewrite my story was by literally writing it down. I have been a lifelong journal-keeper, and I tapped into this strength to help me navigate my lifequake. I would write a brief synopsis of a situation I was struggling with and then go back and read it, challenging myself to imagine reading it from as objective a perspective as possible. Was I painting myself as a victim? Was my low self-esteem showing? Where and how was I letting my narrative limit my perspective? Next, I would complete the following three sentence stems:

The story I am telling myself is …
Another way I might interpret this is …
An opportunity that might arise from this is …

For example, at the end of a tough day with the kids, one that included a fight over brushing teeth, resulting in the loss of a bedtime story and the day ending in tears (for all three of us), I reached for my journal. I vented all of my frustrations on the page. Diving right into my well-carved neural pathways, I quickly traced the bedtime strife back to my husband leaving. After rereading what I had written, I turned to my sentence stems.

"**The story I am telling myself is** that the kids miss their dad; they are being defiant and pushing me away because they blame me for his leaving, their sense of family and security is destroyed, I am a terrible mother." I could get so stuck in this painful place when I let myself, dissolving into despair. It felt like a Herculean task to make the choice to reframe.

"**Another way I might interpret this is** that the kids are exhausted from a long day. They do miss their dad, and they are just letting it all out in the only way they know how. They know it is safe to ventilate their hurt feelings with me because they trust I will still be here for them no matter what." This did not negate the fact that they were feeling the pain of the divorce, but it shifted the blame and shame, forcing me to shed my victimhood, and left the door open for growth.

"An opportunity that might arise from this is that I can open lines of communication and teach the kids how to identify what they are feeling and express themselves, so they will grow up with healthy self-esteem and communication tools." In doing so, I found an opportunity to cast myself as a good mom, helping them learn the skills they will need to learn from the transitions life will inevitably bring their way. Further, I built my own sense of competence as a mother, tapping into the positive feedback loop that left me more confident in my ability to guide them (and myself) through this challenging chapter of our lives.

And, Yet

Two of the most powerful words in the English language, I learned in my study of positive psychology, are "and" and "yet." My old pathways narrated my story that I had tried everything I could to provide my children with a secure family foundation, but it had all blown up. Hence, I had failed. It is the "but" that will trip you up every time. "I had this plan, *but* it fell apart." All that is left after a "but" is devastation and loss.

However, with the subtle replacement of "but" with "and," you learn another way to retrain your brain. "And" provides the opportunity to reframe the narrative. "I tried everything I could to provide my children with a secure family foundation, and…" And what? What comes next? That was up to me. I could get stuck in the "but," or I could challenge myself to find and define the "and." Instead of my story shaping me as a victim and a failure, I could instead be a survivor and hero. "I tried everything I could to provide my children with a secure family foundation, and now I can teach them that families can change and adapt with love."

There were moments when I thought I was in over my head, things I thought I simply could not do. But somehow, each day came and went. With each challenge that seemed insurmountable passing into the rearview mirror, I learned to credit myself with my growing skills. When new ones arrived, I would leaf back through my journal for the last time I had felt the same sense of overwhelm and take note of how I had gotten past it. The next time those feelings came up when I crashed into a moment when I thought, "I just can't do it," I would add the word "yet." Whatever it was I was facing that I felt I simply could not do: go to a cocktail party by myself; take the kids on a "family vacation" without their dad; or – gasp! – go on a date, I would give myself the grace to add the word "yet" to the end of the thought. We are thinking, growing beings – our brains are built for learning. The "yet" pushes the focus toward the learning, nurturing both a growth mindset and an optimism that things will get better.

We can do hard things.
- Glennon Doyle

I've already given examples of how I learned to turn back to former experiences to chart a path forward. It is one of the most success-boosting techniques I know for managing a lifequake. You, too, can mine your own stories for your gold; I promise you, is it there. Think back on a time you got through something that you never imagined you could survive. What tools did you use, whether intentional or not? How did you apply them? What techniques failed you? What lessons can you share with your future self about what worked and what didn't? Write them down – maybe on a sticky note you put on your mirror, maybe as a list in the front of your journal, or perhaps in the form of a letter to yourself that you can read each time life throws you a plot twist. Remember, taking stock in the hard things we do has a double benefit. Not only can it provide a map to guide our future selves to better outcomes, but it also builds our self-confidence and sense of competence in crisis, giving us the strength we need to push through.

In January of 2017, my 85-year-old father fell in the snow while trying to shovel the car out from a snowstorm. While he emerged unhurt from the fall, it set off a cascade of health events and diagnoses that culminated in my siblings and my making the decision that he could no longer live at home with my mother. We moved him 200 miles to an assisted living facility in my town, so I could look after him. The experience of my parents finally separating years after it was too late to improve their lives or our family connection was remarkably sad. It turned out to be an inflection point that caused a deep and painful family rift. Years-old resentments were brought to the fore and exposed. Terrible things were said and could not be unsaid.

For the next two years, Dad was in and out of the hospital and rehab centers so often I stopped keeping count of the days. Months of advocating on his behalf with doctors and social workers, of fighting for his right to return to his assisted living apartment when he improved, of cleaning my car after an episode of incontinence, of apologizing to staff for his demented outbursts, of holding one-way conversations with him when he didn't engage passed. They were exhausting, and they were lonely.

My old narratives and neural pathways pulled at me. The story I sometimes told myself was that my siblings had disengaged and left me alone to manage Dad's health, all the while resenting me for it. Then I would check myself and notice how poorly that narrative was serving me and further isolating me. With intentional effort, I instead chose to notice that each member of my family was hurting as our complicated relationships were laid bare by this crisis. We were like a once-whole piece of glass that shattered on a tile floor, each of us landing in our own sharp and painful corners. I was the fortunate one, I realized. I was the only one in a position to do something proactive and positive in these difficult circumstances. An opportunity was right in front of me to provide my dad with the most dignity and kindness I could while ensuring that he had the best medical care possible.

When my appetite started to flag, it didn't seem surprising. Stress has often had that effect on me. But it quickly went from not feeling particularly hungry to feeling unable to eat. When I did, I could not keep food in my system. In a matter of five weeks, I lost 20 pounds by accident. In my first visit to the doctor's office, she declared I was concerningly underweight, and the tests began. Blood tests, ultrasounds, and biopsies unfolded over a month, during which my heart raced, I continued to struggle to eat, and more weight fell off. My energy followed suit. I was scared for my dad, scared for myself, and trying to keep it all from my children's awareness. It wasn't long before I was called into my boss's office with concerns about how my affect was impacting my work. I left that meeting having received a clear message that my professional future was in jeopardy.

Once again, the very ground seemed to fall out from beneath my feet. My family of origin was in tatters, and my father was suffering the long road toward an undignified death. He needed my time, my problem-solving, and my love at a time when my job was in jeopardy and could not be shortcut. My heart was in pieces, and my own health was scaring the pants off me. I found myself back on the floor, both literally and figuratively. But this time, I had gold to mine. I had no idea how I was going to survive this incredibly long dark season, but I knew that I had done it and how I had done it last time.

I sat by my father for 13 hours on the day he died, knowing he was slipping away. I held his hand and told him that he was not alone, he could rest, and I would always be there. In his delirium, my father told me, for the first time in my life, that I was beautiful. It was probably the morphine talking, **I told myself**. But **another way I could interpret it** was that is my father knew what I was doing for him and wanted me to know he thought it was beautiful. **The opportunity that arose** was a gentle closure to my relationship with my dad and one of the most difficult chapters of my life.

Over two years have passed since that day, and I am keenly aware that another lifequake is on my horizon. It cannot be overlooked that the Covid-19 pandemic has been a global lifequake, and it has had a profound impact on all of us. The fear of illness has been heightened by the despair of witnessing the hate and cruelty of social injustice and inequities laid bare across our country and the world. Awareness of my narrative, reframing my story, and finding an opportunity to be hopeful has become second nature to me now. They have reminded me of my gifts of health and of my financial and emotional security. I have treasured the forced closeness I have had with my two now teenaged children, who are soon to outgrow our home and go on to lives of their own. The opportunity to start a new chapter of my own life is around the corner. I tell my friends, "I have no idea what I am going to do when the kids go off to college … yet."

I no longer resent it when someone compliments me for being resilient. It is both a battle scar and a badge of honor. I agree with Bruce Feiler: there is no such thing as a linear life; the world is too complex, full of ups and downs, left turns, and monkey-wrenches. There are those we see coming, even some we choose. And then there are those that blow in like a hurricane and knock the power out, but just for a while. If we accept and expect that life will be disrupted, that plans will fall apart, we can use these moments for growth. We can seek not to simply bounce back but to bounce forward into a life that is richer and wiser than the one we leave behind. We can rise and thrive.

Amy Rogers | Farmington, Connecticut
aar329@gmail.com

Amy Rogers is a school counselor in Connecticut, focusing on the college admissions process and the progression from high school to college.

She holds a BA from Bucknell University, an Ed.M. from Harvard University, and a Certificate in Positive Psychology from the Wholebeing Institute.

Amy has spent her career supporting others through transition in a variety of roles, including high school, college, and graduate school admission, as well as career counseling and placement. Amy is also a certified Designing Your Life Coach who helps young adults map and pursue their professional goals.

Amy welcomes readers who are looking for support or simply to share stories to contact her directly at aar329@gmail.com.

Living Gratefully With An Attitude of Gratitude and a Compassionate Heart
- Linda Jackson

When we appreciate the good, the good appreciates.

- Tal Ben-Shahar

Cultivating gratitude is a powerful practice to increasing your positivity every day. Gratitude is a state of being thankful and appreciative. Living gratefully balances negativity.

When I was growing up, I remember being reminded to be thankful for a roof over our heads, good meals, and the clothes we wear. At every dinner we said grace, expressing gratitude for the food we were about to eat. My parents weren't always happy, but they were grateful for every comfort we had living in the countryside of Pennsylvania farmland. They wanted us to know that others had much less and being thankful was an important virtue.

As an adult, I learned that being happy is a choice, sometimes, an every moment choice. When I began studying Humanistic Education, went to live at Kripalu, and, then studied Positive Psychology in the CiPP/WBI program, gratitude became my daily practice for balancing my life with more positivity. Barbara Fredrickson in her book, *Positivity*, says that gratitude and other positive emotions increase our positivity ratio.

My life quest has been in search of happiness and peaceful living. Most important has been learning that happiness and positivity are often found within, by the choices I make, and not from stuff or people outside of myself. Gratitude has been the #1 practice I use to focus on what is working and what is good every day.

At the end of 2019, I began planning a month off in 2020 to travel and focus on my photography. A month off was on my bucket list and a small inheritance, an unexpected gift, became the means. The new year came and so did COVID which brought our country to a halt and I joined millions to stay at home with the hope it would allow the virus to fade away. I can get as angry, fearful, and anxious as others and I was all of that in the first week of being at home alone. It soon became apparent that the shutdown would extend beyond a month. One morning I woke up and remembered that I had 'planned' a month off in 2020. Here it was, my month off! I laughed as I realized my request was granted.

Though it wasn't in my vision of a month off, that time was a gift I hadn't expected. I posted a large newsprint on my wall.

Whenever I walked by I took a pencil and noted what I was grateful for. Gratitude opened my heart each time I noticed the good when some days seemed endlessly gray.

That gratitude list created mental space to be creative, productive, and create a routine that brought joy, decreasing feelings of hopelessness, fear, anxiety, and anger. After the first week, I actually found myself enjoying the quiet stillness everywhere. There was so much to notice and be grateful for – the spaciousness of time, clearer air without traffic, walks with my dog, quiet trails in the woods, and so much beauty to appreciate. I even began walking with my camera so I could photograph the beauty I saw and then share that beauty and positivity on social media with others who were also at home.

Gratitude

Gratitude for me is living life mindfully. Looking for what I am thankful for requires me to open my senses, pause, and notice beauty everywhere. Before going to bed, I review my daily gratitude list which acknowledges what worked and what went well. Each gratitude is heartfelt from that very day, such as a good meal, a conversation I had, or a project I worked on. When we focus on gratitude, more thankfulness flows our way.

Authors such as Robert Emmons, Barbara Fredrickson, Tal Ben-Shahar, Sonja Lyubamirsky, and others have all found similar benefits of gratitude. When we are grateful, we celebrate the value of life which magnifies goodness. Gratitude reduces depression by focusing on what is working. Grateful people are more resilient and recover faster from stressful situations. According to Sonja Lyubamirsky, gratitude keeps life fresh by savoring moments. Without appreciation, we stop noticing the good and take life for granted.

Living Gratefully

Brother David Steindl-Rast, a Benedictine monk, speaks of living gratefully. He says that committing to living gratefully invites us to take nothing for granted, to view each day as a gift, and look at challenges as opportunities for gratitude. Brother David says grateful living is approaching life as a gift and viewing the ordinary as extraordinary. He says to notice all that is already present and abundant that we can be thankful for.

Living gratefully is a way of living I strive for. When I step outside every morning, I pause, open my senses and my heart to the blessing of another day. No matter the weather, that pause brings a smile to my face as I step into the day.

When we practice gratitude, we practice being happy with what is. I use a variety of gratitude practices to keep it alive for me. Consider trying some of the practices below for your own gratitude practice and living thankfully.

Cultivating an Attitude of Gratitude Through Greetings and Prayer

Most spiritual and religious practices emphasize gratitude through the use of greetings, prayer, and meditation. I lived at Kripalu Center for fourteen years when it was a residential spiritual community. Each meal and every meeting or gathering began with a moment of silence or prayer in gratitude. As a child, we said grace before every dinnertime. We thanked my mother for making the meal, we thanked the farmers for their work, and we thanked God for blessing the meal and our time together. These pauses reminded me to take nothing for granted.

Loving Kindness meditation is a daily practice I do to notice and to extend compassion and kindness to myself and others. This daily meditation reminds me to be grateful for the gift of life.

I also practice yoga and Qigong regularly. In yoga, a traditional end to each yoga session is honoring the practice by saying, 'Namaste,' an expression of peace and gratitude. When studying Qigong, the instructor would end every class by saying, 'Put a smile on your face.' I love that invitation and use it when I lead a meditation.

Each of these cultivates an attitude of gratitude by honoring the good and extending it to others. What greeting or end do you use or would like to use?

Gratitude Lists

A practice I use is making lists of what I am grateful for. When I spent a year studying Positive Psychology, gratitude lists were taught as a practice that expands goodness. Tal Ben-Shahar, our instructor, said, "When we appreciate the good, the good appreciates." Appreciation is grateful recognition of something. When I review my own gratitude list at the end of the day I feel content and at peace and it is easy to put that smile on my face before going to sleep.

In making a gratitude list, make it heartfelt. With each thing you list, whether it is a good meal, a person, or an event, pause and feel the joy and contentment that comes. I like to write down what I'm grateful for each day so more of my senses are engaged. My COVID newsprint is filled with gratitudes and still hangs in my study as a reminder to live gratefully.

Robert Emmons & Mike McCullough, in a gratitude study that lasted six months, concluded that the gratitude group was the happiest, most optimistic, more likely to achieve goals, were more generous and kind to others, as well as physically healthier. They increased their experience of positivity every day throughout the study by practicing gratitude. I like those outcomes!

Through practicing gratitude, we become benefit finders and notice silver linings day to day. Many silver linings are fun to notice & cherish. If you keep your gratitude lists in a notebook, you can occasionally look back over time to what you are thankful for in your life. You will feel happier as a result.

You get to decide how and when you will keep a gratitude list. I like reviewing my list every day. Some people find that several times a week is enough to keep gratitude fresh. However you choose to keep a list, thankfulness helps to raise your overall experience of positivity.

Gratitude Letters

One of my favorite gratitude practices is writing letters of gratitude. Writing a letter to someone with a focus on gratitude is heart-opening and freeing. During times of despair, grief, fear, and anxiety it can seem easier to give in and give up. That's how it felt when my mother died. I was overwhelmed with grief knowing I could never again call my mother to ask for a recipe, help with a sewing pattern, or to wish her a happy birthday. To remember, I spent a week writing a letter of gratitude to her. I took the time to reflect over my lifetime and expressed in writing all the memories and ways I was grateful for her in my life. I wrote about how I was formed by her and how thankful I was, even for the times I thought she had been unreasonable. I wrote about her strict discipline while growing up and the benefits of that way of parenting. I wrote about my gratitude that she attended every swimming meet and sporting event. As I wrote, I cried over my loss. I laughed over memories of the fun of summer nights playing hide-n-go seek after dark. I smiled over her telling me, 'until it tastes right,' when I'd ask how much seasoning to put in a dish. I cried over feeling abandoned when she and my dad moved across the country to Arizona. I then thanked her for all the times I visited for several weeks at a time exploring the beautiful Southwest. I was grateful for the summers we visited when in Oregon. Once I exhausted everything I wanted to say, I folded it into an envelope and sent it to her in heaven. I could then celebrate who she was in my life. Reflecting on life through the lens of gratitude eased my grief.

Writing that first gratitude letter began a regular practice I've kept up for more than ten years. I've written them to family members, friends, and even people I've had struggles with. Writing each letter takes days as I sift through all of my thoughts and memories. I find balance and perspective when I write gratitude letters.

Another letter I wrote a few years ago was to my ex-husband. Like all the others, I spent days sifting through memories. I honored the fact that we loved each other enough to try marriage twice. I told him all the ways I am grateful for him, his hard-working nature, his love for our daughter and grandchildren, and his wisdom. Even though we know that being married together isn't what we want, we did share a daughter and two wonderful grandchildren. We attended both births, shared in the raising of our daughter, and have shown up for holidays to celebrate family together. After he received the letter, we had a long, heart-filled talk appreciating each other and even apologizing for the challenges we couldn't overcome with each other. I celebrate that we do have an enduring friendship and I know I can call for his advice or help when needed. I am certain that letter of gratitude allowed us to celebrate the love we did have for one another and mend some of the hurts we experienced along the way.

I invite you to write a letter of gratitude to someone. Write about the good in that person and what it means to you. Be detailed, let nothing be left unsaid. Allow yourself time to write and gather your own thoughts from memories. When you are finished, send it, or, even better, read it in person if they are still alive. By writing a letter of gratitude, you open your heart and theirs to the good and what has worked in the relationship. Sending a letter of gratitude extends a deep kindness to that person. We could all use positive appreciation in a world where it seems lacking. Every letter I've written to those still living has deepened our relationship and has been received with joy, surprise, and grace.

Family Gratitude Sharing

A great way to deepen the relationships between families is to find time to share gratitude with one another. Several years ago, my daughter, her husband, and my grandchildren came to live with me for three months as they transitioned from being a military family to the tedious task of job searching and finding a home. We knew there would be challenges as three adults, two children, and two dogs were living in less than 1000 square feet. We chose to focus on what was working over what were obstacles to living peacefully.

Together, we began a ritual of sharing gratitudes at the end of the day. Knowing we were committing to positivity with one another helped us navigate the rough spots. Now, four years later, they continue that practice each night. They now share 'Best, Worst, and Weirdest' experiences of the day. They are richly bonded together in love and shared experiences. I'm so proud of them.

When my grandkids grumble about one another, as children do, I will ask them to pause and tell me two or three things they appreciate about the other. Often, they run off laughing and having forgotten what they were grumbling about.

Three Plusses and a Wish

Another practice of gratitude is one I learned years ago and used when I taught preschool, again when I worked with children at Kripalu, and still with my grandkids. It is called "Three Plusses & A Wish". I was aware that when giving feedback to anyone, it was a habit to focus on what they were doing wrong or should fix and no one felt supported. I instituted the practice of saying three things that are working and are good about the person and, only then, express constructive feedback in the form of a wish. This simple practice of appreciating one another before any constructive feedback changed the energy in the room to a higher level of positivity and support that lasted. I've shared this technique with great success over the years. Everyone feels appreciated and more willing to take constructive feedback to heart.

Grateful Conversations

This practice is one I've recently had the opportunity to practice and one I will continue to use. On New Years' weekend, I learned that my dearest friend for half my life was dying. She was sent home from the hospital with hospice.

My relationship with my friend, Deb, has been founded on positivity. Together, we learned that being positive was the way we preferred to be. We supported one another through some challenging times. We counted on one another to be a shoulder to cry on, a listening ear, and someone to celebrate our successes. Of course, we shared hurts and wounds with one another and, always, the thread of who we were with one another was living gratefully.

When she came home from the hospital with hospice, we knew we had little time together. We shared the shock and the tears of her dying. Mostly, we shared all the ways we were grateful for each other over 34 years. We talked about what we learned together, we laughed over the memories, and we expressed our deep love and gratitude for one another. We passed those last weeks expressing and holding one another in thankfulness. We held each other and cried our last tears with one another in gratitude. Our final words were, "Thank you. I love you."

We had a special friendship that was built on grateful living. I am taking forward from that experience a commitment to continue having grateful conversations. We don't know when we will be with someone for the last time.

Compassionate Heart

Being human includes sorrow, challenges, and suffering. Compassion embraces suffering and creates the space to find our way from suffering if even for a few moments. Compassion is feeling sympathy or sorrow for the sufferings of others. As a health practitioner, I work as a witness to the tolls that fear and anxiety take on the health and well-being of my clients. Some days it seems that everyone is suffering, especially in this time of COVID that has brought suffering to public and global awareness. Sitting with a client and listening deeply is how I cultivate compassion toward each person. We don't need to believe the same values or agree to have compassion. Through listening with my senses and my heart, I extend kindness to others. I try to be compassionate and kind to everyone I meet recognizing we all need compassion as we navigate life.

I have found that the more I practice gratitude, the more compassionate I become in the presence of suffering. I believe that compassion is gratitude in action. Through compassion, we hold space for suffering. We can practice deep listening with all of our senses by pausing and being still with another in their suffering. I can't take away anyone's suffering. I can sit with them and listen to their story, accepting their fears, their anger, or their sickness.

Kristen Neff, in her book, **Self-Compassion**, speaks to giving ourselves compassion and extending kindness within. I am as human as another with my own challenges and suffering. Being quiet and listening inwardly, I can honor my own suffering. I'll sit with myself and ask for what I need at the moment. Practicing self-compassion has allowed me to cry more easily when tears are there. It has also allowed space for all my emotions. Self-compassion is a gift we can give ourselves. It can be as simple as placing a hand on my heart, giving myself a hug, writing in my journal, or taking the time for Yoga Nidra in the middle of the day. Self-compassion is also grateful living.

During the weeks I was with my friend Deb I was aware of the growing emotional turmoil and suffering of her mother who had moved in to be close to her daughter. I often sat with her to listen to her anguish and suffering. I would rub her feet and simply listen. I could only imagine what she was experiencing, yet I could meet her mother-to-mother with a compassionate heart. I could listen and hold space for her tears, her anger, and her fears over losing her only daughter. My life as a mother has been transformed by opening my heart, extending compassion to the mother who was watching her daughter fade away.

Loving Kindness Meditation

Loving-kindness meditation is a simple practice of extending kindness and compassion to ourselves and others. I like to finish my meditation and yoga practice with Loving Kindness meditation.

Here is my personal practice of Loving Kindness.

> *May you be safe*
> *May you be healthy*
> *May you be happy*
> *May you experience peace*

I repeat these lines changing who it may be for. I first choose a person I know, such as "May Anne be safe". Then I'll choose someone I may be struggling with, "May _____ be safe." I'll also expand to everyone, "May everyone be safe." And, lastly, I extend the prayer to myself, "May I be safe." When finished, I sit for a moment in thankfulness. I also extend loving-kindness through my eyes, an act of kindness, a simple hello, a smile, or deep listening.

In Conclusion

Practicing gratitude has gotten me through some rough and emotional times. I know there is always something to be grateful for in every moment. I've learned to notice what's around me and within me that inspires gratitude. Even in the most chaotic crisis or heartbreaking event, there is always something to be grateful for.

Barbara Fredrickson talks about increasing our positivity ratio through positive emotions and positive experiences. By increasing our positivity, the negative decreases. There will always be negative emotions, experiences, and challenges. Positive emotions nurture an attitude of gratitude and a compassionate heart, while daily practice increases our positivity ratio.

We can cultivate habits of gratitude by focusing on what works and what is going well. You can create your own rituals of gratitude that are heartfelt. The practices I presented here are my rituals for living gratefully and extending compassion. Consider keeping a gratitude journal, pausing to express thanks for your next meal, and compassionately and deeply listening to yourself and others. Create reminders for gratefulness if you are new to these practices. We could, indeed, change the world by increasing positivity through attitudes of gratitude and heartfelt compassion. For now, put a smile on your face.

> *Through practicing gratitude, we become benefit finders and notice the silver linings day to day.*
> - Linda Jackson

Linda Jackson | Great Barrington, Massachusetts
https://www.centreforacupuncture.com

Linda Jackson, Lic.Ac., MAcOM, MEd

My mission and calling are to teach as many people as possible practices that nurture and build our positive wellbeing, health, and happiness. I am an acupuncturist, herbalist, author, and wellness coach in private practice in Great Barrington.

With a Master's Degree in both Education and Oriental Medicine as well as certification in Positive Psychology and Life Coaching, I work with individuals and groups to design pathways to health and general wellbeing. As a founding member of Kripalu Center, my work is influenced by spirituality, mindfulness, meditation, and yoga practices that are foundational practices in my own daily life.

If you wish to learn more, please visit my website at centreforacupuncture.com. The best way to reach me for consultations and appointments is to email me at linda@centreforacupuncture.com or call me at 413-329-4738.

A Call to Thrive
- Wendy McLean

The right question can make all the difference.

Asking something a different way can be all that's needed to shift our perspective, make us curious, or propel us to find answers that can change our life. For example, when 'How are you?' becomes instead 'What made you smile today?', a completely new avenue of conversation unfolds. The answer shifts from "Fine" into "Enjoying my family" and something is learned, connections are made. While we might assume that acquiring richer answers is the goal, the better objective is finding the right questions. This is confirmed by the science of Positive Psychology, which has taught me to appreciate how searching for answers to the right questions has influenced my life. It has propelled my journey towards greater thriving, and now I feel called to empower others to find their own

333

questions and their own journey. To that end, a vision of a better internet experience has taken shape in my mind, a project titled *Everyone's Wisdom*. It provides solutions to a problem that others resign to live with, but for which I see an answer. Yet, I'm getting ahead of myself. My story must begin with the person who imparted a gift of seeing solutions, my father.

Ironically, my father's most profound lesson would come after his death. I was 20. A few months had passed in grief and I was trying to get through my senior year of college when, one night, I had a pivotal dream. My dad was there but unaware of me observing him. He was in a cloud-filled room of sorts, and I sensed he was in conversation with someone; someone I could not see. As I watched, he began to see different parts of his life as if on a movie screen, major life events and turning points, decisions he had made and where they had taken him, each passing by in a flash, these moments of joy and sorrow. He began to cry. I rarely ever saw my dad cry in life. He was an engineer by trade, a brilliant scientific mind that developed application systems theories in the early days of computers. Though he was nonjudgmental and unfailingly kind to others, he was also introverted, stoic, and left no room for emotions himself. Yet, here he was in my dream, feeling every emotion of his life to the fullest, and openly sobbing. For the first time in my life, I could really feel my dad. He turned to me at that moment, with urgency in his eyes, and said, "I missed it all. It was all right there in front of me, and I missed it." I woke from that dream with a new question and knew my life perspective would be forever changed.

Why are emotions essential for a good life?

This is the first time I considered that emotions were anything useful beyond basic pleasures. While living, my dad believed feelings muddled clear thinking and got in the way of being a good person; but after his death, he implored me to learn that emotions are the gateway to every gift life has to offer. His lesson came just in time: I would need practice with this new idea and my life was about to provide every opportunity. First, I was beginning to break free from the myth that straight-A perfectionism was the path to success. Maybe I no longer had to pack my schedule or check off every imagined box of achievement, instead I could follow my emotions. Trying first on small low-risk choices - fun with friends over studying, rest over productivity, ease over pressure to excel - this quickly proved to be a better balance. I was rewarded with more ease, less grieving, and higher grades! Little did I know, that was just the beginning.

> *The best and most beautiful things in the world cannot be seen or even touched. They must be felt with the heart.*
>
> *- Helen Keller*

At the same time, love was beckoning. I met my soulmate, and the experience presented an unexpected challenge. The emotion was so visceral, so strong, that it left me breathless and scared at times. This was harder than the fairy tales made it seem, and though the relationship felt great, it also left me feeling incredibly vulnerable. It would be so easy to play it cool and stay safe behind a veil of indifference. Instead, I doubled down on my newfound emotional freedom. I purposefully ignored the warning shots in my head, took the chance that my heart was right, and trusted my intuition that he felt the same. I needed confirmation that my heart was hearing the truth, so decided to admit how raw I felt, "I'm already so in love with you that this would hurt immensely if it ended. Please tell me you feel the same!" With his reassurances, I felt safer falling even more in love. Rewarded again, I next brought emotions to bear on a major life decision: what to do after graduation. Knowing pursuing a doctorate would advance my career but wouldn't make me happy, I abruptly scrapped those plans. Instead, I chose to find work near those I loved most. Though it felt risky not knowing where I was going next, it felt better than betting on an empty prescriptive plan for success. It takes courage to trust in feelings, yet each time I manage to listen to my heart's truth, I become more engaged and excited about life's experiences.

> *And the day came when the risk it took to remain tight inside the bud was more painful than the risk it took to blossom.*
>
> - Anais Nin

As my trust grew in using emotions as my guide, my perspective changed as well. Maybe emotions were not on a continuum of good to bad, but all had equal significance. In the following years, life provided me with a lot of practice. My emotions became a jumble and I struggled to separate the bad from the good. I loved fiercely and also dealt with the challenges of marriage. I worked in corporations with good and toxic cultures. I suffered chronic health issues and discovered the blessing of alternative therapies. Positive emotions rarely happen in isolation. If I try to avoid sadness, I unintentionally cut off happiness as well. Motherhood was

the perfect example of this dichotomy. I found taking care of
two little ones exhausting on every level, while at the same
time I adored every moment they delighted in something
new. I wanted to be the best possible mother for them,
however, I didn't feel up to the task. I yelled at them so often,
even though I didn't want to! I was so desperate to assuage
my anger that I just wanted it all to stop sometimes. Until I
remembered my father's life lesson, "I missed it all." What
might seem like rest, away from all emotion, actually becomes
numbness. No. There must be a better solution.

> *We cannot selectively numb emotions, when we
> numb the painful emotions, we also numb the
> positive emotions.*
>
> - Brene Brown

I clamored for any source of wisdom and found very little
at first. Dr. Spock's answers didn't feel right to me. The
pediatrician's advice felt disconnected. My mom's answers,
outdated. My friends, struggling just as much. So, I turned back
to my heart, and even more importantly, to the heart of my
children. Maybe they had something to teach me. Instead of
trying to control their every behavior so my negative feelings
didn't get triggered, I could try controlling which emotional
story got my focus. When I was triggered, I focused instead on
what I could learn about their story. If there was an outburst,
I practiced allowing my anger to simmer and focused instead
on setting better expectations so they could rise to meet them.
If someone got hurt, I practiced quieting my need to solve it
and focused instead on listening to them so they could find
their own solution. The reward was sweet! I woke each day
with less trepidation, less attachment to what might happen,

more connection to my girls, and more energy! No longer was I scrambling to prevent every negative behavior. I was free to explore each situation with my girls as a learning experience for me, and for them. Slowly, we shifted. We became a team, explorers mining the annoyance, disappointments, and heartache for the joy, compassion, and connection. Was I perfect at it? Definitely not. But I persisted because I knew this was better than becoming numb. I would keep trying to squeeze out all the richness of these experiences for myself and my family. After all, when we love, we are connected, and our life has greater meaning. When we feel excitement, we are driven, and our life has a purpose. With this, I'd taken another step toward greater flourishing: All emotions are to be felt, and each is a source of wisdom, informing our choices and giving us energy toward building a better life. And I would need all this wisdom to answer the next question.

What happens when we die?

Death was made very real with my father's passing, and this question began gnawing at my soul. As the years flew by, I tried to ignore the primal fear creeping further into my silent moments. It took my own brush with death before I could face this question head-on. It was the Spring of 2000. I was pregnant with my first daughter. In a luxuriously long hot shower, I suddenly felt a strange sensation. I knew something was very wrong, and I immediately called out to my husband. He later reported that just the weird sound of my voice was enough to send him bolting up the stairs. He found me on the floor, wet, eyes rolling in the back of my head. I have no memory of this. Not of turning around, or taking a step, or falling through the door, or hitting the tile floor. I wasn't there.

Instead, I was in a dark tunnel with light at the end. I felt calm, at peace, loved. It was enveloping, a place of infinity and healing, such as I'd never known. I started to move towards the light, and a figure stepped into the doorway at the end. I recognized the silhouette as my father and received a message - felt it more than heard it - Oh no, no, no! It's not your time. As my father began to slowly close the door at the end of the tunnel, I felt a tug in my stomach. The next instant, I heard my husband's voice, saying my name. But it sounded strange to my ears. I felt my cheek cupped in his hand, but I couldn't remember where I was. And for a split second that stretched across time, I wondered how I got here when I was just there. It was so comfortable there. So loving. And this hurt! Here in my body. Pregnant. On the floor. Why am I on the floor? "Wendy!" Oh, right! I'm Wendy. Memory flooding back, I remembered I was in the shower, then I felt really strange. Then shock flooded me, I must have collapsed! Oh no! The baby! Is the baby OK? Miraculously, yes, I was physically fine and so was my baby. In awe, I came to appreciate that I had not given a thing for an experience that would give me so very much.

Oh, the experience of this sweet life.

- Dante

The best gift was replacing my fear of death with awe and curiosity. I had felt a bit of what dying was like, and it felt fantastic on the other side! I scared myself a bit, wishing to be in that place again. I knew I had no wish to die, and yet I felt compelled to be back in that healing embrace, another opportunity to escape the hurt, wrapped up in a blanket of pure love and oneness. To fulfill that yearning safely, I researched near-death experiences. First, I learned what I

FINDING UNSHAKABLE HAPPINESS

had witnessed in my dream 16 years earlier was called a life review. My father had reviewed his entire life to learn what he had gained and what he had missed. I felt lucky to benefit from his lessons within my lifetime. That appreciation grew while reading about others' tunnel experiences. They gave my memories greater prominence. I found I could savor my own encounter, bringing forth the feelings of unconditional love and enjoying them in my present life. The gratitude deepened further after reading an account that discerned the essential difference between life and death. Crossing over and being in oneness is more akin to a healing state: There are recovery and reflection, but little action. It is only in living that we have the opportunity and the dynamics necessary for choice, change, and great transformation. Life is where things happen. Rather than Heaven being the singular goal, the pinnacle of experience, life is also a goal, providing the breadth and depth of experience. Life and death, spiraling together, in a much bigger story than I had ever previously imagined.

With greater awareness about death, my entire perspective about life had also shifted, and yet not a single thing had fundamentally changed in my day-to-day existence. Some might even say my newfound perspective was irrelevant because it was all just happening in my head. But I knew it was fundamental. My gratitude for others' journeys took on new meaning, and my faith grew in those things unknown and unseen. I no longer felt judgment towards others' mystical experiences. Who am I to say what's real to you? My reality now included savoring my near-death experience and bringing a little more of Heaven's unconditional love and oneness into my daily experience. Though I didn't know at the time, this marked the beginning of my quest, a call to a better life, which would emerge from my answer to the most challenging question yet.

How can we thrive?

Finding answers to this third question became increasingly urgent along with my eagerness to provide the best possible life for my girls. So, I felt some relief when, in 2008, I found my first answer after reading The *Last Lecture* by Randy Pausche. Randy was a professor who, when faced with a terminal illness, presents his life's wisdom in a last lecture. But his intended audience was not the hall of people hearing him speak, but his young children whom he would have to leave behind all too soon. Through tears of realization, I also would want to leave my girls the wisdom I'd gained in hopes it would provide greater ease, meaning, and purpose in their lives. Similarly, they were too young, and I had to acknowledge that outside of the major religions, no place or method for passing on core beliefs and nuggets of wisdom existed. I wondered then how I could store it somewhere. With that, my idea for a website was born, one that could share what I'd learned and also provide wisdom from its source - the sages of old, the gurus from the East, the science of the West, the academics in the ivory towers, and the average person on Main Street. I wanted it for my girls, and for others too. A place to use the best of technology to share the best of humanity, by everyone and for everyone - a platform called *Everyone's Wisdom*.

My commitment to this project increased along with my growing efforts to grapple with the complexity of what makes people thrive. While on the mission to find a better understanding, I met Ellie, a spiritual teacher and Reiki Master who would quickly become a dear friend. In 2010 we discovered we shared a similar and rather unique approach toward parenting; we both naturally gravitated toward listening to kids, finding joy in connection, and celebrating even their smallest successes. Together we created Conscious Parenting, and for four years we ran classes and planned a parenting section for a future *Everyone's Wisdom* site. The best part was how much fun we had working together, creating something new in service to others. We were as excited about developing what we would teach as we were in teaching. And, we practiced what we preached. We listened to and celebrated each other, which built energy in our relationship and made the work feel effortless. It was an especially poignant lesson for me. I was thriving, despite being an introvert and preferring to work alone, because collaborating with the right person made hard work more fun.

> *Happy people live secure in the knowledge that the activities that bring them enjoyment in the present will also lead to a fulfilling future.*
> - Tal Ben-Shahar, *Happier*

Gratefully, this work led me to Positive Psychology, a scientific approach to understanding human flourishing. I had stumbled across the field while searching for content to augment a Conscious Parenting class, and character strengths was the first tool I found. Their free, scientifically-based survey was the perfect compliment to our class content on children's gifts. I was pleasantly surprised that values like creativity, kindness, and appreciation of beauty were measurable and actionable! I immediately loved it as the first scientific tool for greater thriving I'd ever seen. Within weeks, I had signed up for the first-of-its-kind certification course given at Kripalu Center for Yoga & Health by Harvard professor Tal Ben-Shahar along with top-notch faculty. Later I would better understand my excitement: The course was a blend of curiosity and spirituality, two of my top strengths rarely found in academia. It was everything I had hoped. Instead of looking at what's wrong with people to diagnose and fix them, Positive Psychology looks at what's already working well to maximize it. The science showed how humans are capable of great things when we focus on positive emotions, strengths, and connections with others. Most importantly, the skills for thriving can be learned, so beyond the basics of safety and security, a better life is available to everyone.

Paradoxically, while Ellie and I delighted in incorporating this science of happiness into our parenting courses, I was struggling with a cascade of personal crises that challenged my own well-being. I experienced bursts of debilitating stress. For example, one power outage left my family cut off for almost two weeks. I woke each day intent on simply keeping warm and finding food. But, I just couldn't. The simplest tasks became impossible. The very moment I needed to think creatively, my mind was frozen with stress. I recognized this same pattern repeating in my girls when they were still too young to express what was happening. When signs of their anxiety became generalized and their behavior increasingly frozen over time, I knew we needed to take action. Thanks to the course, I used the lens of strengths to see that their school neglected their top strengths, and I found a new school that would provide a chance to use their strengths again. I had less control over changing the situation for my mother, whose physical health was on the decline. There's nothing more emotionally difficult than holding space for a loved one in pain. I witnessed first-hand her struggle against the mounting toll it took on her body, mind, and spirit over the years. Yet, I also witnessed her resilience, her focus on the simple things she could control. She greeted nurses with kindness, a joke, and a laugh. She kept her teddy bear close, and her sudoku book closer. She repeated her appreciation for every visitor, gesture of love, and a small improvement in her condition. I learned along with her. Letting go of what I couldn't control as the sole caregiver for my girls, my husband, and my mother was essential to my well-being. And, focusing on the smallest things, even in the briefest moments, kept up my energy for the next crises. Maybe when the struggle is in the many little things that pile up and overwhelm, then resilience can be found in the little things too. Maybe thriving in adversity means removing what isn't working if we can, and more importantly, it means inviting in all the little moments worth savoring. Mastering our fates is as much about knowing and creating what we do want, as what we don't want.

> We are not victims of our genes, but masters of our fates, able to create lives overflowing with peace, happiness, and love.
> - Bruce H. Lipton, *The Biology of Belief*

My journey has been a class in how to thrive. My curiosity encouraged me to find answers to some deep existential questions, start a new business with a friend and engage with a new area of scientific understanding. The answers I found enabled me to traverse one of the most difficult periods of my life with greater presence and grace, each circumstance stripping away the extraneous and forcing me to find what lifted me up the most. I now know what makes me thrive.

We hold these truths to be self-evident; All people
are born creative; Endowed by our Creator with the
inalienable right and responsibility to express our
creativity for the sake of ourselves and our world.
- Barbara Marx Hubbard

I am still seeking answers, soaking up anything that seems remotely connected to human flourishing and creativity from many disparate fields. I've infused what I've learned into developing Everyone's Wisdom®, a collaborative platform to help people share knowledge and thrive. Thus, my own call to thrive overflows as an opportunity to help others do the same. Here are the questions and answers I'm currently working with as I develop Everyone's Wisdom®:

- How can we provide knowledge and solutions to people when they need them most? We already have most answers we need to solve any problem. A new internet platform can empower people with the freedom to seek answers, explore shared knowledge, and take their own steps toward a better life.

- How can we use the best of technology to enable more creativity? By storing knowledge and solutions in a network, the mind is freer to be at its best. People can focus more on learning, creating new associations, solving problems, and collaborating with others.

- What encourages humans to be altruistic and persist toward innovation? Humans naturally want to share and help others. A web experience designed to allow people to connect across the place, time, and chosen topic of interest will enable more of the cutting-edge solutions urgently needed in the world.

No matter what he does, every person on earth
plays a central role in the history of the world. And
normally he doesn't know it.
                                    - Paulo Coelho, *The Alchemist*

We were all meant to flourish. The fact that we are not all thriving isn't a universal truth we must resign ourselves to, but rather a call to action of the role we each have to play. By asking, 'What will help me thrive more often?' we start the journey toward the answers and the wisdom that will improve our lives, and that of our families and communities too. I hope my story has inspired you on your path toward your best. This journey is worth every effort because you matter. Your best in the world matters. Your wisdom is the new revolution. Only you have the passion, direction, strengths and vision to know what works best for you. Only your story can resonate and lift others who share your perspective. Now more than ever, we certainly need our best solutions working for us. It is imperative if we are going to rise together, flourish together, and have a future together. It's our call to thrive.

Wendy McLean | New York
https://www.everyoneswisdom.com

Wendy is an entrepreneur who has created Everyone's Wisdom®, Conscious Parenting Seminars™ and Pencil Portraits. Always inspired to help others thrive, her career has led her from strategic planner to treasurer, from web manager to parenting coach, from seeker to speaker and back again. Now she brings all that together as Founder of Everyone's Wisdom, a web-based platform under development for curating the knowledge, connections, and collaborations that enable the best in humanity. Wendy has two daughters and lives north of New York City with her husband and cat.

Resilient Medicine: A Sensible Approach to Wellbeing

- Dr Samantha Eagle

There are moments in our life that are pivotal–that change the lens through which we view the world. It was three years after my medical school graduation, and I was a young physician establishing an independent practice. While attending a specialty conference on thyroid health, an unexpected keynote speaker had a profound impact on the way I would approach patient care.

The lecture started off unlike others. Instead of the usual subject title and personal credentials being projected on the screen as attendees took their seats, the enormous blank screen displayed a slightly irregular black blob in its center.

When the audience quieted down, the lecturer stood before us and asked: "What do you see?" The answers began to flow from the participants and there were descriptions of the uneven shape. "I see a black dot." "I see a mass with irregular borders." "I see a dark hole."

The speaker, feigning puzzlement, looked up behind him, turned back to the audience and said "That's interesting because what I see is a large white screen which happens to have a black spot.

The presenter was Bernie Siegel, MD, renowned pediatric and general surgeon and Yale professor. He founded Exceptional Cancer Patients, which "helped to facilitate personal lifestyle changes and personal empowerment of the individual's life." (berniesiegelmd.com). Dr. Siegel's simple imagery impacted my thinking in a multitude of ways. His focus was on the totality of the composition and not the imperfection. As physicians, we are trained to identify and describe the black dot, but he shifted this construct to the entire picture. That was a holistic approach–and one that I could embrace. We are oriented to treat the black dot and don't necessarily recognize the power of other physiological functions more numerous than that imperfect spot. The surrounding blank screen represented the body's innate physiology and the place where healing can occur.

I remind myself about this lesson every day. When sitting with patients, I am mindful of the whole being before me. Often, it was a particular symptom or ailment that motivated them to schedule a visit. However, it is never far from my thoughts that most of their body is functioning, with essential physiology such as metabolic and other cellular activities continuing. The body is embedded with these ongoing processes and they support its resilience. A Google search to define the word resilience states it is "the capacity to recover quickly from difficulties; toughness." A second definition is more visual: "the ability of a substance or object to spring back into shape; elasticity." (both from *Oxford Languages*). Each definition, when applied to the medical arena, can help a patient who is struggling. They may learn how to remain optimistic, having hope because of their innate powers. Recognizing their body is trying to heal, they could develop a positive, can-do attitude, despite the rigors of medical regimens.

How reassuring that our body is imbued with resilience. It has a natural, built-in capacity to adjust or recover from much of what life brings. Symptoms are often the body's attempt to correct an imbalance, or dis-ease. The word disease initially did not refer to an illness. Instead, it was defined as "a condition of the living animal or plant body or one of its parts that impairs normal functioning and is typically manifested by distinguishing signs and symptoms." (from *Oxford Languages*). If we interpret the components of the hyphenated version, its meaning changes again. "When disease was first used, it literally referred to 'lack of ease or comfort' rather than to how it is used today to refer to sickness or problems with bodily function. Disease can still be used today to mean 'uncomfortable,' but there is usually a hyphen, as in 'dis-ease.

It is notable that, for decades, our language has recognized the power of mind over body with words that are probably familiar to all of us. The term *psychosomatic illness* refers to the mind's (psyche) influence on the body (soma) and how our thoughts and perceptions can affect our physiology. If we are stressed, unhappy, feel hopeless, depressed and view our life with despair and negativity, we might experience worsening health.

Another powerful result of our thoughts is called "placebo effect." Placebo effect is often considered when a medication is being evaluated. In some cases, the outcome is believed to be generated by one's mind and assumptions of response, be it positive or negative. "A placebo is anything that seems to be a 'real' medical treatment -- but isn't. It could be a pill, a shot, or some other type of 'fake' treatment. What all placebos have in common is that they do not contain an active substance meant to affect health."

We should not minimize how stunning the placebo effect is – it can change one's physiology, without use of a drug or other agent. The term is derived from Latin and means I shall be pleasing (Wikipedia). The way we respond to something is determined by numerous factors, including beliefs, expectations and even life circumstance. After briefly exploring the two previously mentioned dynamic influences of thought, it seems timely to mention the burgeoning field of Positive Psychology and its effect on physical health. Psychological approaches have generally focused on analysis of problems, understanding and finding solutions to emotional duress and unhappiness. Psychological therapies now include guiding patients to an optimal sense of well-being through shifts in attitudes and lifestyles, creating balance for a more positive view of their world. An aspect of this is having a sense of purpose and ability to remain optimistic when life hits hard. We are all capable of tuning into our healthier selves when we rid our mind of toxic thinking. We begin to see strengths and abilities we have not yet utilized. Appreciating the value of a positive mindset can help in the healing process. I hold that as a starting point for new patients as I bring Positive Psychology into the physical realm.

As a naturopathic physician with a focus on Functional Medicine, I see application of the holistic perspective of disease presenting in various ways. For example, let's explore fever. The rise in temperature is not just a symptom needing to be managed, but rather, is a sign that the immune system is operating in a healthy way. Fever may be caused by a microbe, be it from an external source or an internal imbalance. It reflects the body's wisdom that something is "off" and has numerous biological processes which serve to rebalance. Yes, our body is resilient and often self-correcting. However, when the body is overwhelmed and medical help is required, a resilience-focused physician will recognize that they can use the body's own mechanisms advantageously. Let's harken back to fever. It is helping kill offending microbes by mobilizing a specialized part of our immune system (white blood cells), which do the job. We would not want the body's defenses to be continually tapped, but perhaps a fever is good medicine in specific situations. Enter the role of an open-minded physician, because there would be fewer options available to a patient without one. A resilient physician could explain this physiology and perhaps encourage a patient to bear with it for a while (unless the fever is extremely high). A patient with resilience might accept the idea and find a way to cope, using a Universe of tools. They could view it as the body doing what it evolved to do for survival. Therefore, a patient might choose to rest, keep hydrated and not suppress the fever. The resilient patient is one who becomes informed and empowered.

Recently, I was waiting for word from a long-time patient of mine, who was meeting with an oncologist after having a biopsy. As the reality of the situation was becoming evident in her work-up, my role was to get her through challenging, fear-packed days until we had answers. While we both recognized the likely diagnosis, I knew from her personality that she could muster internal strength and resilience in facing her challenge. It called to mind my own experience with the black dot – which I shared with her.

Instead of the typical phone call, I received an email from her. Upon opening the message, I was surprised to see a photo of her soaring through the air on a swing, smiling. She wrote "My smile is the byproduct of resilience. This was immediately after hearing that I have Stage 4 cancer. I was too upset to drive, to go home, go out – so I went for a walk knowing I needed to decompress." She elaborated "Resilience, for me is: self-care, believing in your own ability, resourcefulness – find the right tools (swing), ability to change your perception, celebrate the small pleasures, seeing all the wellness around the black dot."

Early in my career, I began to pay attention to the personalities and belief systems of patients who fared particularly well when faced with challenging and, at times, devastating medical diagnoses. A pattern began to emerge. I noted the traits and behaviors of those patients were: remaining optimistic, identifying what is positive or joyful, finding gratitude, making good choices for their well-being, regrouping to accommodate a new lifestyle for their health. That's a whole lot of characteristics to hope for, and not all patients have the ability or will to respond in those ways. I asked myself, is there a single concept with a broad range of perspectives and actions that could describe something so remarkable and inspiring? Then, it hit me – those patients and our medical team have a common attribute – resilience. Their resilience, whether patient or practitioner, has huge implications which could affect outcome. In each medical situation, one follows evidence-based protocols appropriate for specific patients. However, within that guideline, the practitioner focused on fostering resilience will address more complex issues with an open mind and the resilient patient will embrace what is positive, hopeful and possible.

Hoping means seeing that the outcome you want is possible and then working for it.
- Bernie Siegel

Where can one start? The short answer is making proactive choices for a healthier life no matter what one's current state of wellness happens to be. In my practice, we like to say we'll meet you where you are and take you where you should be. Including a nutrition plan optimal for one's condition is a good beginning. We help individuals make small, sustainable changes for better health. We all have heard the call to "eat more fruits and vegetables," but the change needed may not be that simple or the patient might have no interest in complying. At that point, the practitioner has to be clever and perhaps change the patient's point of view.

I recall an overweight, diabetic male patient who came to me for dietary counseling. The first words out of his mouth

FINDING UNSHAKABLE HAPPINESS

were "I hate vegetables." Not a great start to a new patient visit... He claimed he only made the appointment because his other doctor referred him for a consultation. His situation was serious because his diabetes was not under control. I would not give up and decided to take another tack. I asked him about his life and what brings him joy. He smiled and said his two grandsons made him happy. Now, I had something to work with, although he remained resistant to anything else I brought up. As he began to trust my intentions, I suggested that he must be a role model for his grandsons. I said show them that you are not going to let your condition beat you down. Teach them to be resilient. I hit the jackpot with that one. He opened up about how concerned he was about his health and wanted to be around to see them grow up. I asked him if ignoring an important part of diabetes treatment was a way to ensure that. His resistance all but disappeared and, as the visit continued, he became more interested in self-care. Ultimately, he walked away with a good beginning for weight loss and managing his diabetes with proper nutrition. He was in a positive state of mind and willing to follow the diet – even though it included vegetables.

Nature provides us with an amazing model of equilibrium. To see the cycle of seasons – the frozen ground of winter giving way to the optimism of spring and the abundance of summer – is to know true balance. Unfortunately, many of us bombard our bodies every day with a blend of toxic substances or behaviors. Unhealthy substances may be in the food we eat or in the air we breathe. Sometimes the stress and emotional imbalances that are byproducts of busy lives become our toxins. When an unhealthy lifestyle has a tight hold on us because of finances, relationships or mindset, we are setting ourselves up for unhappiness and feeling trapped.

We risk worsening health if we do not change our ways. Feeling optimistic, hopeful and empowered lightens our emotions. It is being able to do the dance as life throws curve balls. That is the ultimate definition of resilience. Naturopathic doctors work to reconcile two competing influences – the fundamental potential of our body to repair itself, and the stressors to which we are subjected. We create a plan for better health that gives the body's natural functions the ability to perform as they are designed. It is how I came to recognize that I practice what I call Resilient Medicine because the conventional model of treatment does not allow for the wide range of patient differences, beliefs and needs.

> *Patients want to be seen as people. For me, the person's life comes first; the disease is simply one aspect of it, which I can guide my patients to use as a redirection in their lives. When doctors look at their patients, however, they are trained to see only the disease.*
>
> - Bernie Siegel

A patient in my practice, a woman in her seventies, recently told me a story about a physician encounter many decades before. As a young woman, she developed painful and debilitating symptoms and her primary care practitioner could not arrive at a diagnosis. He sent her to a specialist and she spent over an hour in the waiting area before getting to see the doctor. Once she entered the consultation room, he hurriedly looked over her questionnaire, fired off a few questions, did a brief examination and said laboratory work was required.

She told him she wanted to explain what happened to her and what she believed was the onset of her disease. He responded he did not have time to hear her story and he did not have time to figure out how she became ill. The doctor was writing prescriptions and said, "This is how we treat your symptoms. See how they work and come back in two weeks." The visit ended and she felt unheard, alone and frightened. The ensuing part of her journey with chronic illness entailed exploring other options and finding a physician who listened.

How could her experience have been different? There are many contributing factors to illness that a physician, stuck in a groove, cannot take the time to explore. Unfortunately, medicine is sometimes set up for assembly line patient care because it is most efficient, even if not most effective. The specialist, with whom the older patient consulted, saw only the black dot. It was how he was trained, and that determined how he would treat and bill for services. Sometimes addressing symptoms is sufficient, and the body is able to heal because the therapy is helpful. However, there could be a point of diminishing returns the longer the symptoms are suppressed, and the ailment still underlies the patient's physiology. The body gives out, new symptoms develop and the patient gets sicker. A physician recognizing the concept of Resilient Medicine takes into account the many aspects of a patient's life before suggesting regimens. Is the patient's lifestyle one that could be causative of the condition? Do they have access to a healthy living and working environment, good nutrition, stress management? The practitioner does not see the treatment simply as one prescription away from relief. Rather, the physician approaches care with sensible, do-able options for the patient's well-being. In Naturopathic Medicine, we use the body's own healing mechanisms, whenever possible, to create a treatment plan. Sometimes patients have to learn to love themselves enough to take care of themselves and not give up. It is a matter of helping the patient see they have the strength and resilience to get through the challenge, even if they have been dealt a devastating blow, such as a diagnosis of cancer.

Negativity creates physiology. Most people know that dwelling on anger, fear or perhaps just a world-weariness can plummet us into feeling stressed, depressed or helpless. Mental health professionals are well equipped to assist patients who are in the grip of doom and gloom. As a physician, I have to recognize the changes which may occur in the body when one has spiraled into a sad, anxious or hopeless state of mind. What patients might not realize is that their perspective on life can affect them at the physical level. A chain reaction may occur that produces more symptoms. Our thoughts, positive or negative, have consequences for the body. We can appreciate the "fight or flight" mechanism when faced with a threatening situation. It is a built-in response necessary for survival. Our heart and breathing rate increase, energy is released, muscles become tense and we can take action. Attention changes so we focus on the threat before us. Even digestion decreases. You don't hear the birds singing when a bear is in your path. You don't need digestive processes when you may become the meal.

However, ongoing mental stress taxes our adrenal glands (which produce adrenaline and cortisol) and high blood pressure along with other physiological changes might develop. Importantly, our brain could be affected, too, and set us up for depression and even addictive behaviors.

What is remarkable about our mental state is that we are in the driver's seat to change it and therefore change our physiology. Some of us have a natural gift of resilience to process experiences and work through traumas, sadness or feeling out of control. A resilient person might find they can accept a new normal once illness has its onset. Other people have to work harder to develop ways to cope with adversity and find an outlook and behavior that will promote a sense of well-being. None of it is easy and often one has to go through a grieving process when poor health has severely affected their life. The Elisabeth Kubler-Ross definition of the grieving process is mainly associated with loss of a loved one. It outlines denial, anger, bargaining (with a higher source), depression and ultimately acceptance. An important aspect of grieving is that one not get stuck in any of the first four stages, which become their new normal. Everyone experiences loss of health differently. Mobilizing strength, hope and the will to prevail could take some coaching. The goal would be to release negativity and help a patient become their own advocate to regain optimal health.

When people become ill, it's hard to imagine they could find happiness as their world is crammed with doctor visits, diagnostic tests and medical therapies. Some people do. They find a new purpose in getting well and perhaps helping others confront their illness. Or, they see what and who is in their life as being gifts. Everyday experiences become precious. Their will to recover is focused and more important than petty gripes or disappointments. They have resilience that helps them and their physician explore ways to support healing. Patients may hit walls with current treatments. They become driven and find new options, feeling they can defeat their diagnosis. One learns how to manage and cope with what comes at them, resilience becomes a way of life. That symbolic black blob need not determine their fate. Being positive creates another physiology, a better one – and may just play a crucial role in reclaiming health.

No matter what the statistics say there is always a way.

- Bernie Siegel

Samantha K. Eagle | Brattleboro, Vermont
https://biologichealthcare.com

Dr. Samantha K. Eagle is founder and Medical Director of Biologic Healthcare in Brattleboro, VT. She has a Naturopathic Medical Doctorate and a Master's Degree in Human Nutrition. Her focus is on Functional and Lifestyle Medicine with an Integrative approach. She provides specialty care for digestive/nutritional issues (interest in diabetes), rheumatic conditions and weight normalization.

Dr. Eagle's background in teaching undergraduate biology inspired her attention to patient education. Commitment to giving patients access to information and treatment options fostered her passion for Lifestyle Medicine. Recognizing the economic challenges to healthcare, she has introduced her patient-centered model to national audiences of practitioners.

Dr. Eagle is a medical consultant for an international corporation that develops comprehensive screening tools to create personalized representations of an individual's health. Their programs have extensive applications for large and small companies and organizations. The end goal is to inspire people to make lifestyle changes that positively influence their wellbeing.

IN CONCLUSION

Unshakable Happiness Found

-Donna Martire Miller

In conclusion: I wish to say Bravo to everyone involved with this book, and that includes you, the reader! We are all engaging in the happiness revolution of our times.

I will let you in on my secret ...

I was not always happy, far from it. My children and grandchildren will tell you that I cried at the tiniest things. Little did they know that those tears were my moments of joy, watching them in school performances or seeing them on the holidays, going on short vacations with them ... yes that always brought tears of joy to my eyes because otherwise, I was simply lost living in the daily grind. I spent many years ignoring my authentic voice. I lived according to what the culture of the day was telling me.

My self-prescribed belief system looked something like this: Work hard, withhold love when angry, point out what your children do wrong, and correct them (and if I did not, well, shame on you is what the voice told me). Food is the pleasure everyone looks to; it will solve any problem. As my daughter said ... mom, you were a food pusher, and the most immense hurtful belief was...God is vengeful ... Therefore, I felt hopeless and doomed.

In those years, the whispers of my soul tried to rise, but I did not listen. I lacked the tools to believe it was possible to be any different. I gained weight, disconnected from a sense of self, and only noticed the faults and problems around and with me that needed to be fixed, which overwhelmed me. I felt hopeless, I became depressed and anxious, I developed health disparities that were killing me ... I needed to find out about happiness and the corresponding health benefits.

Make the most of yourself ... for that is all there is of you!

- Ralph Waldo Emerson

As I reflect back, whether I was raising my children, performing in front of a crowd of thousands as a blues singer, working in the Human Services field, providing trauma-based intervention to children suffering from abuse and neglect and their families, or teaching at the university, there have been many opportunities to give and receive happiness, love, and connection. However, I did not always recognize them. Or understand how vital that recognition would be to human flourishing.

Simultaneously there were many painfully tender moments where I felt like a misfit, an imposter, alone, misunderstood, sad and frightened. I can see now that I had settled for believing that this is all life would be. I never felt at peace; accomplishments were not what I was striving for, although, at the time, that is what I thought was the driving force.

What was I missing? True Happiness was the answer. Oh, I had fleeting moments of joy, but I could not hold on to those peak moments for long, and I would go back to feeling like my life was similar to a hamster on an exercise wheel. I began to search for it in others, thinking someone else who seemed happier must have the answers. I would realize later that the energy I put into giving others and their opinions so much control over my life was where the deep-seated pain of not being seen for who I was and the subsequent feeling of utter loneliness was rooted.

This emotional discomfort became the catalyst for some serious soul searching. I began to discover my true desires. I wanted to know myself better and be known and loved for who I was. Don't we all? I wanted to be happier. That is when I learned about Positive Psychology and the science of happiness. Wholebeing Institute, Led by Tal Ben-Shahar and Megan McDonough, utilized the Research experiments conducted by doctors Martin Seligman, Sonia Lyubomirsky, Mihaly Csikszentmihalyi, Carol Dweck, Barbara Fredrickson, Christopher Peterson, Ryan Niemiec, and many others that have been mentioned in the Author's stories in this book to teach us evidence-based tools to practice to experience human flourishing and provide us with the "way" power to actively pursue a happier life!

According to Dr. Seligman, this research aimed to catalyze a change in our thinking from a preoccupation not only with repairing the worst things in life to "also" building the best qualities in life. He and the rest of the professors/ scholars/ researchers/ and authors are the real pioneers of the science of happiness. They are to be gratefully acknowledged for bringing all of us these tools!

When psychologists talk about happiness or subjective wellbeing, they mean the experience of frequent positive affect, a sense that life is good and worthwhile. I wanted to learn what I could do to help myself and everyone I loved or cared for. Here is what I know to be true from my own life experience and from teaching this to others.

Using a positive lens to view life by is not lying to ourselves. It is a choice that we make to activate what is possible. I once believed that if I worked very hard at something, I would be successful, and then I would be happy. I now realize from learning about positive psychology that the opposite is true.

Research shows that when we are happy, it increases our chances of success. When we can see our life as a blessing and become more grateful, neuroscience shows that our brains become more engaged. We no longer seem to sleepwalk through our days on what is now termed *autopilot*. We have an opportunity to use a *beginner's mind* even in the most mundane situations, shifting our perspective to something more pleasing. It is a way to bring us into alignment with our life. It is our way to bring more and more personal integrity into our way of being.

When we can be more positive, our brain chemistry gives us that juicy dopamine and serotonin hormone that actually get the oxytocin going! This lowers our stress hormone cortisol and makes us more motivated and creative. I have found that having a positive attitude has improved my closest relationships and given me a foundation of hope, vision, and belief in my ability to accomplish goals. This positivity outlook has had a noticeable ripple effect on those I love, work with, care for, and within the community that I work and that I live in.

Sometimes I still catch myself listening to an old negative narrative my inner critic starts to state. It is natural to do so, this is a habit, and like anything else, it takes practice. I then have to remind myself that those thoughts are not based in reality. Today *is* different, and the evidence that I have to prove that - is in what I have discovered that matters to me and choosing to focus and build upon that. Before learning about the science-backed happiness strategies, I would have fixed my belief on what my mind was telling me. Now I have control over these thoughts, and I am better prepared to make intentional choices aligned with my values and character strengths. I can choose to use this knowledge in any situation.

Neuroscience research has shown that it is not the external reality that shapes us but the lens through which your brain views your life that shapes our reality. If we can change our fixed mindset to a growth mindset, look for what we value in how we view things, we can increase our ability to be happier and more optimistic.

I am currently teaching a course in Human Services at a local University. We are studying a book called the *Happiness Advantage* by Shawn Achor. We are learning that by practicing mindfulness and raising our level of positivity in the present moment, the brain experiences a positivity boost. It then focuses better, intelligence rises, and creativity rises. Best of all, energy increases when mindfully being positive instead of negative, neutral, or stressed.

According to research, writing just three things you are grateful for at the end of the day begins an upward spiral of positive emotion. In a 30-day gratitude challenge (in 30 days, science shows that we can build a new habit), the brain starts to scan our days, not for the negative but for the positive first! It helps minimize bad moods and allows us to get back to our authentic truth. At a deep level, expressing gratitude is that feeling of knowing we are in alignment with meaning and purpose in our life. It is key to finding our happiness, health, and wellbeing.

Positive reminiscence - writing about a positive experience you've had recently allows your brain to relive it. In this way, you increase your positive emotional state.

Exercise teaches your brain that taking action is essential. It is very well documented that movement in any form is the best antianxiety and antidepressant out there!

Meditation allows your brain to get relief from anxiety or the overwhelming chaos created by our long to-do lists and multi-tasking. Meditation lowers blood pressure and provides a host of other health benefits. In Megan McDonough's book *A Minute for Me*, I learned that meditation can be done anytime, anywhere with little effort and enormous benefits!

Random acts of kindness are deliberate conscious acts of kindness. Even giving a smile to a friend or the cashier at the grocery store increases happiness for everyone concerned!

I now realize that it is not the job of anyone else to make me happy, nor can I blame God or life. I am happier today because these incredible leaders in the field of positive psychology were courageous enough to teach this rigor`ously researched science of happiness and its strategies.

My happiness and healthier living prescription started with knowing who I am at my best and reaching towards that daily. From recognizing and savoring what I find lovely and beautiful. From being grateful for this life and everyone in it.

From learning how to let go of what hurts and to find forgiveness or compassion when possible. From discovering character strengths and building upon them to cope and be resilient. From constantly being open, embracing a growth mindset, learning something new about myself. From music and dance, yoga, and long leisurely walks with a friend. From accepting reality, in life, there is no avoiding suffering completely. From deeply loving the God of my understanding and knowing that God is love. From deeply loving others and sharing whatever I have or know with them. I had to learn to love and accept myself, have the courage to be messy, admit mistakes, ask for forgiveness, accept the lessons and walk forward with the knowledge I needed to engage in a life worth living in every moment left that has been given to me.

You have more power and control over your happiness than you can imagine! Right now, you may or may not be happy. Happiness may be fleeting for you, here today or gone tomorrow, or perhaps you are a pretty happy individual, born that way! Positive Psychology is based on broadening and building what is working in your life. If you are happy, you can be happier! If you wish to make happiness more consistent in your life, you can!

If you are looking to increase your happiness, you can! If you want to be happy and can't find your way, I hope the stories in this book have inspired you to take some action in that direction. I know that you, too, can listen to the whispers of your authentic self, create a life that holds happiness for you and for those you love. Finding your pathway to happiness will happen as you begin to see your value and utilize some of these strategies to create a good and pleasurable life filled with meaning and purpose.

In this way, as the authors in this book have said, you will discover the way you were meant to show up in this world, and will lead others in their search for unshakable happiness.

> *Being happy is not a fatality of destiny, but an achievement for those who can travel within themselves.*
>
> - Pope Francis

I wish you well, I wish you peace, I wish you love and happiness … *Finding Unshakable Happiness.*

Donna Martire Miller, M.S. CIPP, is devoted to teaching, writing and speaking on subjects that increase happiness and make life worth living! Her career has been devoted to facilitating educational growth in both traditional and non-traditional settings. She holds a Master's degree in Counseling and human resource development. Donna is certified in Positive Psychology from Kripalu with Wholebeing Institute, where she then became teacher's assistant. She is also certified in Positive Psychology Coaching, Teaching for Transformation, Mindfulness and Strength based practices through UPenn, VIA and Wholebeing Institutes. She has additional certification in Women's Wellness and Meditation from Deepak Chopra, Wayne Dyer and UCLA. Donna trained with Kripalu Faculty Megha Nancy Buttenhiem, graduated from "Let Your Yoga Dance" as an instructor.

She is an international Keynote speaker, trainer, and a presenter at National Conferences. Donna held The Executive Director position for 30 years at HELP FOR KIDS a positive parenting, family-strengthening Center in Southern Connecticut. As Founder of Happily Ever Actions™ she provides people with actionable strategies, thought-provoking insights and evidenced based tools toward optimal living. She considers her greatest accomplishment to be motherhood and enjoys spending time with her adult children and grandchildren. When Donna is not writing and authoring her books on Happily Ever Actions, she can be found teaching meditation, let your yoga dance or singing with a blues band!

Happiness is the ultimate currency!
- Tal Ben-Shahar

Joseph Bologna lives in Connecticut, where he enjoys his family, photography, and writing. From a very early age, he began to create the path that would take him around the world as a photographer. Currently, he has expanded his reach as an author. He is a founding partner in Happily Ever Actions, a business that teaches happiness and wellbeing strategies.

Joseph has visited 26 countries and has taken over 90,000 photos. His work can be seen in travel magazines, private companies, and businesses. He has been peer awarded numerous times and is considered a top 10 popular photographer in View Bug. His recent accomplishments include the summer of 2020 people's choice award, the 2020 top shot, and the 2021 top shot, elite awards. He is currently collaborating on a three-book series featuring selected photographs and original writings.